Lessons from Modernism

Lessons from Modernism

Environmental Design Strategies in Architecture 1925–1970

Kevin Bone, Editor
with Steven Hillyer
and Sunnie Joh

Essays by
Daniel A. Barber
Michael Ben-Eli
Alan Berman
Kevin Bone
David Rifkind
Carl Stein

The Cooper Union Institute for Sustainable Design
The Irwin S. Chanin School of Architecture of The Cooper Union

The Monacelli Press

This publication is a development of the exhibition
Lessons from Modernism
Environmental Design Considerations
in 20th Century Architecture
1925–1970
on view at The Cooper Union
January 29–March 23, 2013

Curated and designed by
Kevin Bone
Steven Hillyer
Sunnie Joh
Sara Jones

The exhibition was presented by
The Irwin S. Chanin School of Architecture
of The Cooper Union and
The Cooper Union Institute for Sustainable Design
and made possible with generous assistance from
The Stavros Niarchos Foundation

Published in the United States by The Monacelli Press.
All rights reserved.

Library of Congress Control Number 2013955485
ISBN 9781580933841

Designed by Yve Ludwig

Printed in China

www.monacellipress.com

Acknowledgments

Over the years, I have challenged my design and seminar students to identify and describe environmental design innovations in architecture. That file of projects came to include many examples from the early years of the modern movement. When the Cooper Union Institute for Sustainable Design was established in 2009, we began to explore projects that we would like to pursue, and the idea of examining environmental design in modern architecture was always on the list. By 2010 we had blocked out the basic outline of this project. It can be described in three stages, all of which benefited from the efforts of a group of dedicated Cooper Union people: the research, the exhibition, and this publication.

In preparing the exhibition, many people helped make this project a reality, and we owe them a great debt of thanks. Then Dean of the Irwin S. Chanin School of Architecture, Anthony Vidler, provided enthusiastic encouragement for this work as well as the vitally important support of the School of Architecture. Associate Dean and current Acting Dean Elizabeth O'Donnell stepped in and worked with us on grant applications and provided editorial guidance throughout the exhibition and publication. Two other colleagues at Cooper Union were partners in this project from the onset and contributed in countless ways, throughout the research, planning, exhibition design, and preparation of this publication: Steven Hillyer, Director of the School of Architecture Archive, and Sunnie Joh, Program Director at the Institute for Sustainable Design. Kenneth Frampton's moral support was immensely helpful, and indeed, over several sessions with me, Kenneth helped establish the range of projects that should be represented.

The research and development stage of the exhibition was exhaustive, and many colleagues and members of the extended Cooper Union family made significant contributions. The core research for this project was done by myself, Steven Hillyer, and Sunnie Joh. Significant contributions were also made by Lydia Xynogala, who prepared the material on Constantinos Decavallas, including original interviews with the architect. For the work of Iannis Xenakis, Lydia made a site visit to the location and produced original photography of his project. Lydia Kallipoliti, a Senior Associate at the Institute at the time, provided general research oversight and developed arguments for the didactics in the exhibition. Sotirios Kotoulas spent six months combing through hundreds of possible projects and helped us establish the original selection of about fifty projects we considered for the study. Carl Stein, author of his own study on modernism, preservation and sustainability, *Greening Modernism*, came to many of my seminars where he generously worked with students on studies of possible projects for inclusion. Emmy Mikelson, Senior Associate for Public Programming and New Initiatives at the School of Architecture, provided editorial guidance throughout the production of the exhibition didactics. Albert Appleton, Senior Fellow for Sustainable Entrepreneurship to the Institute for Sustainable Design, and Visiting Professor in Sustainability at The Cooper Union, contributed writing to the exhibition. Oliver Antoniu, Zulaikha Ayub, Ali Dur, Melanie Fessel, Yael Hameiri, and Yoon-Young Hur all researched various projects.

Sara Jones, Senior Coordinator of Special Projects of the Architecture Archive, was a critical partner who oversaw every aspect of the exhibition design and graphic identity. Patrick McElnea, the Archive's Collections Assistant, did the remarkable model photography and graphic production work that was so important to both the exhibition and this publication. Patrick Robbins, Associate to the Institute, worked on text, fact checking, and image permissions, and provided invaluable services on behalf of the success of the exhibition. Derrick Benson and William Hood further assisted with image permissions and fact checking for this publication.

Many people assisted in the production stage of the show. The numerous detailed drawings and models were produced by a remarkable team of current and former students of architecture at The Cooper Union. Daniel Wills oversaw a team that included Adrian De Silva, Karim Ahmed, Eduardo Alfonso, Visar Aliu, John Angelo Alonzo, Lori Beppu, Charlie Blanchard, Vincent Hui, Chia Chou, Jeremy Jacinth, Benjamin Johnson, Aikaterini Kefalogianni, Minas Konstantinou, Katerina Kourkoula, Andrew Lam, Jennifer Lee, Matthew Maiello, Harry Murzyn, Andrea Pinochet, Dan Schillberg, Wes Rozen, and Lydia Xynogala.

In the fall of 2012, I taught a class devoted to the subject of this study. The students made significant contributions to advancing the work: John Angelo Alonzo, Charlie Blanchard, Kristy Chiu, Sam Friedberg, Benjamin Johnson, Andrew Lam, Matthew Maiello, Phong Nguyen, Alice Yang Ong, Alexa Reghenzani, Andrea Recalde, Chris Taleff, and Wan-Jen Tsai.

Professional groups also assisted in the preparation of the exhibit. Thanks to Bone/Levine Architects, which generously supplied space, printers, research support, logistics, model shops, and substantial financial support. Our appreciation goes out to Joseph Levine, who encouraged our activity underfoot, and Molly Iannarelli who helped in countless ways throughout the development of the exhibition. Special thanks are due to Barbara Wronska-Kucy for her inspired analytical drawings of building sections examining the construction and performance characteristics of the projects, and to Paul Deppe for his contributions to that effort. I am grateful to our friends at Situ Studio for their fabrication of the landscape components of the models and for sharing their excellent analysis of the Frank Lloyd Wright projects that were featured in the show.

The exhibition and publication were both made possible by the generous support of the Stavros Niarchos Foundation, an organization that seeks to inspire a building culture that has a future. Additional support was provided by friends, family, and associates: Elinor Giobbi, the Koeppel Family, Joe Levine and Jane Cyphers, Citizens for Water, Dan Malloy, Steve Cortazzo, and Kemper Systems USA. Thank you all. And we must ultimately acknowledge and thank the Rudin Foundation, for their visionary generosity that allowed for the establishment of The Cooper Union Institute for Sustainable Design. Without them none of this would have been possible.

Deeply felt thanks to the contributing authors of the essays in this book (many of whom also contributed didactics to the exhibition): Alan Berman, David Rifkin, University of Florida, Daniel Barber, University of Pennsylvania, Michael Ben-Eli, Director of the Sustainability Laboratory, and Carl Stein. All were generous with their time and talent. Many thanks to Elizabeth White, our editor at The Monacelli Press, and her staff for their great work, and Eugenia Bone, who contributed editorial expertise throughout the project.

Kevin Bone, Director
The Cooper Union Institute for Sustainable Design

Contents

Lessons from Modernism
Kevin Bone
11

Reviewing Modernism through
the Lens of Sustainability
David Rifkind
17

Climate Map with Projects
28

New Dwellings for Bordeaux
Le Corbusier + Pierre Jeanneret
30

Open-Air School
Johannes Duiker
36

Night Shelter for the Homeless
Affonso Eduardo Reidy +
Gerson Pompeu Pinheiro
42

Karuizawa Summer House
Antonin Raymond
46

Weekend House
Albert Frey + A. Lawrence Kocher
52

Housing at Sunila Pulp Mill
Alvar Aalto
58

Jacobs House I
Frank Lloyd Wright
64

Houses in Space
Amancio Williams
70

House Over the Brook
Amancio Williams
76

Jacobs House II
Frank Lloyd Wright
82

Building for the Emprezas Gráficas o Cruzeiro
Oscar Niemeyer
88

Maison Tropicale
Jean Prouvé Workshops
94

Soholm 1
Arne Jacobsen
100

Bachelor Flats
Bronek Katz + Reginald Vaughan
106

Dexter M. Ferry Jr. Cooperative House
Marcel Breuer
112

Walker Beach House
Paul Rudolph
118

Munkegaard Elementary School
Arne Jacobsen
124

Cocoon House
Paul Rudolph + Ralph Twitchell
130

Pavilion on the Lagoon Rodrigo de Freitas
Affonso Eduardo Reidy
136

Valéria P. Cirell House
Lina Bo Bardi
140

Siedlung Halen
Atelier 5
146

School of Plastic Arts, National Arts School
Ricardo Porro
152

House on a Cycladic Island
Iannis Xenakis
158

House II in Kavouri
Constantinos Decavallas
164

Vacation House on Aegina
Constantinos Decavallas
170

Timeline, Selected Projects, 1925–1970
178

Lessons from *Lessons from Modernism*
Daniel A. Barber
188

Modern Legacy/Sustainable Culture
Carl Stein
196

The Search for a Healthy Living and
the Roots of Modernism
Alan Berman
201

Towards a New Architecture?
Michael Ben-Eli
207

Notes on Materials
218

Index
221

Lessons from Modernism

Kevin Bone

Today architecture finds itself at a crossroads. The green building movement is gaining momentum, but the elite expressions of the profession, the grand architectural speculations that characterize our time and its supporting critical establishment, tend to address green building as a technical specialty that is best dealt with by consultants, no different than code conformance or an engineering problem. Or worse, the very idea of an ecologically based, climate-oriented design agenda is seen as a threat to the discipline of architecture. Those arguments have a great deal of influence in both university studios and in the field, which is unfortunate because they are wrong.

As the twenty-five works here clearly show, beautiful, innovative, and inspired design can engage and work with the agencies of nature. Great architecture can express that design agenda in the identity of the work. Indeed, our times suggest there cannot be great architecture made today—not truly influential, important, and modern architecture—that does not effectively address our unfolding epoch of environmental travails.

To meet the challenges of imagining a more efficient, less consumptive, and less environmentally dangerous human enterprise, twenty-first century architects, engineers, planners, and builders are applying new technological and digital strategies and exploring the possibilities of emerging innovations. But in conjunction with the pursuit of technological solutions, we should remember that the knowledge embedded in previous architectural investigations is an important resource.

Architects have previously looked to history for inspiration and guidance in response to environmental issues. In the 1960s, in reaction to the terror of the atomic age and the ugliness of rampant unplanned development, scholars including Bernard Rudofsky, a visiting critic and professor of architecture and art at Yale University, examined vernacular constructions, traditional building methods, and the catalogue of indigenous techniques for insights into designing for a more livable world. But the heart of the twentieth century, the modern age, and the vast body of architectural experimentation associated with modernism, has been largely ignored in the quest for environmental design solutions.

Lessons From Modernism looks at twenty-five examples of modern architecture created between 1925 and 1970 that approach design problems in ways that today would fit the definition of green architecture or sustainable design. These works incorporate environmental strategies that are integral to the architecture and solve critical problems of comfort, use, and economy by recognizing and adapting to natural forces. None of them satisfy all the criteria of today's green building best practices (a moving target in any case), nor would they qualify for certification under any of our many systems for evaluating environmentally appropriate architecture. But these projects do present a catalogue of architectural sensibilities that accomplish much of what green design aspires to do. Together they reflect a range of project types, environmental design ideas, and solutions to the challenges of different sites and climate zones.

While the motivations of the modern architects were very different from those in the design community today, there are important common challenges. The modernists addressed problems of health and hygiene in a growing population of urban dwellers, fuel and energy shortages, material availability, and building costs, issues that confront present-day designers as well, though for different reasons. As such, the integration of architecture with natural phenomena was as vital to the early modernists as it is to the current green building movement. Indeed, these early works portray an essential sensibility that promotes designing with nature as an ally, and it is this sensibility that every student of architecture should acquire if we are to address contemporary issues of climate change and ecological degradation, and create more environmentally compatible human settlements.

Much of early modern architecture was executed before the advent of mechanical equipment to regulate interior atmospheric conditions. To make buildings more livable, more useful, and more comfortable, architects developed strategies that emphasized passive heating, passive cooling, natural lighting, and natural ventilation. Architects realized climate regulation through plastic solutions: the incorporation of sunscreens and layered facades, the optimization of building forms and building orientation, the use of water basins, natural shading, and planting programs for cooling, and the provision of sheltered outdoor space and protected gardens to expand the comfort zone of the buildings. These are design ideas that produced both better-performing buildings and distinctive architecture.

Many of these buildings demonstrate an aesthetic of simplicity. Small in scale and inexpensive to build, they have remained valuable and useful because of the adaptability of the spaces. The modernist project pursued structural innovation. Engineering and building construction methods aspired to maximize efficiency and minimize the use of materials. Site-design strategies sought to promote integration with the setting, to embrace the natural surroundings, limit disturbance of natural landscapes, and reintroduce green ways and natural landscape into urban environments. All are informed by the climates of a given site and most profoundly, all respect the universal and elemental relationship of the architecture to the daily and annual patterns of the sun. These are projects where the architecture responds to the solar dictates of place.

As Le Corbusier observed, "This tiny pathetic adventure, lived out daily by a tiny leaf, by the billions of tiny leaves that form part of the complex existence of hedgerows or great forest, always obeying and turning their faces to the great warm star, proclaim the fundamental law of this earth we live on: that the sun is our dictator."[1]

As the earth travels through its yearly orbit, the relative orientation toward the sun at any given location on the earth changes by a few degrees from day to day. This is the reason that the length of every day varies slightly from the day before and the day after. The relationship between the rotational axis and the orbital plane also determines the angle at which sunlight will strike the surface of the earth throughout the year. This angle is called the angle of solar incidence, and it is critical because the angle at which the incoming solar ray strikes the surface of the earth determines the amount of solar energy that a given place will receive. The closer to perpendicular the angle of solar incidence, the greater the solar energy gain, as is the case in the equatorial regions. The more acute the angle of declination (the lower the sun is in the sky), the less solar radiation hits the earth's surface, as in the extremes of northern and southern latitudes. This changing in the angle of incidence is the primary driver of seasonal change.

For each of the projects in this book there is associated solar information. On the site plans, red lines mark the route of the sun through the vault of the sky on four benchmark days: the winter solstice, the spring and fall equinoxes (the two equinox sun paths are the same), and the summer solstice. The larger circle around the solar paths represents the horizon, and shows where the sun rises and sets for each designated path. Three sections show the intersection of the building and the sun at noon, illustrating the maximum sun angle for each of the benchmark days and how the architectural work addresses the sun in these various states.

These projects address conditions in four primary climate zones: northern, temperate, arid, and tropical, and associated subzones. Architectural work in the northern zone, where responding to cold is more important than managing the limited summer heat, is represented in two projects by the Danish architect Arne Jacobsen, and one by the Finnish master Alvar Aalto. Both architects experimented with the garden rowhouse typology, a planning approach that allowed for individual dwellings to be nestled together. The compactness of the volume reduces heat loss and minimizes the amount of surface area exposed to the cold. Natural lighting is import-

1. Le Corbusier, *The Radiant City,* trans. Pamela Knight and James Palmer (New York: Orion Press, 1967), 78.

ant but in the cold, low-light winters of Scandinavia, the amount of glass must be restricted to conserve heat, so glazing was used sparingly. The designs allowed for the most interior illumination at the best times of day, yet occupied a limited amount of the total exterior envelope.

Temperate zones present architectural challenges related to the wide range of thermal conditions that may be present, from deep cold to extreme heat. This book examines nine projects designed to perform well under both summer and winter conditions. Because of the swing in temperatures and the lower range of solar angles, many of these temperate-zone projects are conceived to invite the winter sun in, helping to warm the spaces, but also offer protection from solar gain by shading open wall areas from the hot, high summer sun. The temperate climate has many days when temperatures allow for a mingling of outside and inside use of space, and the temperate-zone projects explore this flexibility in plans that freely connect indoor to outdoor areas. Plan configurations dictated by climate forces, like minimizing exposed surface areas in cold northern zones or providing narrow, well-ventilated spaces in the hot, humid tropics, are not as important in the temperate zones, and as a consequence more complex architectural forms and diverse plans emerged. These open, experimental plans are perhaps best exemplified by the many prairie-based residential works by Frank Lloyd Wright. The Jacobs House, the first of Wright's Usonian projects, is an L-shaped form, with the protective enclosure of the L facing south and east, and the living areas opening onto sheltered gardens. The house and the outdoor spaces defined by the L create a microclimate, retaining the warmth of the low winter sun and buffering the house from the northern wind. The glass that admits the warmth of winter sun is protected from the high sun of summer by the broad horizontal overhangs characteristic of Wright's prairie work.

Arid zones are characterized by long periods of daytime heat and a wide swing in the diurnal temperature differential. The dry climate creates a clear night atmosphere that promotes high levels of night sky radiation, a process that can dramatically cool the evenings. Building strategies in hot arid climates often rely on a building envelope with a heavy mass that absorbs and retains the cooler air and provides a comfortable interior throughout the day. The sensuous form of Iannis Xenakis House, with its thin slot windows and small square openings, is an example of this strategy.

The tropical and subtropical zones, typically characterized by hot, humid weather that lasts year-round, present a particularly demanding architectural problem as buildings need protection from strong, high sun and effective methods to maximize natural ventilation during hot days and hot tropical nights. Walls and roofs must be fully protected from the sun but still allow light and air to enter. Ventilation issues are often resolved by siting elongated structures perpendicular to prevailing breezes. This allows crosscurrents to pass completely through the building. Plans (and cross-sections) are devised to avoid blocking airflow through the interior spaces. Outside walls are often shaded with arcades, sunscreens, recessed windows, sun shelves or louvers, and are oriented to limit the amount of wall surface exposed to the sun, and in the case of buildings that are elevated, the airflow under the structure contributes to cooling at night. Being lifted off the ground also limits ground level radiant heat from passing into the materials of the building. Building for the humid tropics, unlike building for hot, dry climate zones, typically does not utilize thick walls because the nights are not cool enough to lower the temperature of heavy construction. Lightweight structures work best. Buildings with limited exterior wall mass, such as Prouvé's Maison Tropicale, do not hold as much heat, and the building elements cool down more rapidly in the evening.

The combined problem of limiting heat gain to the walls and roofs of the structures and promoting maximum natural ventilation can be contradictory design parameters, but the modern architects responded with magnificent architecture. The double roofs, multi-layered and articulated facades, brise-soleils, sun shelves, deeply shadowed openings, and ventilated roofs addressed these problems, and these elements have become iconic expressions of the era, defining many of its most important works.

These architectural solutions for tropical environments are particularly germane as questions of comfort and habitability, if addressed through conventional mechanical means, will continue to increase demand on the use of fossil fuels and hasten the resultant damage associated with reliance on those fuels. The question of how to build for the tropics is crucial in the twenty-first century. Currently, 40 percent of the earth's population, or about 2.7 billion people, live in tropical zones, many in sub-standard conditions. By 2060, 60 percent of the total global population—5.4 billion people—will be living in tropical regions, including the nations around the Bay of Bengal and throughout Equatorial Africa. The majority is expected to become urbanized.

Beyond architecture that recognized and worked with regional climates, there are other experiments that present useful insights into environmental design. Le Corbusier's New Dwellings for Bordeaux, his 1925 work that proposed modestly scaled, multifamily housing in an agrarian master plan, is frequently studied for its honeycomb architecture, atelier type spaces, and hanging gardens. However, the agricultural component of this project is equally important. Rather than imagining a garden community where each dwelling is given some ground space for yard and garden use, the proposal for the New Dwellings included central common lands dedicated to agriculture, with ample space for farmland and orchards to be shared by the community. The project is a seminal form of urban agrarianism and a workable alternative to the wholesale displacement of productive cropland for low-density suburban enclaves.

Priorities for outdoor learning spaces shaped the 1929 project for The Open-Air School in Amsterdam by Dutch architect Johannes Duiker. This design for a small neighborhood elementary school expressed Duiker's desire for a healthier, more hygienic society, with classrooms that were linked to a south facing, outdoor, open-air learning terrace. Duiker's aesthetic of simple spaces filled with light and air argued for the health and happiness of the children and proposed a practical alternative to the dark, heavy masonry school houses typical of Holland at the time. In our own culture, the outdoor classroom trend is rapidly growing, stressing the value of teaching students out of the classroom and addressing the challenges of educating digital-age students who have little exposure to the natural world.

Contemporary green arguments about the materiality of buildings stress the importance of using locally sourced materials from regional supply chains. Antonin Raymond developed his Karuizawa Summer House based on the sectional diagram of Le Corbusier's Errazuriz House in Chile (1930), a concrete and masonry structure designed for an arid desert site. The Raymond house, built for the subtropical location, is built with timber and thatch. Both the columns and beams of the house are round, hand-polished timbers, a traditional Japanese material vocabulary used to express the space planning ideas of Le Corbusier. None of the wood was painted and the materials were all local. As Raymond noted, "The aggregate for concrete retaining walls and other concrete parts of the building was the lava stone dug up from the ground . . . [T]he roof a thatch of 'karamatsu' [a locally sourced material] . . . When the reed curtains were let down, the whole thing was like a primitive African chieftain's quarters."[2]

Lina Bo Bardi's Casa Valéria Cirell (1958) in São Paolo, Brazil is also modeled on a Corbusian precedent that transforms the original concept by means of vernacular construction methods. Casa Cirell, like Raymond's summer house, directly adopts the formal prototype of Le Corbusier's 1924 design for mass-producible artisan dwellings. Bo Bardi transforms the white simplicity of the Corbusian model into a unique and handcrafted object. Rubble-faced masonry walls, timber-framed thatched roof verandas, and hardwood lattice sunscreens are all used to fit the project to the São Paolo environment. The ideal vision of a pure and optimized dwelling on an abstracted flat ground is transformed into a house that seeks to embrace its climate, its physical setting, its architectural heritage, and its local culture.

The very argument of modernism that put forth a case for buildings stripped of excess and designed to find their beauty in function and space is in accord with the green manifesto that declares one should use what one needs, and not more. Early modern architects rejected the ornamentation and stylistic standards that characterized much of the design of the late nineteenth century. The heavy materiality of building embellishment was deemed unsuitable for the modern world. The modernists sought to employ simplicity and utility and to exclude non-functional elements and the excesses they represented. This aesthetic, or really these values, inform the contemporary green building movement.

There are numerous other projects that could have been explored in this book, many of which would have undoubtedly furthered the thesis. To provide a larger context, twenty-nine additional projects are presented briefly in the timeline of the period from 1925 to 1970. We hope that these and still other projects will find their way into future analyses by architects and students of architecture.

The goal of this study is to inspire an examination of a broader body of work through the lens of the environment. It is our hope that these lessons from modernism will influence a culture of architecture that seeks not only to do less harm, but inspires a new mandate for the practice of design.

2. Antonin Raymond, *Antonin Raymond: An Autobiography* (Tokyo: C.E. Tuttle, 1973), 134.

Reviewing Modernism
Through the Lens
of Sustainability

David Rifkind

Imagine a history of modern architecture organized around the theme of sustainability. In contrast to more familiar accounts of modernism, which emphasize social reform, technological determinism, or aesthetic concerns, such a history might examine projects and movements in terms of the way they managed material and energy resources. Movements with conflicting aesthetic concerns might find themselves linked by a common attitude toward landscape and habitat preservation. For example, architects normally viewed as sharing an affinity for social reform might find themselves at odds over how to sustain vibrant and diverse communities. An environmental history of modern architecture would cut against the grain of the movement's paradigmatic narratives.

An environmental history of modern architecture would bring greater nuance to our understanding of the importance of technology to the development of architecture in the last two centuries. Modernism is not just an uncritical embrace of mechanisms and materials; it also recognizes that *techne*, a poetic practice of interpretation and discovery, includes an ability to harvest and shape climate and resources in a manner that sustains both human life and the natural environment. Such a history would emphasize the radically new (in the early twentieth century) concern with human health that propelled an interest in brightly lit, well-ventilated, and easily cleaned interiors, and it would devote ample space to the landscape architects who chose native species over exotic ones and sought to preserve sensitive habitat.

The roots of sustainability were always present in modern architecture, though rarely brought together as comprehensively as in contemporary architectural practices. Modernism's responses to ecological concerns appear instead as a series of fragments, organized around such themes as material efficiency, climatic responsiveness, healthy living and work environments, and the integration of open green space into cities. Yet at the same time modern architecture included a host of environmentally and socially destructive practices, such as suburbanization and resource intensive building methods. To complicate our environmental history of modernism, many projects display both tendencies simultaneously, making it necessary to trace with great precision the degree to which a richly diverse range of built environments engaged nature and society both positively and negatively.

The complexity of framing a history of modern architecture through the lens of sustainability can be illustrated by examining the career of Le Corbusier. He advocated an unprecedented integration of the built and natural environments, seemingly investing modernism with an ecological awareness, but he treated landscapes as objects of contemplation from, rather than continuous with, their architectural counterparts. He framed the landscape through expansive windows or presented it from the remove of rooftop gardens whose scarce vegetation recalled the broad peastone paths and neatly geometric pools of the French baroque landscape. At the same time, Le Corbusier designed interior spaces filled with light and freshened with breezes drawn through ample fenestration, reflecting a concern with health provoked by recurring contagions like the 1918–19 influenza pandemic. Le Corbusier's contradictions are even more pronounced at the scale of the city, where he promoted lushly vegetated parkland as an integral component of urban space but failed to recognize the city's role in promoting social and cultural vitality through a rich mix of uses in each neighborhood. Taken as a whole, Le Corbusier's oeuvre demonstrates a paradox common to most of his contemporaries: a passionate concern with certain aspects of sustainability married to a curious disregard for others.

What criteria should we use to assemble a taxonomy of sustainable modernism? It is neither possible nor useful to draw a line dividing "sustainable" and "unsustainable" buildings, cities, and landscapes. Instead, every work ought to be assessed in terms of degrees of sustainability, and the way we judge these projects and their designers has a lot to do with what kinds of sustainability we prize most. Let us begin with the major categories of ecological and social sustainability, which overlap but are not identical, and then fill out our catalog with concerns about resource use, landscape and habitat preservation, human health, and community development.

Abundance and Scarcity

The very materials of modernism can be seen as antithetical to ecological concerns. Glass, steel, and concrete—the archetypal materials of the

Sun and Wind

The Gallicism "brise-soleil" entered English through the work of Le Corbusier, who began using sunshading devices as an integral component of his work around 1933.[7] Designed to shade windows from direct sunlight, and thus keep heat and glare from interior spaces, the brise-soleil quickly emerged as a motif in modernist buildings around the world, especially in the tropics and the Mediterranean region. Le Corbusier recognized the utility of the brise-soleil in temperate climates, too, where carefully designed shading devices would exclude the heat of the high summer sun while admitting the warmth of the low winter sun.

The device's most triumphant early use came in the Rio de Janeiro office tower built for Brazil's Ministry of Education and Public Health by a team of architects led by Oscar Niemeyer and Lucio Costa (1935–43).[8] Their brilliant design incorporated a vast brise-soleil with operable fins across the entire north facade (the sunny side of a building in the southern hemisphere), which they contrasted with an uninterrupted expanse of glass on the south facade. Combined with a narrow floor plate, the building's extensive glazing fills the offices with indirect light, which reduces the need for artificial light while eliminating glare and heat gain, and offers unimpeded views over the city and surrounding landscape.

Along with harnessing indirect light and passive solar heating, many modernists embraced natural ventilation for both practical and aesthetic reasons. Maxwell Fry and Jane Drew, who worked with Le Corbusier at Chandigarh, employed elegant screens across the long facades of simple block buildings, which cooled the ambient air before drawing it through the structure. Fry and Drew developed their climatically responsive buildings in the humid tropical context of the British Gold Coast colonies (later Ghana and Nigeria), as did faculty and students of the Architectural Association's department of tropical architecture, who experimented with cross ventilation, indirect natural lighting, and other strategies calibrated toward making pleasant habitable spaces using a minimum of energy resources.[9] Buildings like those designed for the campus of the University of Ibadan (1949–60) exemplified the climatic construction principles Fry and Drew elaborated in such books as *Tropical Architecture in the Humid Zone* (1956).[10]

Fry and Drew were among many architects who synthesized modern construction techniques and planning strategies with traditional means of lighting and cooling buildings in the years between 1930 and 1970. Victor and Aladar Olgyay published another influential book, *Design with Climate: Bioclimatic Approach to Architectural Regionalism* (1963), and Fry and Drew's colleagues in London, such as Otto Koenigsberger and James Cubitt, built important structures throughout the rapidly dissolving British Empire.[11] These architects demonstrated a remarkable sensitivity to traditional settlement patterns, which they respected in housing and urban planning schemes across the tropics.

The need to shade buildings from the tropical sun and to increase prevailing breezes led to the development of another modernist gesture:

7. Christopher Mackenzie, "Le Corbusier in the Sun," *Architectural Review* (February 1993), 71–74.

8. Valerie Fraser, *Building the New World: Studies in the Modern Architecture of Latin America, 1930-1960* (London: Verso, 2000). Kenneth Frampton and Yukio Futagawa, *Modern Architecture 1920–1945* (Tokyo: A.D.A.Edita, 1989).

9. Rhodri Windsor Liscombe, "Modernism in Late Imperial British West Africa: The Work of Maxwell Fry and Jane Drew, 1946–56," *Journal of the Society of Architectural Historians* Vol. 65, No. 2 (June 2006), 188–215.

10. Maxwell Fry and Jane Drew, *Tropical Architecture in the Humid Zone* (New York: Reinhold, 1956).

11. Victor Olgyay and Aladar Olgyay. *Design with Climate: Bioclimatic Approach to Architectural Regionalism* (Princeton, N.J: Princeton University Press, 1963). Otto H. Koenigsberger, "New Towns in India," *The Town Planning Review* Vol. 23, No. 2 (July 1952), 94–132.

the parasol roof. Exemplified by the roof of the High Court in Chandigarh (1955), the form emphasizes the sheltering role of the roof during monsoon rains, extending outward to shade the building from the mid-day sun and curving downward to accelerate the prevailing breezes.[12] In the hands of Paul Rudolph (see his unexecuted International Bazaar building for Miami's Interama fairgrounds, 1966–67) the parasol became a highly poetic formal response to significant climatic challenges.[13]

Energy and Efficiency

Architects have been in the forefront of incorporating renewable energy in the built environment. In 1948 architect Eleanor Raymond collaborated with scientist Mária Telkes of the MIT Solar Laboratory to build the first inhabited house using active solar technologies. Built in Dover, Massachusetts, with funding from philanthropist Amelia Peabody, the house was heated entirely by a system that employed molten salts to store the sun's thermal energy. The Dover house was not Raymond's only experiment with emerging technologies; she also designed one of the first houses built primarily of plywood, a much more efficient use of wood, which was erected in 1940.[14]

Architects were also among the early adopters of photovoltaic technologies. In 1966, the Ogami Lighthouse in Japan's Nagasaki Prefecture became the first building in the world powered entirely by electricity from solar panels. This came just twelve years after Bell Laboratories developed the first practical silicon-based solar cells and five years after the pioneering United Nations Conference on New and Renewable Sources of Energy launched a worldwide conversation on the need to find ways to power the world without despoiling it. Yet while architects began employing solar panels in the 1960s, few incorporated photovoltaics as a formal component in their designs. In contrast, sun shading devices like elaborate screens and projecting trellises would continue to appear in modernist works well into the 1970s.

Renewable energy technologies were prominent in intentional communities that emerged from the countercultural movements of the 1960s. Their remote sites often lent themselves to small-scale wind power installations in addition to photovoltaics, both of which combated the increasingly visible problem of air pollution in the post-war period. Drop City, a pioneering community founded in Colorado in 1965, included a solar hot water heating system that was widely emulated. While communes represent a retreat from the modern world in some respects, they nonetheless reaffirmed the utopic aspirations of modern architecture in others.[15]

Drop City, for example, featured the use of geodesic domes, demonstrating the high esteem in which Buckminster Fuller was held outside the mainstream of architectural practice. Fuller's driving concern was efficiency, and he approached the design of the built environment from the standpoint of how to use such finite resources as materials, energy, space, and time in the most efficient way possible. His designs for Dymaxion houses and vehicles, realized only in a series of prototypes, were successful responses

12. The extensive literature on Chandigarh includes Ernst Scheidegger, Maristella Casciato, and Stanislaus von Moos. *Chandigarh 1956: Le Corbusier, Pierre Jeanneret, Jane B. Drew, E. Maxwell Fry* (Zürich: Scheidegger & Spiess, 2010).

13. Robert A. Gonzalez, "The Fair City of Interama: Flash in the Pan or Unbuilt Utopia?" *Journal of Architectural Education* Vol. 62, No. 1 (September 2008), 27–40.

14. Eleanor Raymond and Doris Cole, *Eleanor Raymond: Architectural Projects, 1919–1973* (Boston: The Institute, 1981).

15. Simon Sadler, "Drop City Revisited," *Journal of Architectural Education* Vol. 59, No. 3 (February 2006), 5-14.

to the problem of resource scarcity in an advanced industrial society. The geodesic dome is the apotheosis of his work; universal in its applicability (and thus at odds with site-specificity), the geodesic dome offered a model of sustainability through the highly efficient use of materials, adaptability to diverse programs and sites, and ease of reuse.[16]

The countercultural movements of the 1960s and 1970s largely abandoned the historical avant-gardes' belief in broad social transformation, yet they maintained that earlier generation's utopian aspirations. Paolo Soleri conceived of Arcosanti (1970–present) as a self-sustaining city (a vision that has proven difficult to attain).[17] Built largely of locally available materials in the Sonoran desert of Arizona, Arcosanti demonstrates the legacy of Wright's Usonia as transmitted through the nearby Taliesin West.

Preservation

Historic preservation is an underappreciated component of sustainability. After all, demolition and new construction usually require far more embodied energy and material resources than rehabilitating an existing structure. Modernism's cult of the new—starting with the Futurists' call to demolish all cultural institutions as part of a constant process of destruction and renewal—prized invention over conservation. As a result, the historic preservation movement that emerged after the 1963 demolition of New York's Pennsylvania Station is often seen as a repudiation of modern architecture.[18]

Yet modernism includes some excellent examples of preservation and adaptive reuse. Interestingly, many were conceived by Italian architects, such as Carlo Scarpa's Castelvecchio Museum in Verona (1959–73), the Italian firm BBPR's conversion of the Castello Sforzesco in Milan into a museum (1956), and Lina Bo Bardi's SESC Pompeia cultural center in São Paolo (1977–82). More recently, designers have tackled the large-scale redevelopment of industrial sites with a remarkable sensitivity toward preservation, resulting in such popularly and critically acclaimed projects as Latz+Partners' transformation of a steel mill into the Landschaftspark Duisburg-Nord (1990–2001), the renovation of FIAT's Lingotto factory by Renzo Piano Building Workshop (1983–2003), and the High Line in New York City by James Corner Field Operations, Diller Scofidio + Renfro, and Piet Oudolf (1999-2011). Many of these buildings and landscapes represent the kind of industrial projects that inspired the International Style, and so their preservation constitutes a poetic return to origins for modernism.

Health

A concern with human health is one of the key aspects of sustainability that played a central role in many strains of modernism. The squalid living conditions of western cities in the late nineteenth century spurred urban reform movements, like the City Beautiful, that examined how urban form could help ensure public health. Epidemics like the devastating global flu

16. Joachim Krausse, and Claude Lichtenstein, eds. *Your Private Sky: Discourse* (Baden, Switzerland: Lars Müller, 2001).

17. Paolo Soleri, *Arcosanti: An Urban Laboratory?* (San Diego, Calif.: Avant Books, 1984).

18. A good revision to this conventional view can be found in Randall Mason, *The Once and Future New York: Historic Preservation and the Modern City* (Minneapolis: University of Minnesota Press, 2009).

pandemic of 1918–19 set in sharp relief the need to rethink architecture's role in safeguarding its users' physical wellbeing. Le Corbusier argued that architecture could combat the spread of microbes with increased natural lighting and ventilation, and by employing smooth, non-porous surfaces and eliminating the dust traps of traditional ornament. Le Corbusier lifted his buildings off the ground on concrete pilotis, freeing the inhabited spaces of the ground's dampness. He proposed transforming the city into a lushly vegetated public park interspersed with buildings in order to immerse each resident in an atmosphere cleansed of pollution and contagion.

Le Corbusier's concern with salubrity was shared by many pioneering modernists, who found a receptive audience in progressive circles world-wide. Los Angeles physician Philip Lovell commissioned two houses, one by Rudolph Schindler (1921–22) and the other by Richard Neutra (1927–28), which featured ample day lighting and ventilation, along with a variety of outdoor spaces where Lovell and his family could exercise and sleep.[19] Both residences confirmed their designer's belief that architecture could sustain human health. The basic principles of increasing residents' access to sunlight and fresh air, while minimizing the use of materials and forms that might harbor microbes and pollutants, would underpin the design of new housing throughout the twentieth century.

Urbanism

The story of urban planning and regional development is central to the history of modern architecture, and includes some of the strongest successes and greatest failures from the vantage of sustainability. Urban reform efforts, ranging from the utopian socialism of Charles Fourrier to the City Beautiful movement to the participatory planning of the 1960s, sought to improve the lives of city-dwellers by transforming or replacing the fabric of the urban environment. Many of these efforts produced communities that exemplify sustainable principles like walkability, proximity to services, and access to green space. Others, however, such as the low-density sprawl of postwar suburbanization, have produced some of the greatest challenges to a sustainable future.

The Garden City movement sought to create a balance between the cultural richness available to residents of densely populated cities and the restorative potential of access to parks and the open countryside. The principles laid out by the movement's founder, Ebenezer Howard, were widely implemented and often synthesized with other urban reform movements.[20] Garden cities use smaller lots, carefully designed streets, and effective zoning to enhance walkability, which reduces residents' dependence on vehicular transportation and increases the personal interactions that foster a sense of community. Often connected to a nearby metropolis by public transit, garden cities offer a sound model for urban planning.

Yet modernism is often associated—and rightly so—with unsustainable urban planning and regional development, especially in the United States where postwar modernity coincided with suburbanization and the

19. See the chapters on Schindler and Neutra in Thomas S. Hines, *Architecture of the Sun: Los Angeles Modernism, 1900–1970* (New York: Rizzoli, 2010).

20. Ebenezer Howard, *Garden Cities of To-Morrow: (being the Second Edition of "To-Morrow: a Peaceful Path to Real Reform")* (London: G. Allen, 1902).

broad adoption of privately owned automobiles as the primary mode of transportation. The sprawling suburbs of the Americas, Australia, South Africa, and, increasingly, of newly developed nations around the world, comprise one of the built environment's greatest threats to the planet's ecological and social stability. Ground transportation in suburban settlements produces inordinate levels of greenhouse gas emissions, landscapes are indiscriminately altered, wildlife habitats are displaced by paving and lawns, and the social alienation that accompanies such dispersed areas erodes any sense of community.

Suburbia's principle problems include the separation of residential neighborhoods from the civic, cultural, and commercial functions that bring vitality to communities, and the devolution of the city street from a place of civic discourse to a conduit for vehicular traffic. Recognized now for their deleterious effects on the environment and the body politic, both of these conditions were advocated as progressive solutions to the perceived congestion and insalubrity of traditional cities by the architects and planners of the *Congrès Internationaux d'Architecture Moderne* (CIAM).[21] The Athens Charter, published by CIAM after their 1933 meeting, called for the reorganization of modern cities according to four functions, three of which—housing, work, and recreation—would be segregated into separate districts linked by the fourth, circulation.

The radical transformation of the city proposed by CIAM emerged from an earnest concern with improving the lives of its residents. Rationalized traffic networks were intended to bring greater efficiency to the metropolis and thus make high quality housing and services more broadly accessible. Zoning practices like setting structures back from the street fostered improved public health by bringing more light and fresh air into buildings. The consequent open spaces were to be filled with gardens and parks, turning the ground plane into a vast carpet of greenery punctuated by buildings.

Yet the physical separation advocated by CIAM enabled segregation on the basis of race and class, exacerbating tendencies fueled by changing social conditions in the second half of the twentieth century. Whereas the bourgeois metropolis of the nineteenth and early twentieth centuries filled the space between work and home with collective places of assembly and discourse, the postwar suburb offered only residential districts and office parks stripped of their vital social and commercial functions. New spatial relationships reflected altered social relationships, and rarely in a good way. This transformation was particularly visible in the series of bedroom communities named Levittown, which successfully harnessed modern logistics and finance in the service of regional development, with the full range of consequences both ecological and sociological.[22]

Yet not all twentieth-century urban planning stripped the city of its social functions. The Garden City movement's concern for balancing cultural richness with access to wholesome greenery influenced the *siedlungen* designed by Ernst May in Frankfurt.[23] Interwar planning efforts in the United States included projects like the Regional Planning Association's design of Radburn, New Jersey, as well as a series of greenbelt

21. Eric Mumford, *The CIAM Discourse on Urbanism, 1928–1960* (Cambridge: MIT Press, 2000).

22. Joan Ockman, "Mirror Images: Technology, Consumption, and the Representation of Gender in American Architecture since World War II," in Diana Agrest, Patricia Conway, and Leslie Weisman, *The Sex of Architecture* (New York: Harry N. Abrams, 1996), 191–210.

23. Susan R. Henderson, *Building Culture: Ernst May and the New Frankfurt Initiative, 1926–1931* (New York: Peter Lang, 2013).

towns and homestead developments (like Roosevelt, New Jersey) that infused the city with the full range of spaces intended to foster cultural and social connections.

Conclusion

How would an ecological history of modern architecture conclude? There is no shortage of excellent criticism and theoretical writings about sustainability in the built environment. As a discipline, architecture, particularly in the last twenty years, has played a leading role in making ecological stewardship a part of public discourse. The benchmarking programs of the United States, Canada, and the European Union are all examples of this bellwether stance. The principles elaborated by William McDonough and Michael Braungart in their pioneering book *Cradle to Cradle* provide a blueprint for the design disciplines going forward.[24] From the vantage of professional organizations, industry leaders, and academia, sustainability would seem to have emerged triumphant in its ubiquitous presence in architectural discourse.

This is true in practice too, where ecological and social sustainability are foreground concerns for the profession. A broad range of award-winning projects around the world, from the community-built schools of Diébédo Francis Kéré to the vegetated skyscrapers of Ken Yeang, speaks to the central importance of ecological balance, environmental stewardship, and social engagement in contemporary architecture.[25] These concerns are not limited to architecture, either. Throughout the design disciplines, including urbanism, landscape architecture, and interior design, sustainability has emerged as a compelling set of interests with a profound impact on the built environment.

Yet one theme that emerges from this outline of sustainability in modern architecture is that of unintended consequences. The ecological benefits of an energy-efficient building evaporate if the structure is only accessible by private automobile. Climate-responsive buildings may serve clear social goals, but those benefits are diminished if they fail to repair the surrounding urban fabric. We need to recognize the complexity of every project and to balance our criticism by acknowledging that buildings are rarely either completely sustainable or unsustainable and that every work can be measured in degrees of sustainability.

One benefit of an environmental history of modern architecture is that it challenges the hagiographic canon of modernism's "master builders" by examining in depth the development of regional schools, like that of William Wurster and Joseph Esherick, giving due consideration to marginalized pioneers, like Eleanor Raymond, and placing greater emphasis on the ecological concerns of neglected innovators ranging from Paul Rudolph to Ralph Erskine.[26] Such a history would give due recognition to important innovators of key technologies, such as the Living Machines system developed by Tom Worrell. Such a history would dispel the narrative of modernism as a relentless attempt to dominate nature.

24. William McDonough and Michael Braungart. *Cradle to Cradle: Remaking the Way We Make Things* (New York: North Point Press, 2002).

25. On Yeang, see Ken Yeang, *Designing with Nature* (New York: McGraw-Hill, 1995). On Kéré, see Andres Lepik, *Small Scale, Big Change: New Architectures of Social Engagement* (New York: Museum of Modern Art, 2010).

26. On Wurster, see Marc Treib and David Gebhard, *An Everyday Modernism: The Houses of William Wurster* (San Francisco: San Francisco Museum of Modern Art, 1995).

Modern architecture was never the monolithic entity characterized by its critics. In all fields of cultural production, modernism is better described by Octavio Paz's phrase, "a tradition against itself."[27] The diversity generated by this ongoing process of self-criticism and re-invention has left us a legacy that requires careful dissection and evaluation. By cutting against the grain of existing studies of modernism, this environmental history recovers a neglected current of environmental sensibility coursing through modern architecture.

27. Octavio Paz, *Children of the Mire: Modern Poetry from Romanticism to the Avant-Garde* (Cambridge, Mass: Harvard University Press, 1974.)

Climate Map with Projects

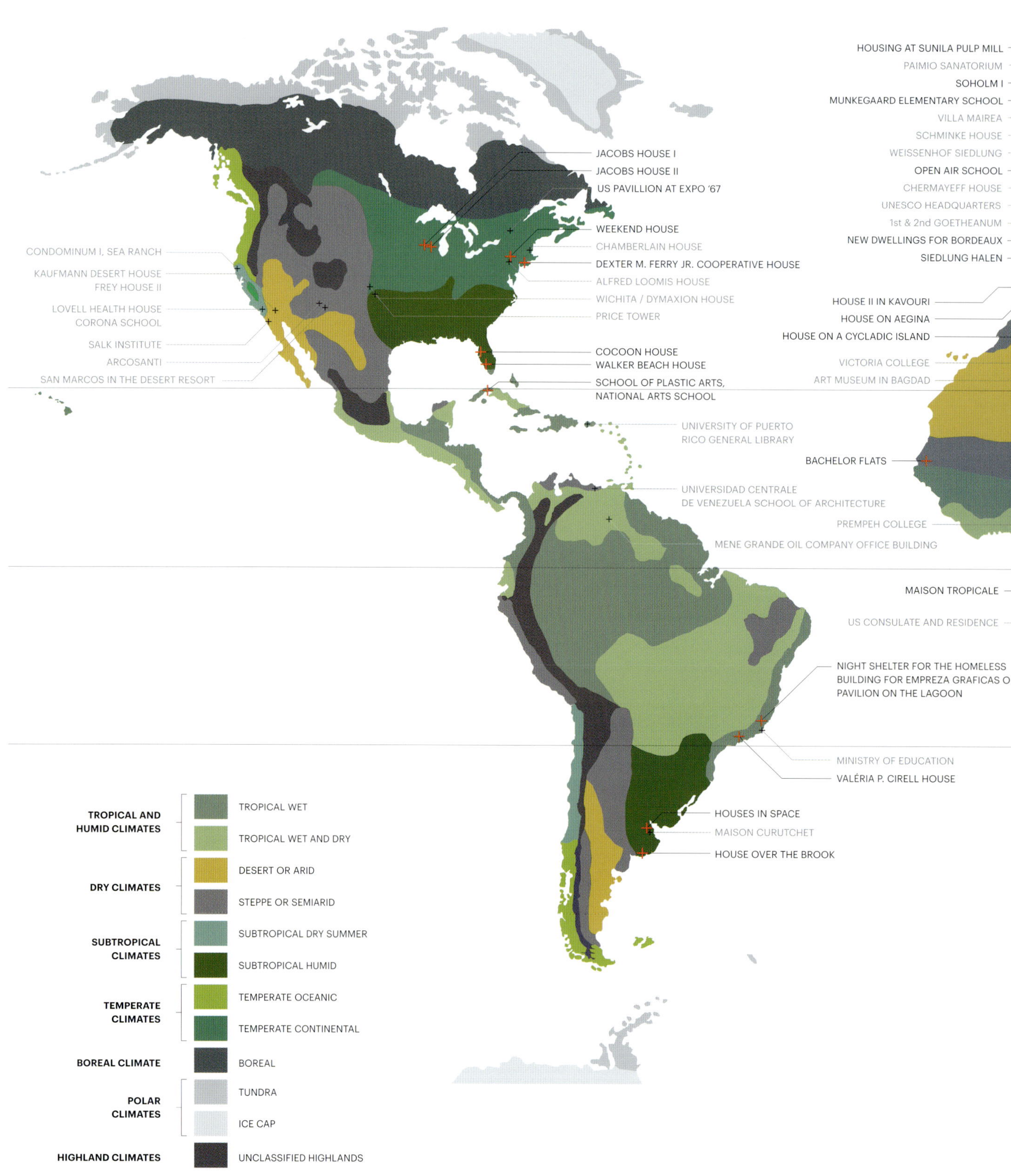

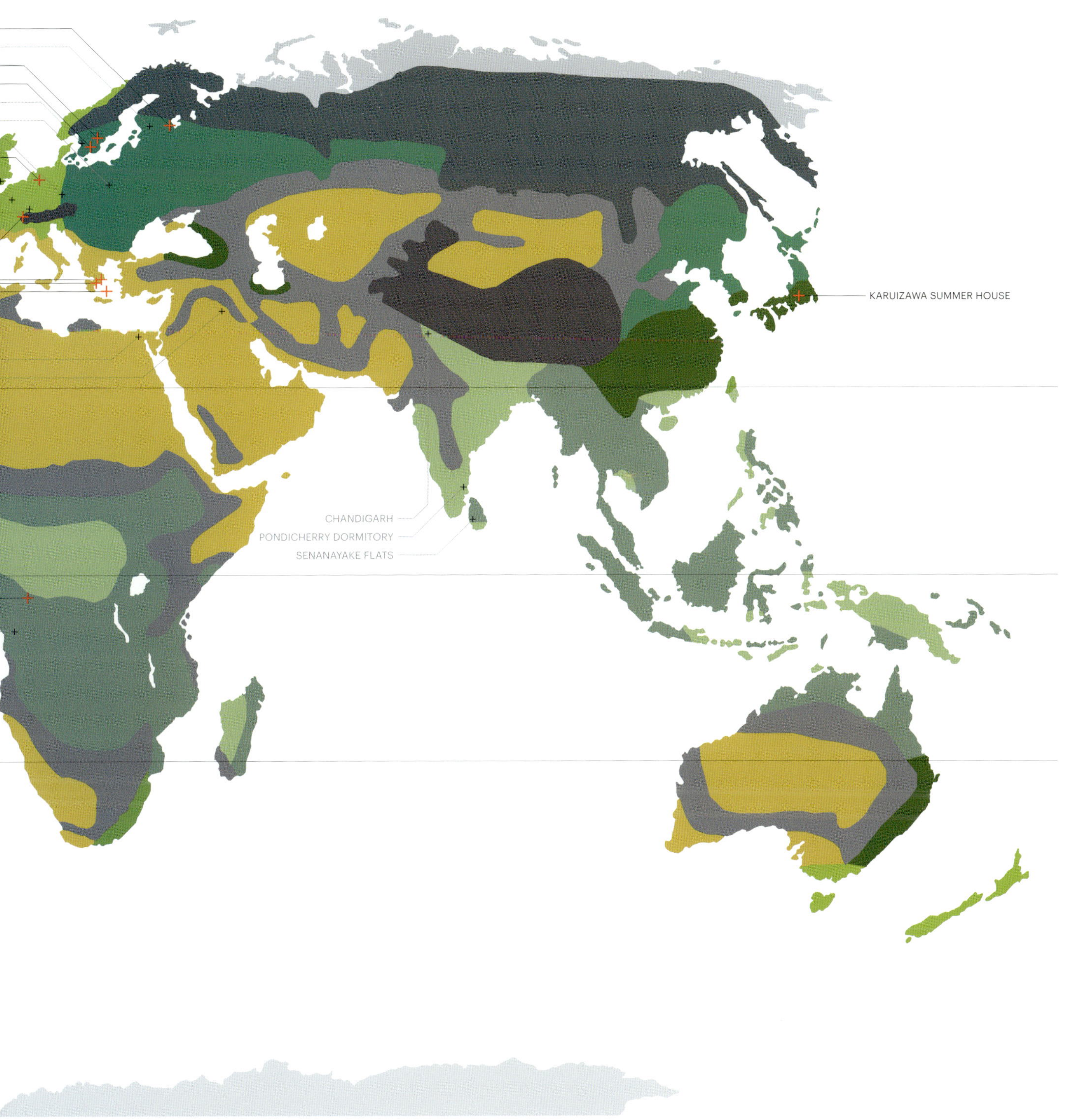

KARUIZAWA SUMMER HOUSE
CHANDIGARH
PONDICHERRY DORMITORY
SENANAYAKE FLATS

New Dwellings for Bordeaux
Le Corbusier + Pierre Jeanneret

YEAR
1925

LOCATION
Bordeaux, France
(not built)
44°49'N 0°35'W

CLIMATE ZONE
Temperate Oceanic

PROGRAM
Multifamily Housing

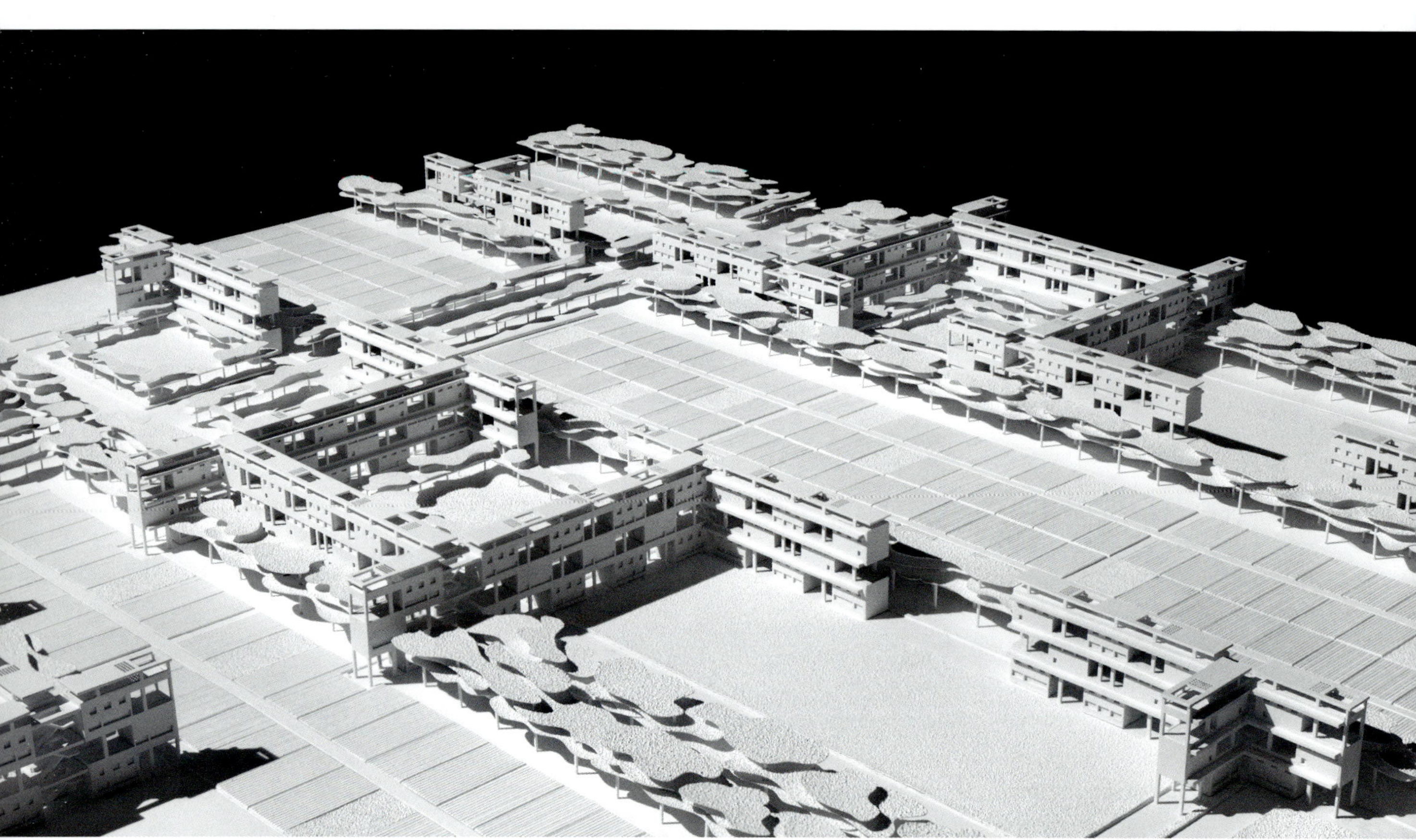

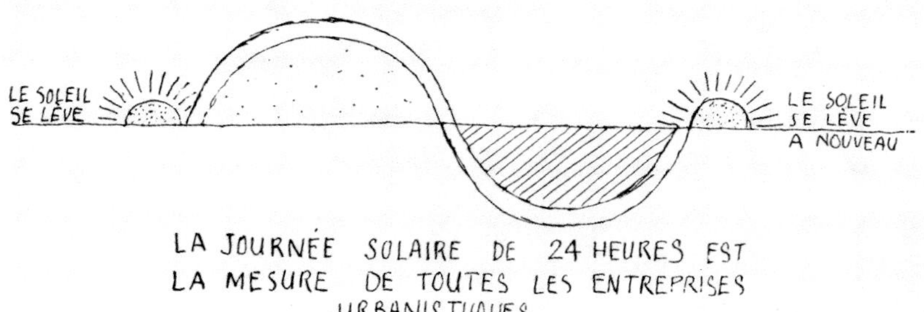

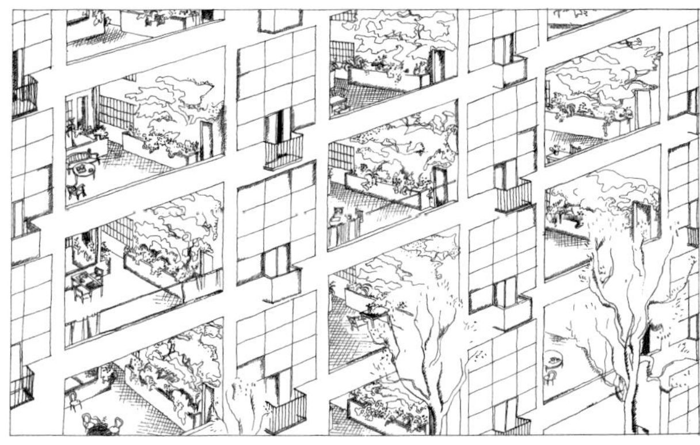

The New Dwellings for Bordeaux are part of a mass-produced building typology that Le Corbusier termed the "Freehold Maisonettes." In this unbuilt project, prefabrication was advocated for its potential cost savings, improved quality of construction, and for the speed at which it could be assembled. The maisonettes are modest in size but generous in architectural amenities. Each unit consists of two floors, a double-height space, and a terrace garden, a feature Le Corbusier called the "hanging gardens." The parti takes the prototype of the stacked dwelling unit and uses it in a low-rise, multifamily housing community integrated into an agrarian master plan. This agricultural component is a useful model for today's urban agrarianism movement. Rather than imagining a garden community with individual lawns and flowerbeds, Le Corbusier proposed large common areas devoted to agricultural use. The landscaped settings include not only row crops in the central farm areas but also precincts designated for orchards, outdoor recreation fields, and ball courts. The variety of outdoor spatial conditions includes not only the productive agricultural fields, but also smaller scale courts that give a communal dimension to the

expansive master plan. There are few specifics about the size and location of this proposed work in Corbusier's text, but there is the suggestion from the site plan and perspective rendering that the project is imagined as having no specific limits, as the images show no edges to the complex. Instead, the buildings are depicted as passing off the edge of the drawings, indicating the possibility that the repetitive architectural pattern could be expanded across the flat gridded landscape.

In addition to the integration of this productive agricultural landscape into a housing project, the maisonettes themselves incorporate several noteworthy design features. The "honeycomb" building block, in which volumes and voids alternate in a vertical checker-board configuration, provides every apartment with a planted terrace for outdoor family living. These gardens have direct light from two sides of the building, creating a more appropriate growing environment than a small, isolated terrace. The honeycomb pattern allows for increased natural ventilation and increased daylight in the units, as all sides of each dwelling are part of the exterior envelope. Le Corbusier's drawings for the hanging gardens of the Freehold Maisonettes show

PRIMARY SOLAR PATHS AND CORRESPONDING SECTIONS

Bordeaux, France

44° North Latitude

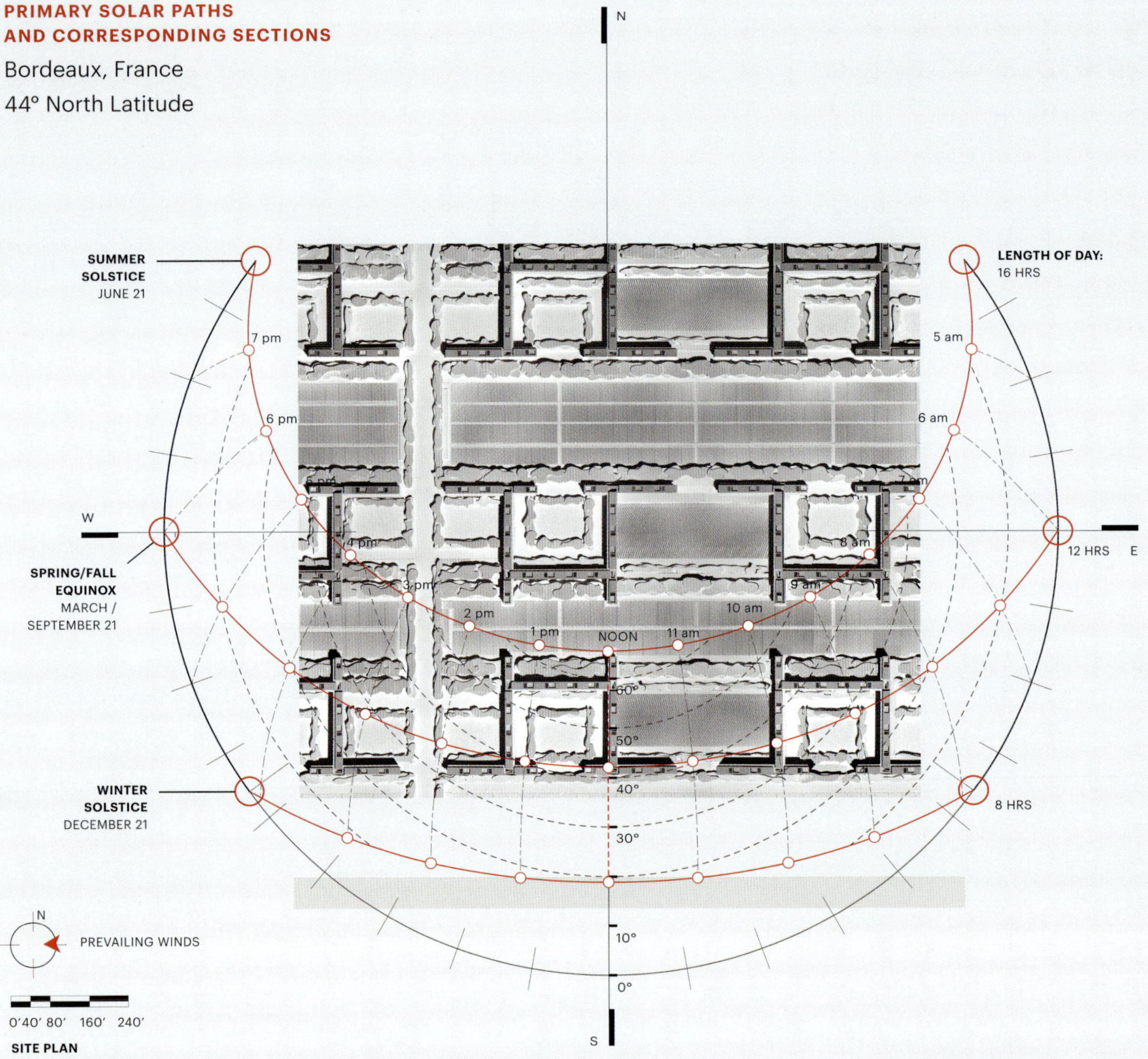

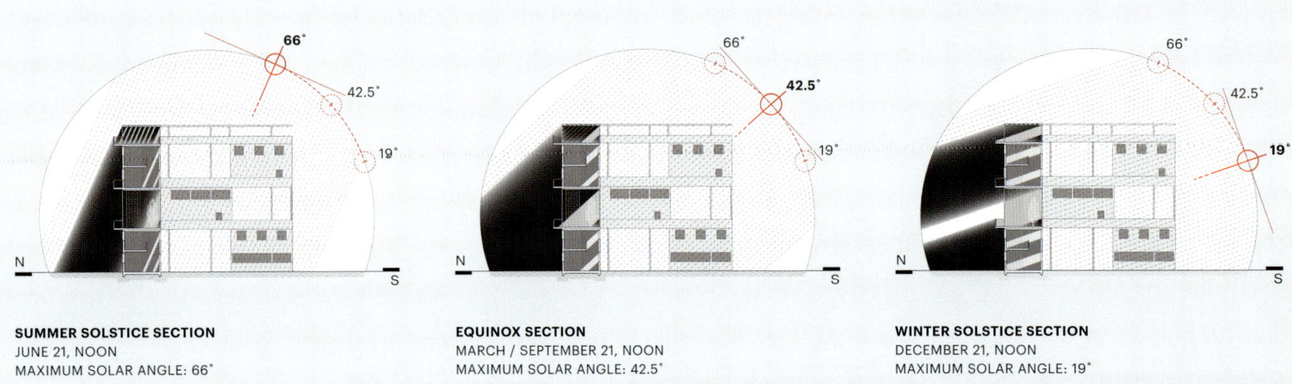

SUMMER SOLSTICE SECTION
JUNE 21, NOON
MAXIMUM SOLAR ANGLE: 66°

EQUINOX SECTION
MARCH / SEPTEMBER 21, NOON
MAXIMUM SOLAR ANGLE: 42.5°

WINTER SOLSTICE SECTION
DECEMBER 21, NOON
MAXIMUM SOLAR ANGLE: 19°

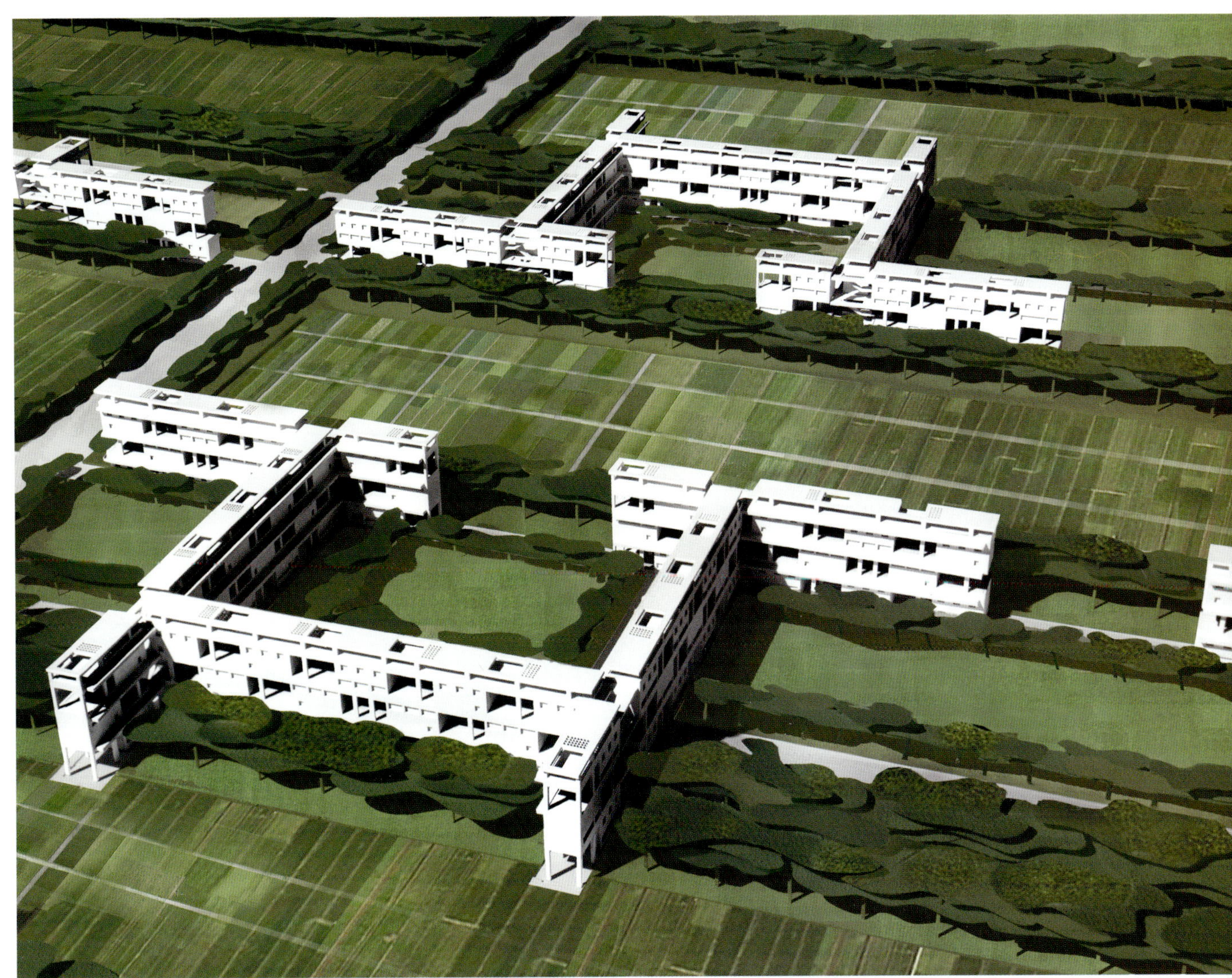

recessed windows in the terrace areas, a detail that would shelter the large expanses of glass from direct sun. The roofs of the buildings were designed as outdoor terraces shaded by elevated sunshades (brise-soleil) and pergolas. This shading not only makes the roof usable for residents, but also reduces the heat gain to the building. Circulation to all of the dwellings is from the exterior via open walkways and stairs. These open circulation elements support the ideal of natural ventilation and natural light on all sides of the units, eliminating enclosed corridors.[1]

1. Le Corbusier, *Towards a New Architecture* (Mineola, NY: Dover, 1986), 246–53.

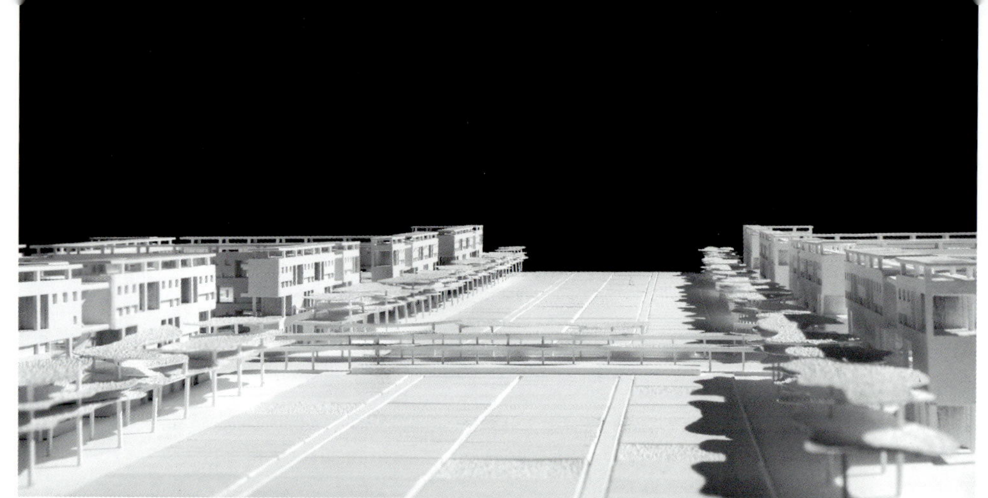

Open-Air School
Johannes Duiker

YEAR
1930

LOCATION
Amsterdam, Netherlands
52°20′52″N 4°52′27″E

CLIMATE ZONE
Temperate Oceanic

PROGRAM
Elementary School

Dutch architect Johannes Duiker was a leading figure among a group of modern architects who worked to address better hygiene and healthier living at a time when Europe was ravaged by tuberculosis and other diseases. His design for the open-air school demonstrates the ways sunlight and exposure to the outdoors can act as major components of a healthier life. Duiker's approach was very clear: "There are ordinary schools which breed the patients and open air schools in parks which attempt to heal them . . . Our approach to life in the fresh air will be on a higher plane. Modern techniques permit the restriction of material to a minimum and make it possible for us to warm such spaces, which are almost entirely open, without any difficulty, so that children need only be lightly clad to spend their time here!"[1]

The school was originally sited in a park setting, but lack of funding forced the municipality to locate it within the courtyard of a housing block. Primarily square in plan, the building is positioned 45 degrees off due north to take advantage of the maximum solar gain during the winter months. The ground level consists of the main entry, gymnasium, an administrative office, and one classroom. The plans for the upper floors are broken into quadrants, with one classroom located to the east and west, and a shared, semi-enclosed outdoor class-room facing south. The north quadrant is an open void, allowing light and air into the interior. The south-facing covered terraces can be used as outdoor classrooms during warmer months. To maximize their usage, Duiker installed radiant heating on all of the terraces.[2]

The structure is comprised of thin, flat concrete slabs with tapering beams and columns just within the perimeter of the building. The columns, located at the mid-point of each structural bay, allow the corners of the school to be fully open, thereby increasing natural light. The exterior walls are almost entirely of operable glazing, which allows ample amounts of sunlight and cross ventilation. Metal window framing is used minimally and detailed in such a manner that the steel sections are turned inward. This, in combination with the extensive use of glazing on the facade, creates a sense of lightness and transparency. Duiker also designed an entrance building for the enclosed courtyard of the housing block, which contains two apartments, a bicycle shed, and a workroom.

1. Johannes Duiker, *B. Bijvoet und J. Duiker 1890–1935* (Zurich: Organisationsstelle für Ausstellungen des Institutes GTA an der ETHZ, 1975), 85.

2. Robert Vickery, "Bijvoet and Duiker," *Perspecta: The Yale Architectural Journal* 13/14, (1971): 155.

PRIMARY SOLAR PATHS AND CORRESPONDING SECTIONS

Amsterdam, Netherlands
52° North Latitude

SITE PLAN

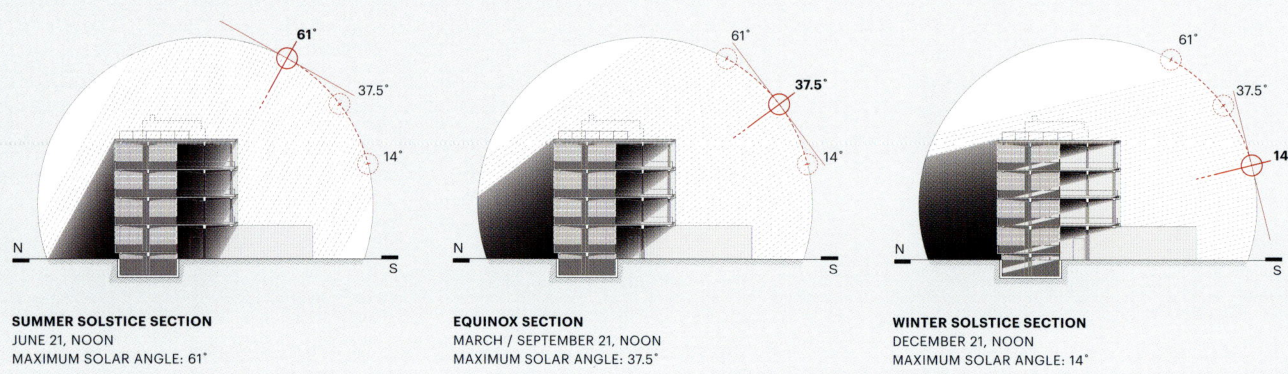

SUMMER SOLSTICE SECTION
JUNE 21, NOON
MAXIMUM SOLAR ANGLE: 61°

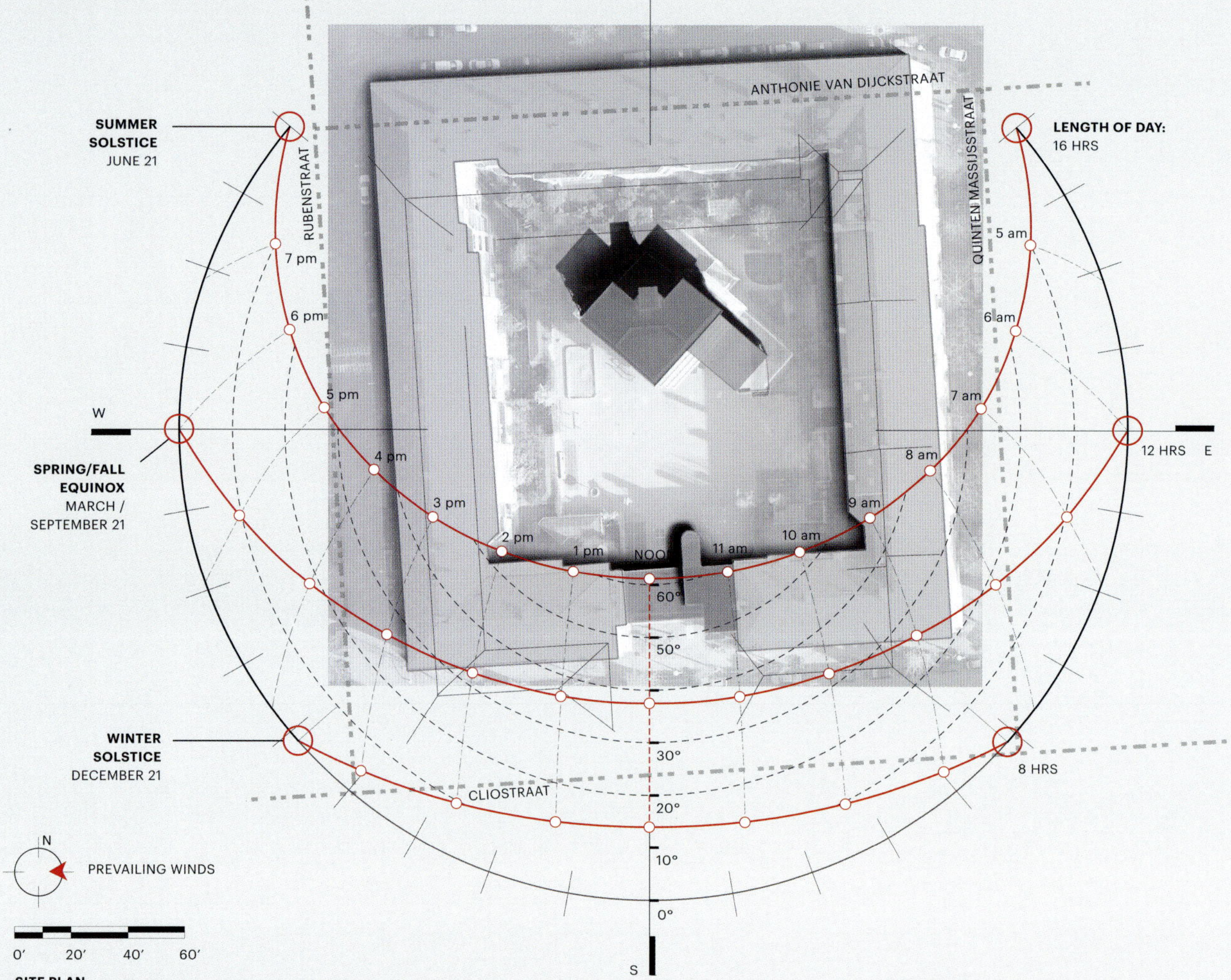

EQUINOX SECTION
MARCH / SEPTEMBER 21, NOON
MAXIMUM SOLAR ANGLE: 37.5°

WINTER SOLSTICE SECTION
DECEMBER 21, NOON
MAXIMUM SOLAR ANGLE: 14°

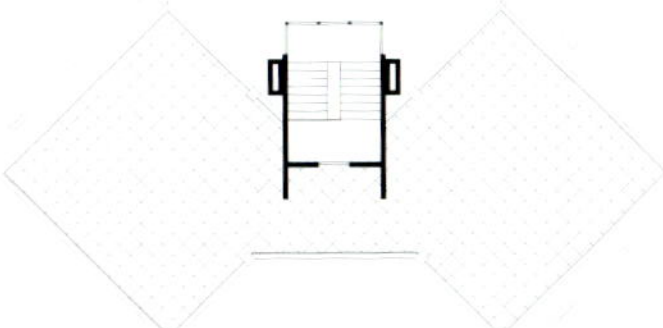

ROOF LEVEL

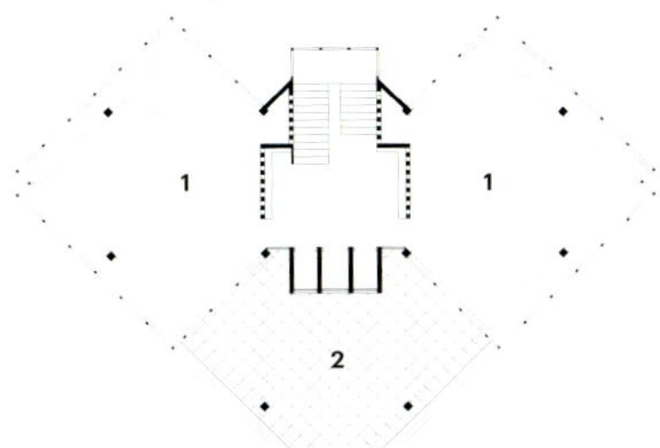

LEVELS 2–5

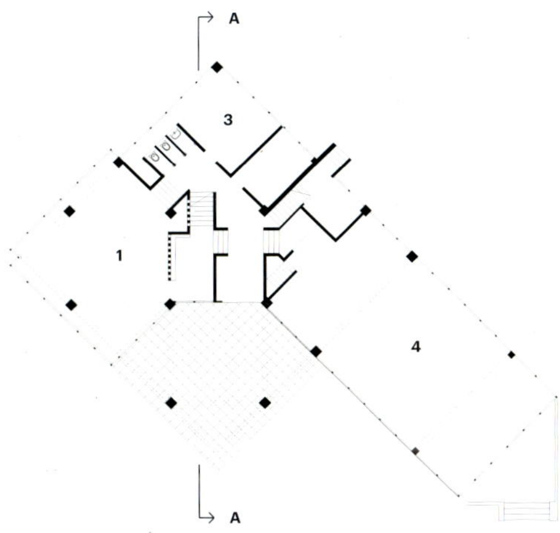

GROUND LEVEL

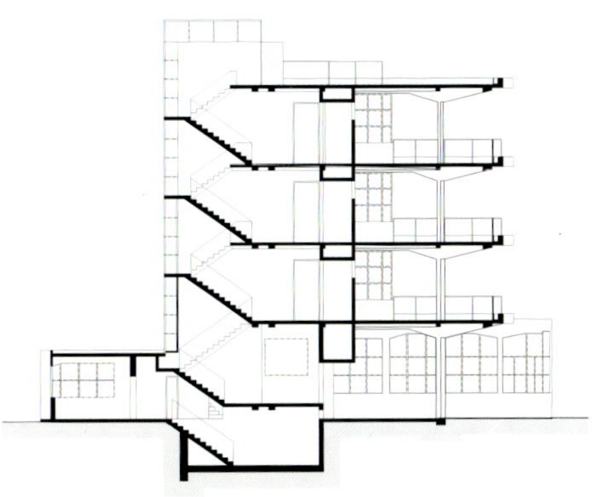

SECTION A – A

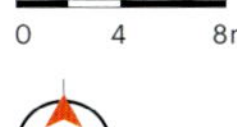

1 Classroom
2 Open-air classroom
3 Administrative office
4 Gymnasium

Night Shelter for The Homeless
Affonso Eduardo Reidy + Gerson Pompeu Pinheiro

YEAR
1931

LOCATION
Rio De Janeiro, Brazil
22°53′41″S 43°11′27″W

CLIMATE ZONE
Tropical Savannah

PROGRAM
Homeless Shelter

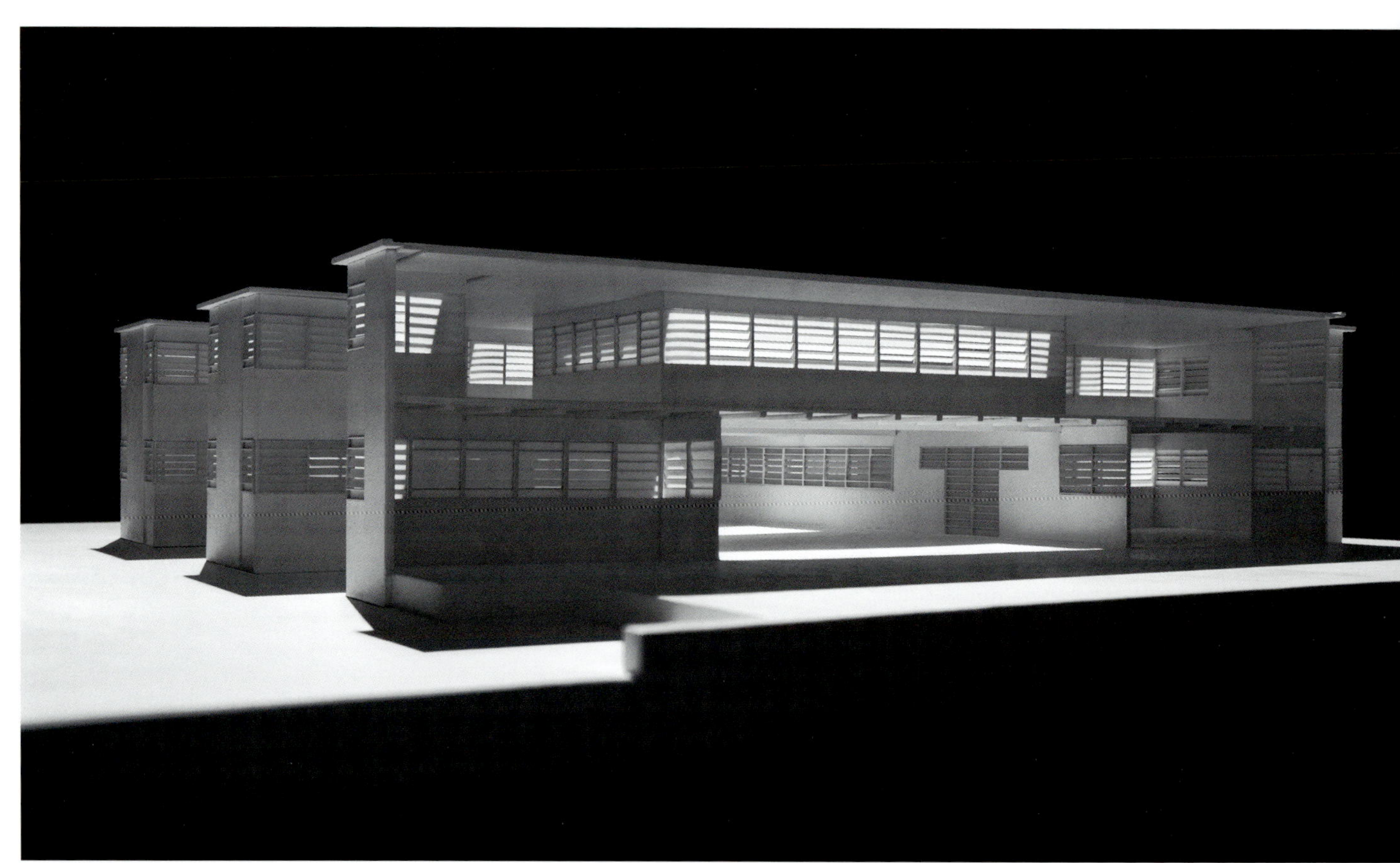

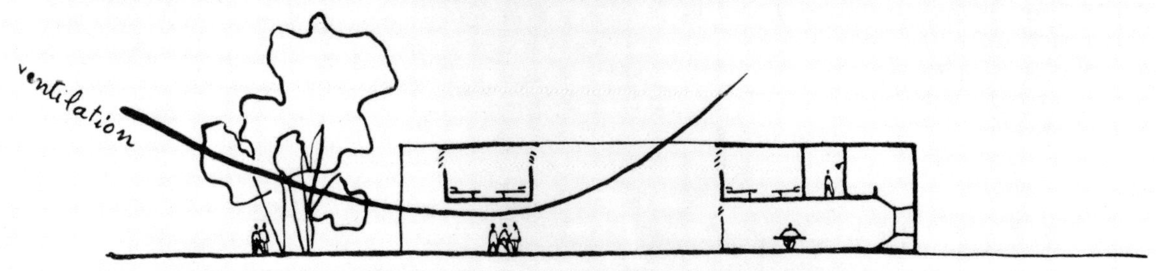

The night shelter for the homeless (Albergue da Boa Vontade), designed by Affonso Eduardo Reidy and Gerson Pompeu Pinheiro, marks the beginning of a new direction in architecture in Rio de Janeiro through its elemental geometric form, operable facade system, utilization of a concrete flat slab construction, and open, central plan.

The building is simple, yet formally powerful, consisting of twin bridges suspended over an outdoor court. The elevated dormitories span a core patio area, creating a shaded communal space. The building has no recognizable window openings. Continuous horizontal bands of operable glass louvers at both levels allow for maximum natural ventilation and softly filtered natural light to the interior spaces. The system of louvers, establishing a generous connection of interior to exterior, provides the ample flow of light and air that the architects considered essential to promoting health and hygiene. Even the iconic T-shaped entry door is an invention that provided not only a place of passage into the building, but its all-glass construction illuminated the lobby space within.

The emphasis on airflow, shaded urban space, and regulated interior sunlight offers a low technology solution to the issue of comfort in the tropical climate of Rio de Janeiro. The floating dormitories, in addition to creating a shaded outdoor microclimate, define a large space that acts as a discrete zone where the homeless can convene with some decorum in this heavily populated urban environment.[1]

The project, which was unanimously selected by the jury of a national competition, provides dignified shelter for the needy while also acting as "a natural school of hygiene," encouraging free movement of the occupants between the outside urban environment and the enclosed interior courtyard.

1. Klaus Franck, "Hostel for Homeless Persons, Rio de Janeiro–1931.32," *Affonso Eduardo Reidy–Bauten und Projekte* (Stuttgart: Verlag Gerd Hatje, 1960), 12.

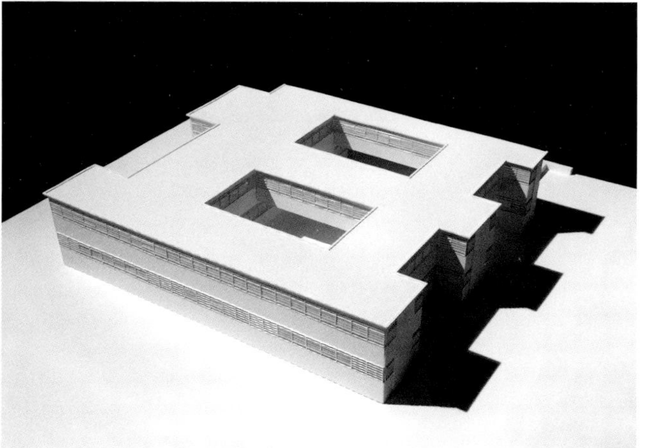

1 Courtyard ventilation
2 Exterior shading blind
3 Cross ventilation
4 Stack effect
5 Solar reflective roof structure

PRIMARY SOLAR PATHS AND CORRESPONDING SECTIONS

Rio De Janeiro, Brazil
22° South Latitude

SITE PLAN

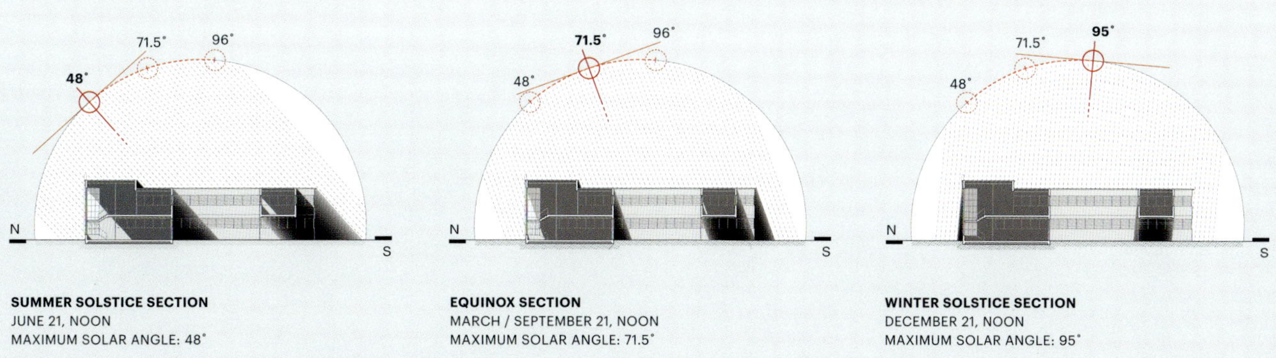

SUMMER SOLSTICE SECTION
JUNE 21, NOON
MAXIMUM SOLAR ANGLE: 48°

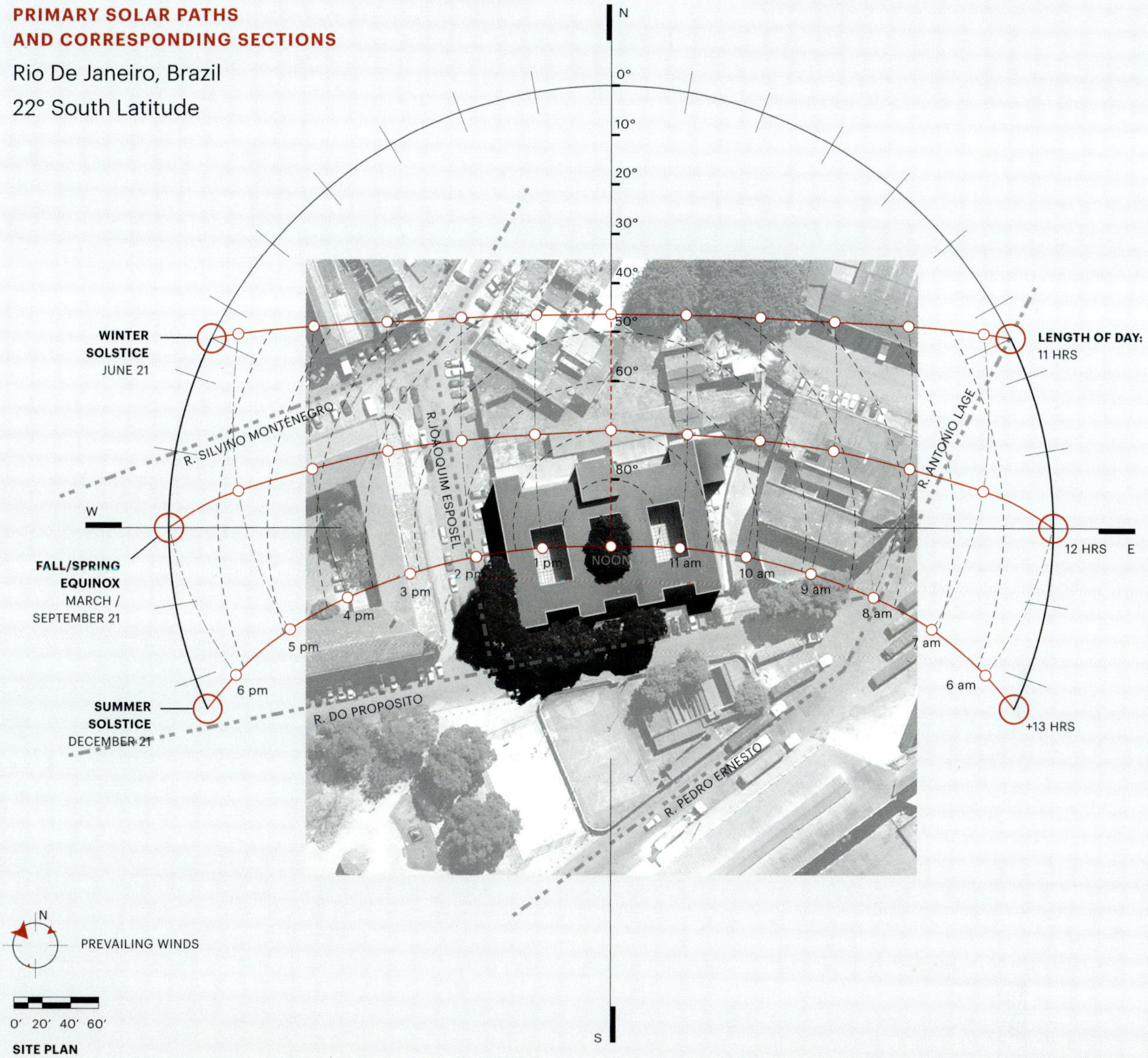

EQUINOX SECTION
MARCH / SEPTEMBER 21, NOON
MAXIMUM SOLAR ANGLE: 71.5°

WINTER SOLSTICE SECTION
DECEMBER 21, NOON
MAXIMUM SOLAR ANGLE: 95°

Karuizawa Summer House
Antonin Raymond

YEAR
1933

LOCATION
Karuizawa, Nagano
Prefecture, Japan
36°19′44″N 138°35′40″E

CLIMATE ZONE
Humid Subtropical

PROGRAM
Summer Residence

The summer house is sited on a plateau in a mountainous region one hundred miles northwest of Tokyo, an area popular with first-generation urbanites seeking to return to the countryside after the Great Kanto Earthquake of 1923.[1] The east to west plan takes full advantage of the solar exposure and surrounding views. As Antonin Raymond noted, "The winters being sunny, the sun's rays are used for heating the house, making it advisable to have large southern openings. On the north and west sides, however, openings are reserved for summer cross ventilation and lighting only."[2]

Raymond installed his patented sliding door system on the east and south facades. This technique described as *shin hazushi,* uses tracks for sliding doors and windows that are independent from structural members. The doors and windows can retract completely out of view into an adjacent recess, removing the barrier between interior and exterior. Bedrooms in the eastern wing facing the rising sun are enclosed with this system. The kitchen and corridor connect the bedrooms to the main wing, which is adjacent to a central dipping pool. The pool supports evaporative cooling, as the natural airflow rises through the house, pulling the water-cooled air inward. The water, flowing from a well on the north side of the house, supplies the kitchen, bathroom, and pool, which is allowed to overflow when filled. The spilling water drains downward across the yard, into the pond on the southern side of the site. The main living space, with a view of Mount Asama to the west, opens to the south using the *shin hazushi* technique.[3] In his own description of the house, Raymond remarked, "I shall never forget that first meal; the scent of the new wood; the immaculate table of freshly planed *hinoki*; and the grays and reds of the simple glazed ware upon it. The sliding doors had slid away, and the whole plain and distant mountains, ridge behind ridge, lay before us as part of the space we were in."[4]

The house is a traditional post-and-beam structure employing local materials and Japanese joinery. The aggregate for the concrete retaining walls is locally excavated lava stone. Thatch covers a standard galvanized metal roof to reduce noise during heavy rain and heat gain during the summer months. The house is elevated on posts to allow air circulation below. Reed blinds and thatch overhangs provide another means of environmental control.

Raymond modeled the house in part after Le Corbusier's unbuilt design for Maison de M. Errazuriz in Chile (1930), employing a butterfly roof and internal ramp, with the two architectural elements aligning at the hinge point, as in Corbusier's iconic cross section for the Chilean project. Raymond demonstrates how local strategies of construction and materiality can be used to adapt modernist architectural concepts to various locations and climates.

1. Kawazoe Noboru in *Edo/Tokyo Encyclopedia*, Shinzo Ogi, ed. (Tokyo: Sanseido, 1987), 124, as cited in Ken Tadashi Oshima, *Constructed Natures of Modern Architecture in Japan 1920–1940*, Ph.D. diss., Columbia University Graduate School of Arts and Sciences, 2003, 206 (UMI number 3104839).

2. Antonin Raymond, *Antonin Raymond, His Work in Japan 1920–1935* (Tokyo: Jônan Shoin, 1936), 76.

3. Ken Tadashi Oshima, "Designing from the Hearth: The Architecture of Antonin Raymond," *The Japan Architect* 33, (1999): 7.

4. Antonin Raymond, "Toward a True Modernism," *New Pencil Points* 23, (1942), 78, cited in Oshima, *Constructed Natures*, 9.

PRIMARY SOLAR PATHS AND CORRESPONDING SECTIONS

Karuizawa, Nagano Prefecture, Japan
36° North Latitude

SITE PLAN

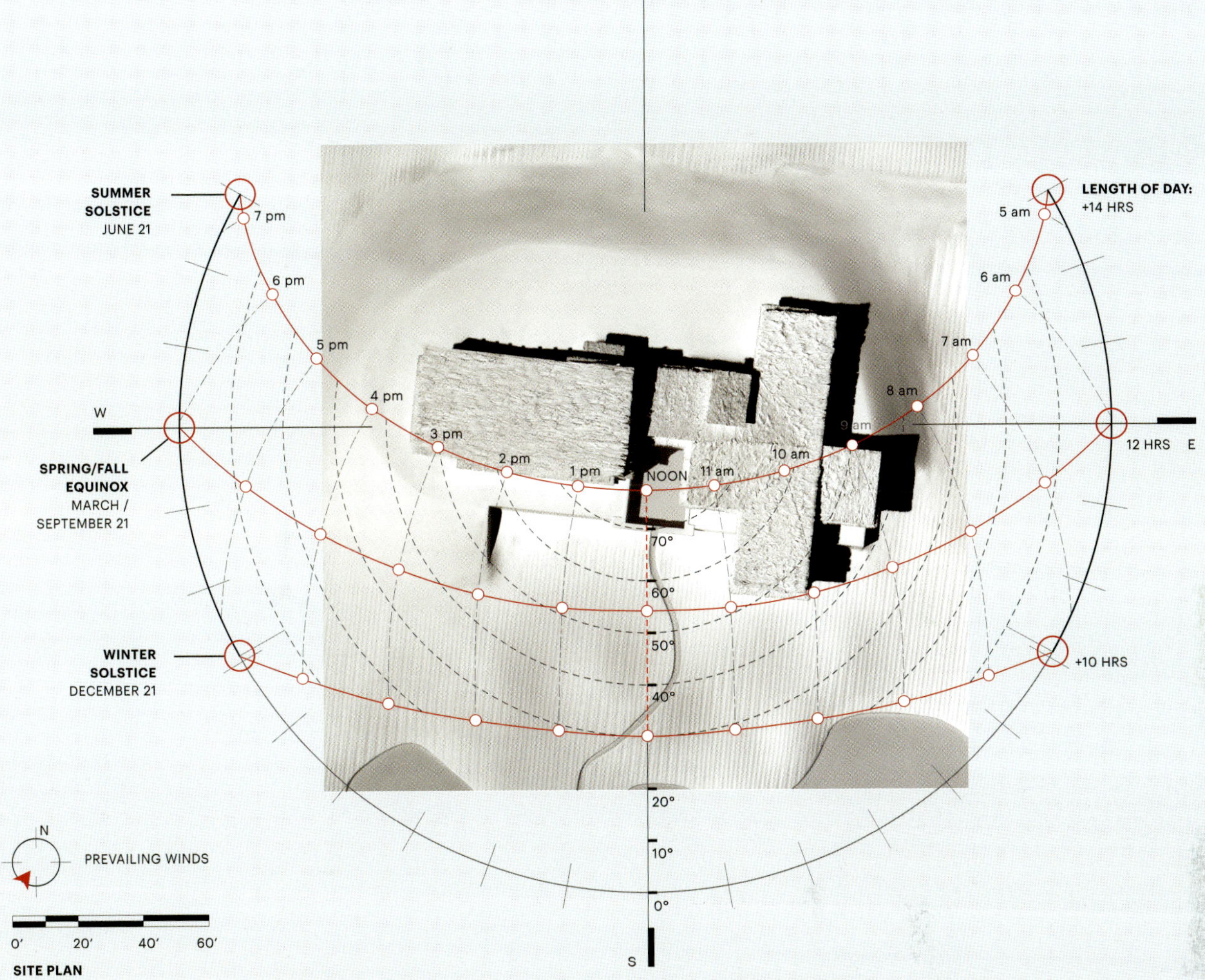

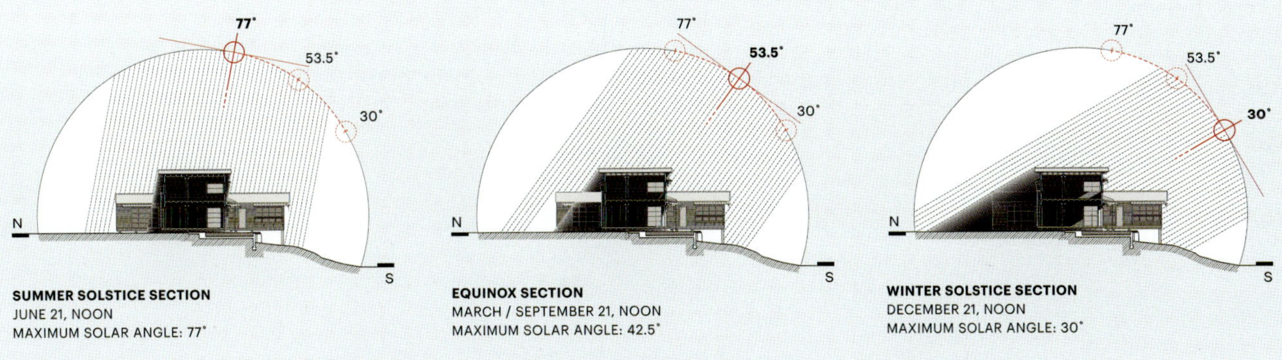

SUMMER SOLSTICE SECTION
JUNE 21, NOON
MAXIMUM SOLAR ANGLE: 77°

EQUINOX SECTION
MARCH / SEPTEMBER 21, NOON
MAXIMUM SOLAR ANGLE: 42.5°

WINTER SOLSTICE SECTION
DECEMBER 21, NOON
MAXIMUM SOLAR ANGLE: 30°

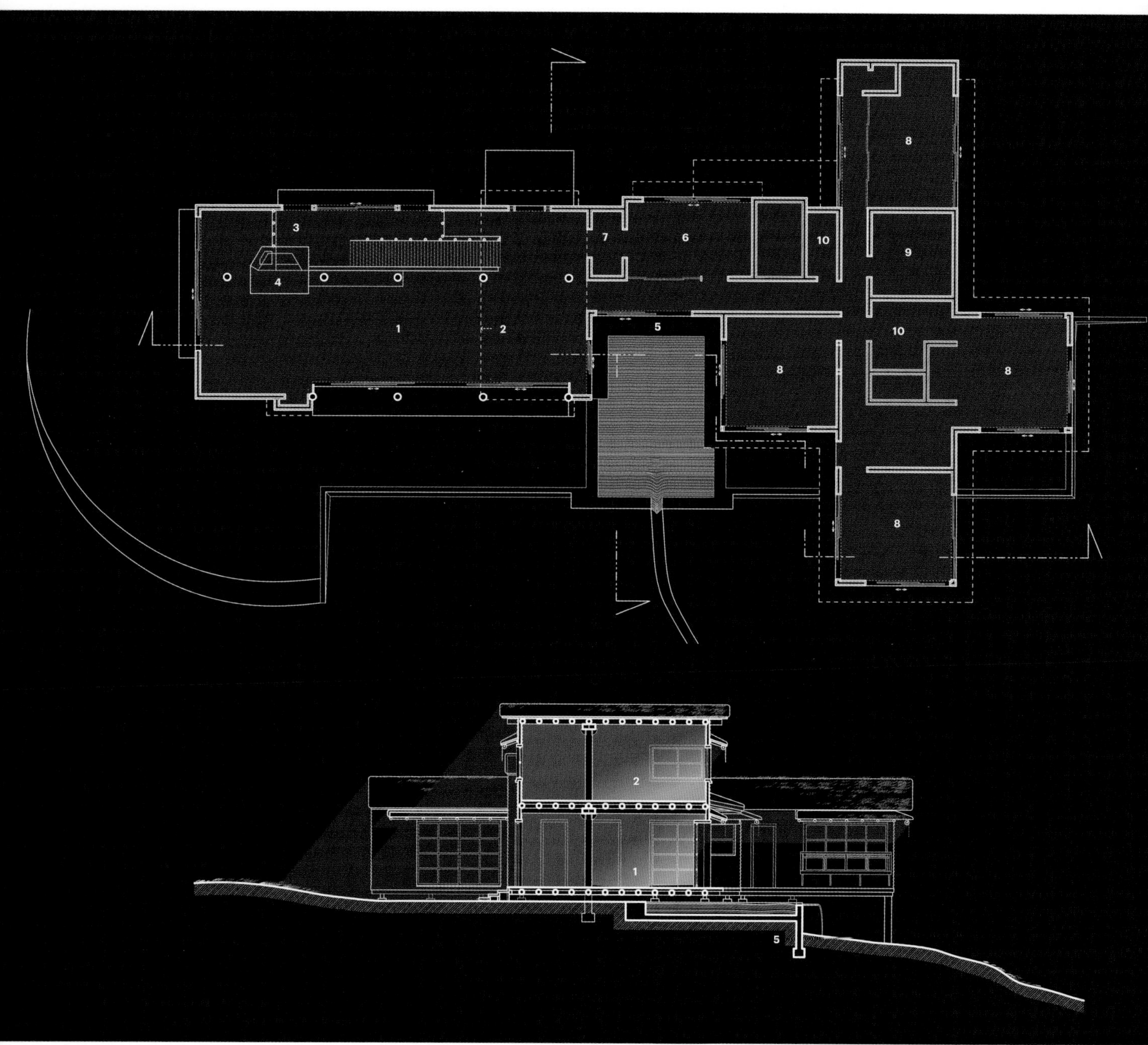

1 *Living room*
2 *Mezzanine above*
3 *Ramp*
4 *Fireplace*
5 *Pool*

6 *Kitchen*
7 *Pantry*
8 *Bedroom*
9 *Bathroom*
10 *Storage*

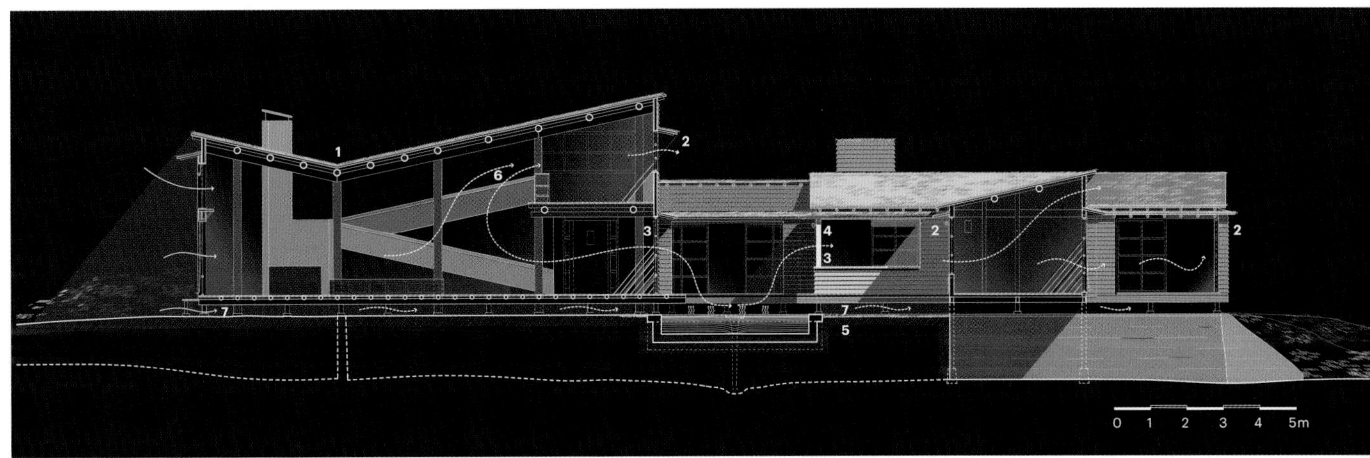

1 Thermal absorption organic roof matting
2 Shading overhang
3 Operable sliding door/ window ventilation
4 Door and window shading blinds
5 Evaporative cooling pond
6 Induced ventilation
7 Elevated building ventilation

Weekend House
Albert Frey + A. Lawrence Kocher

YEAR
1934

LOCATION
Long Island, New York
40°53'26"N 73°16'46"W

CLIMATE ZONE
Temperate Continental

PROGRAM
Weekend Residence

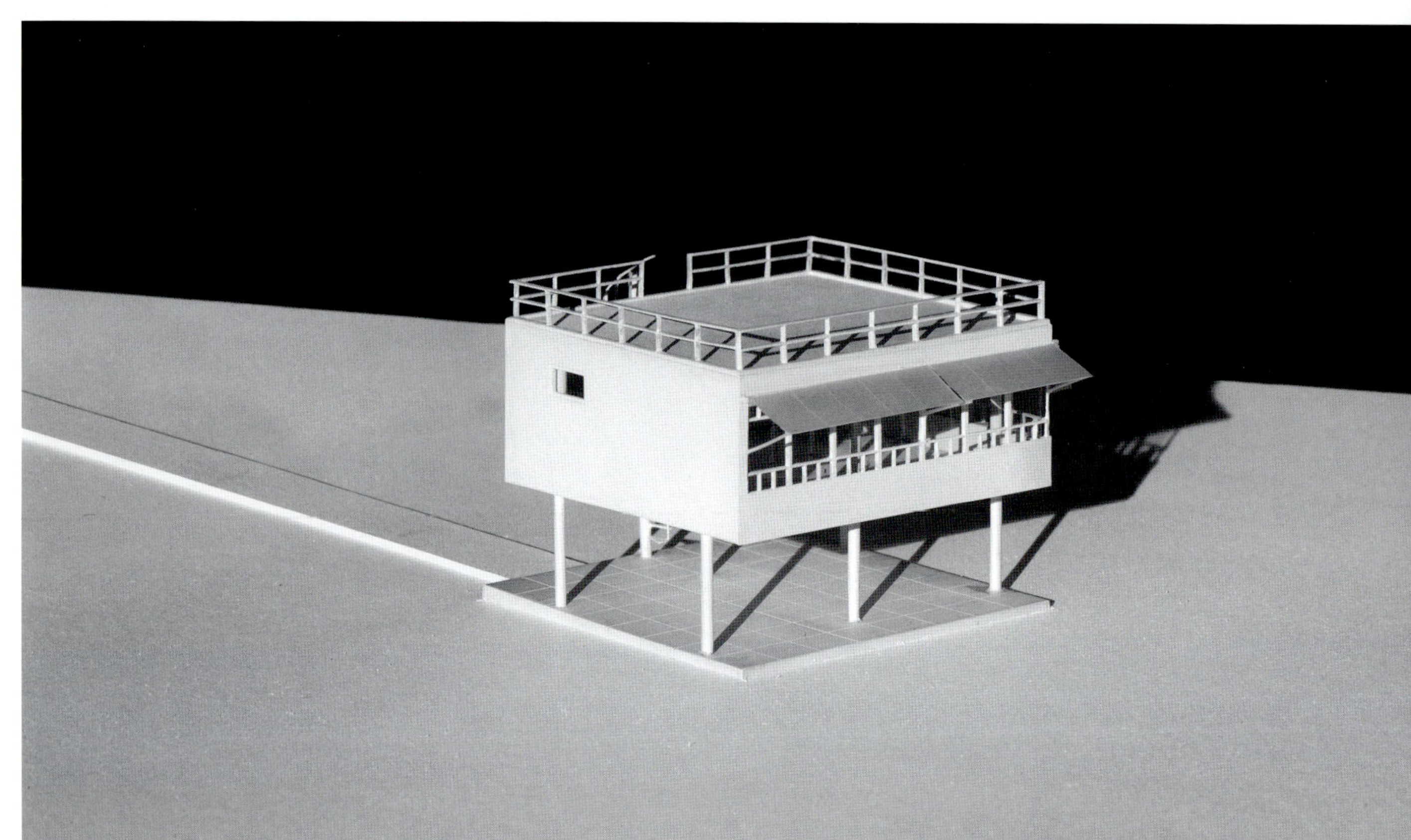

Designed by Swiss architect Albert Frey and his American partner, A. Lawrence Kocher, the weekend house was built in a wooded area approximately one mile from the North Shore of Long Island and thirty miles from the owner's primary residence. The modest structure, now demolished, occupied a minimal footprint. The structure comprised six slender steel columns measuring four inches in diameter and grounded on concrete foundations. These supports served to elevate the main living space above the ground plane to afford optimal views and take advantage of offshore breezes. The lower level served as a carport and shaded garden. The main level and only interior space was a 500 square foot open plan. Curtains mounted to a ceiling track were used to separate the living, dining, and sleeping spaces as needed. The roof doubled as both a sun deck and place to sleep during the summer months. All three levels were accessible by an exterior circular stair.

The house was situated to afford maximum benefit from the trajectory of the sun. A retractable canvas awning along the roofline of the southern and eastern facades provided shade during the summer months. The low solar path during the winter months allowed light to enter and warm the interior space. In contrast to the generously glazed south and east walls, the northern and western facades were each punctured only by a single small window.

The house was an experiment in the use of lightweight materials. Redwood framing was used to construct the floors and walls, which were then insulated with paper-backed aluminum foil between the joists and studs. The foil, commonly used for industrial purposes, increased thermal efficiency by reflecting heat. Compressed fiberboard further insulated the roof and interior floor. The exterior wood sheathing was first painted and then covered with canvas. The marine canvas was applied in horizontal strips and sealed with oil paint before being finished with aluminum paint to optimize reflectivity to sunlight.[1] The house, providing only the minimum spatial needs of a weekend dwelling, took advantage of both the space below the elevated volume and the roof area to realize all useful benefits from this small enclosure. The range of experimental materials sought to minimize costs and improve performance.

1. Alfred Roth, ed., *The New Architecture: Presented in 20 Examples* (Zurich: Les Editions d'Architecture, 1948), 12–14.

PRIMARY SOLAR PATHS AND CORRESPONDING SECTIONS

Long Island, New York

40° North Latitude

SITE PLAN

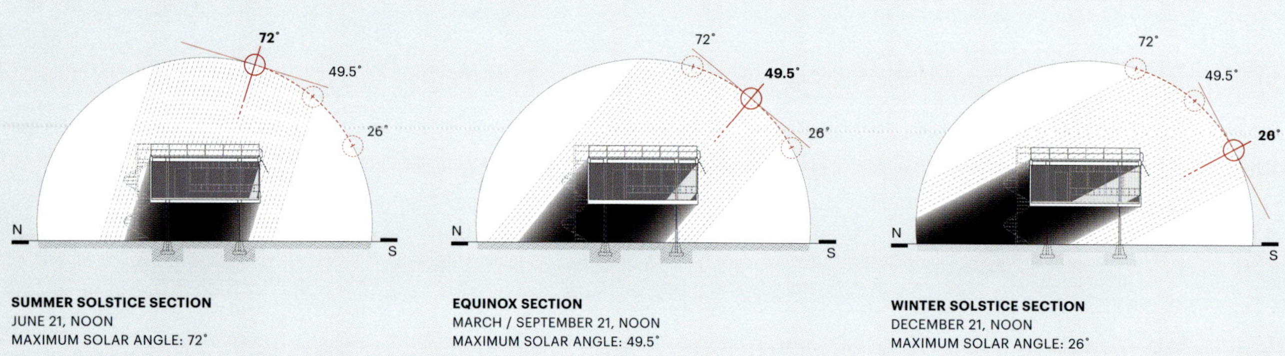

SUMMER SOLSTICE SECTION
JUNE 21, NOON
MAXIMUM SOLAR ANGLE: 72°

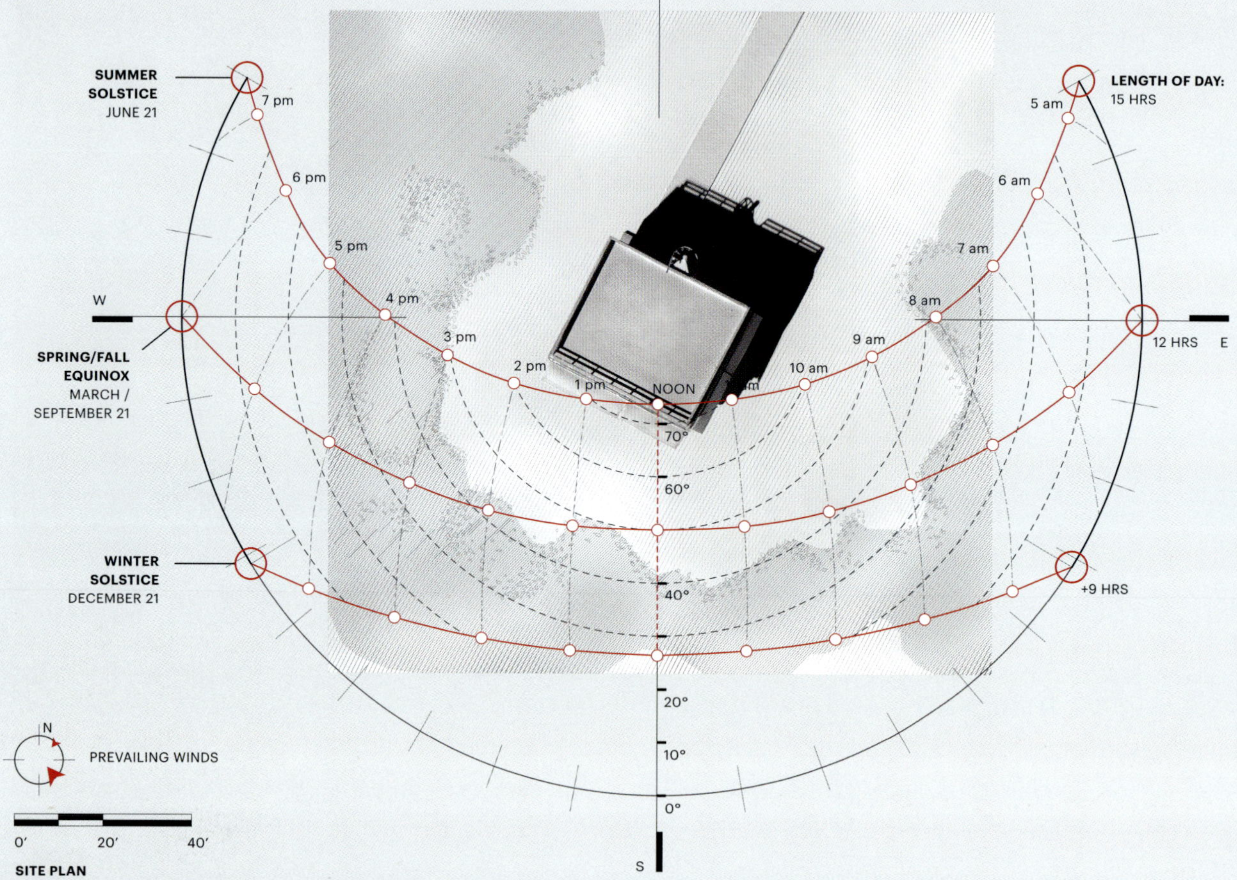

EQUINOX SECTION
MARCH / SEPTEMBER 21, NOON
MAXIMUM SOLAR ANGLE: 49.5°

WINTER SOLSTICE SECTION
DECEMBER 21, NOON
MAXIMUM SOLAR ANGLE: 26°

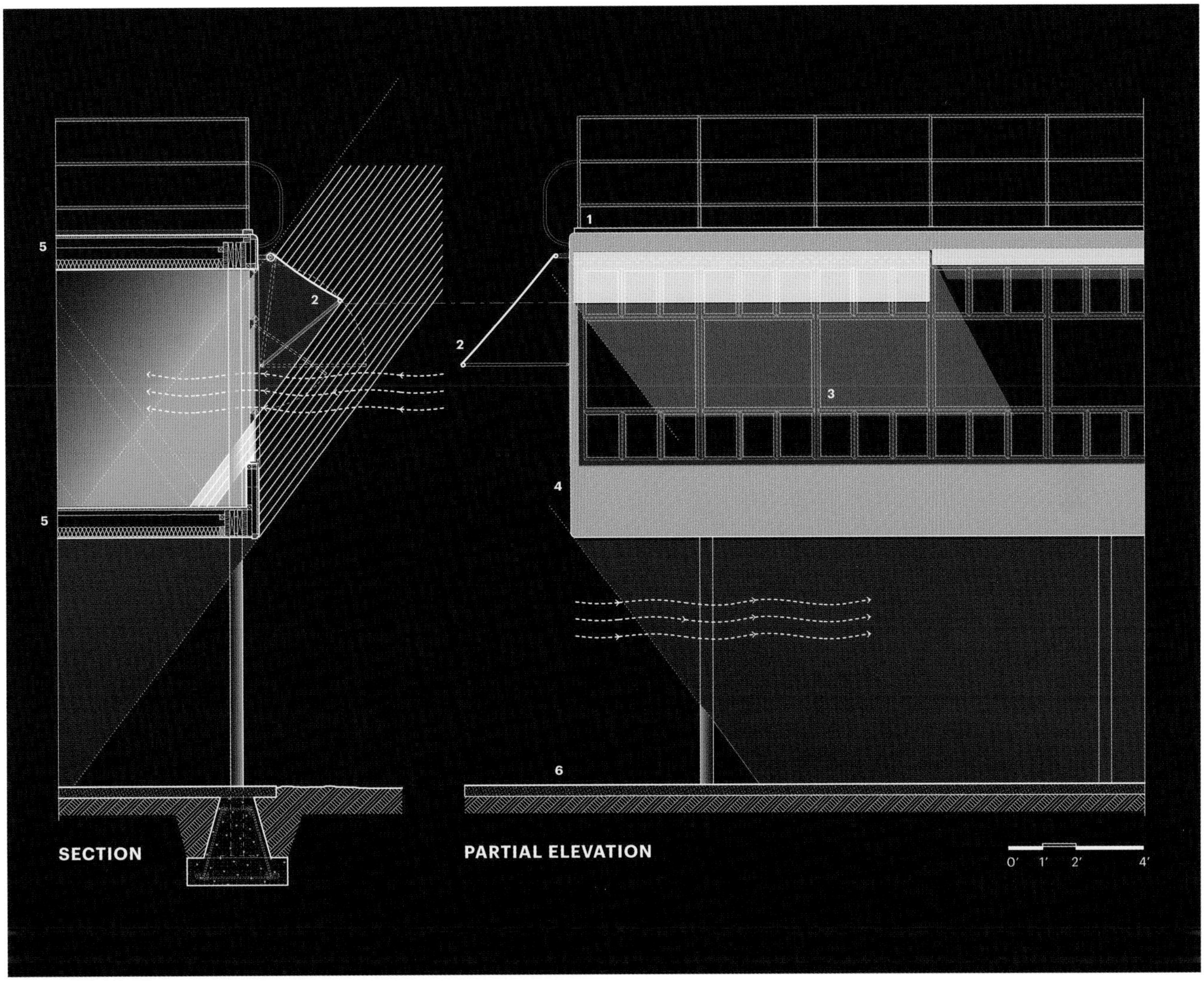

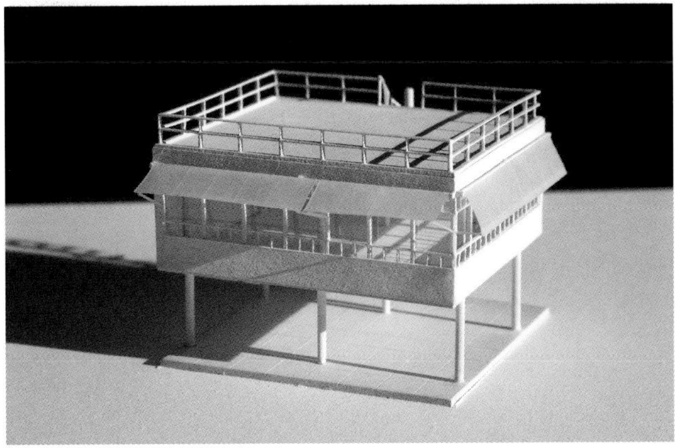

1 Canvas roof terrace
2 Operable canvas awning
3 Operable window
4 Reflective canvas
wall surface
5 Insulated ceiling/floor
6 Open ground floor ventilation

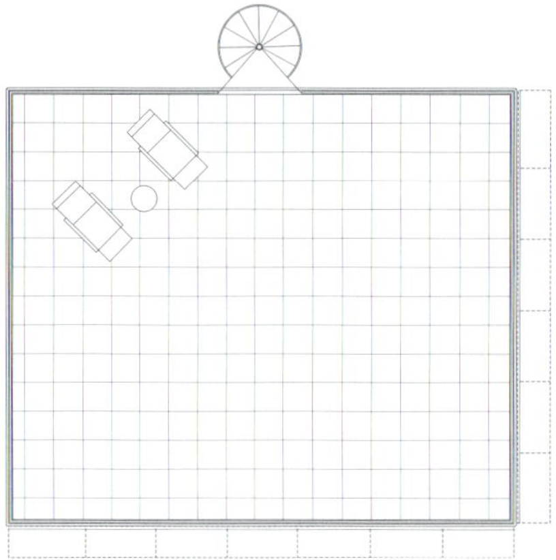

ROOF LEVEL

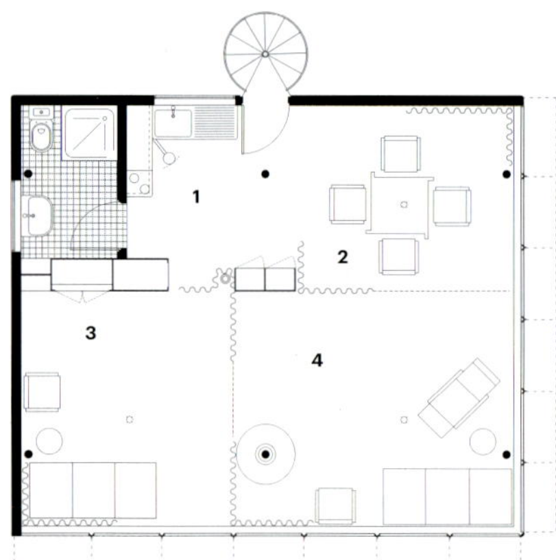

MAIN LEVEL

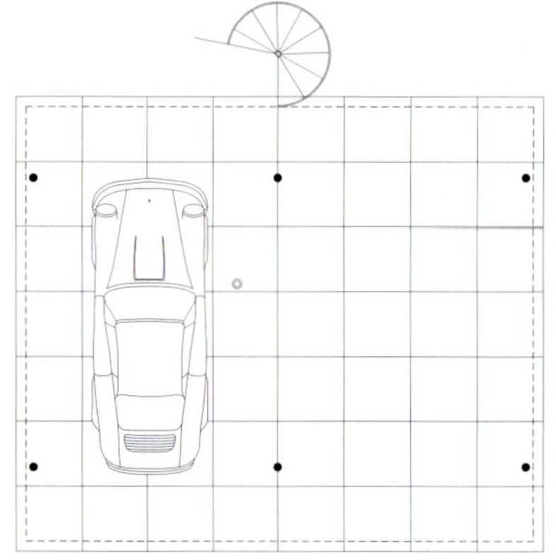

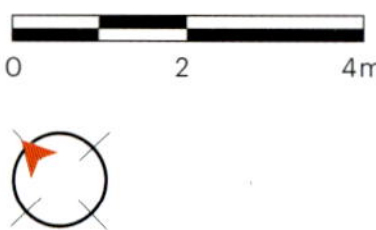

GROUND LEVEL

1 Kitchen
2 Dining area
3 Bedroom
4 Living area

0   2   4m

Housing at Sunila Pulp Mill
Alvar Aalto

YEAR
1936

LOCATION
Kotka, Finland
60°29'35"N 26°57'22"E

CLIMATE ZONE
Continental Boreal

PROGRAM
Workers Housing

Alvar Aalto designed the master plan for the Sunila Pulp Mill, a community of industrial and residential buildings at the mouth of the Kymi River in the port town of Kotka, Finland. The dwellings at Sunila, a small group of row houses for supervisory personnel, were one part of this massive island complex. The expansive mill site, with topography composed of steep hills and valleys as well as rock outcroppings and pine trees scattered throughout, was zoned into several districts. Seeking to leave the natural features of the site as undisturbed as possible, Aalto specified, "Only the south slopes of the hills are for dwellings, the valleys are traffic ways and gardens. On the north slopes the pine forests shall remain undisturbed."[1]

The master plan included living quarters for the mill's extensive population of administrators and workers. A collection of twenty buildings employed a variety of row house and apartment block designs. Decentralized power generation and an underground utility distribution system provided flexibility in the site plan layout, allowing the arrangement of the housing structures to follow the contours of the south-sloping land. The cluster of five row houses, known as the dwellings, was arranged in a staggered pattern with the main facades oriented southwest-to-west to maximize afternoon daylight and emphasize the views toward the waters of the Gulf of Finland. Long stepped walls fan out down the slope to create terraced garden areas in front of each house.[2]

The transparency of the south-facing elevation provides passive heating from the low Nordic winter sun, while recessed openings and entrance niches at the ground level, retractable canvas window awnings on the upper stories, and an abundance of surrounding vegetation shield the higher summer sun and prevent overheating. Balconies allow natural light and air to enter the upper floors. The north elevation remains mostly closed, with only a few small openings to prevent thermal heat loss. Through the application of precise and inventive architectural strategies, this project, built using only common materials and methods, was able to become a superbly balanced formal composition, one that takes full advantage of the seasonal conditions and that beautifully integrates these dwellings into their natural surroundings.

1. Alvar Aalto, *Alvar Aalto* (Zurich: Verlag für Architektur, 1963), 96.

2. "Sunila Finland," European Union Modern Movement Neighbourhood Cooperation, accessed January 29, 2013, http://momoneco.kotka.fi/sunila.html.

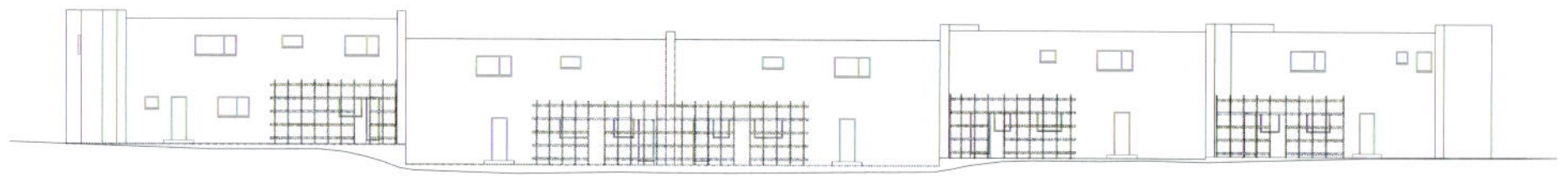

NORTHEAST ELEVATION

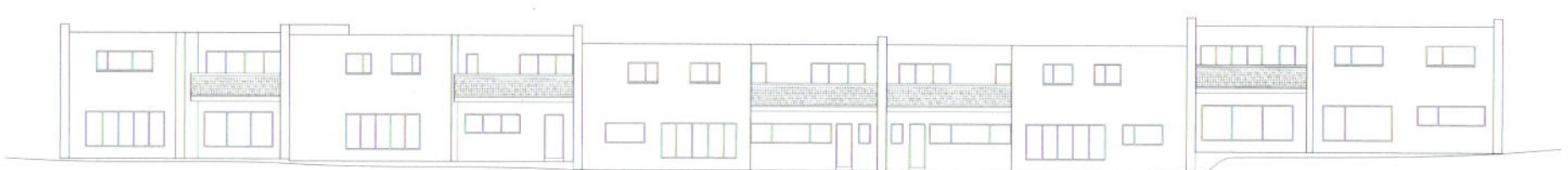

SOUTHWEST ELEVATION

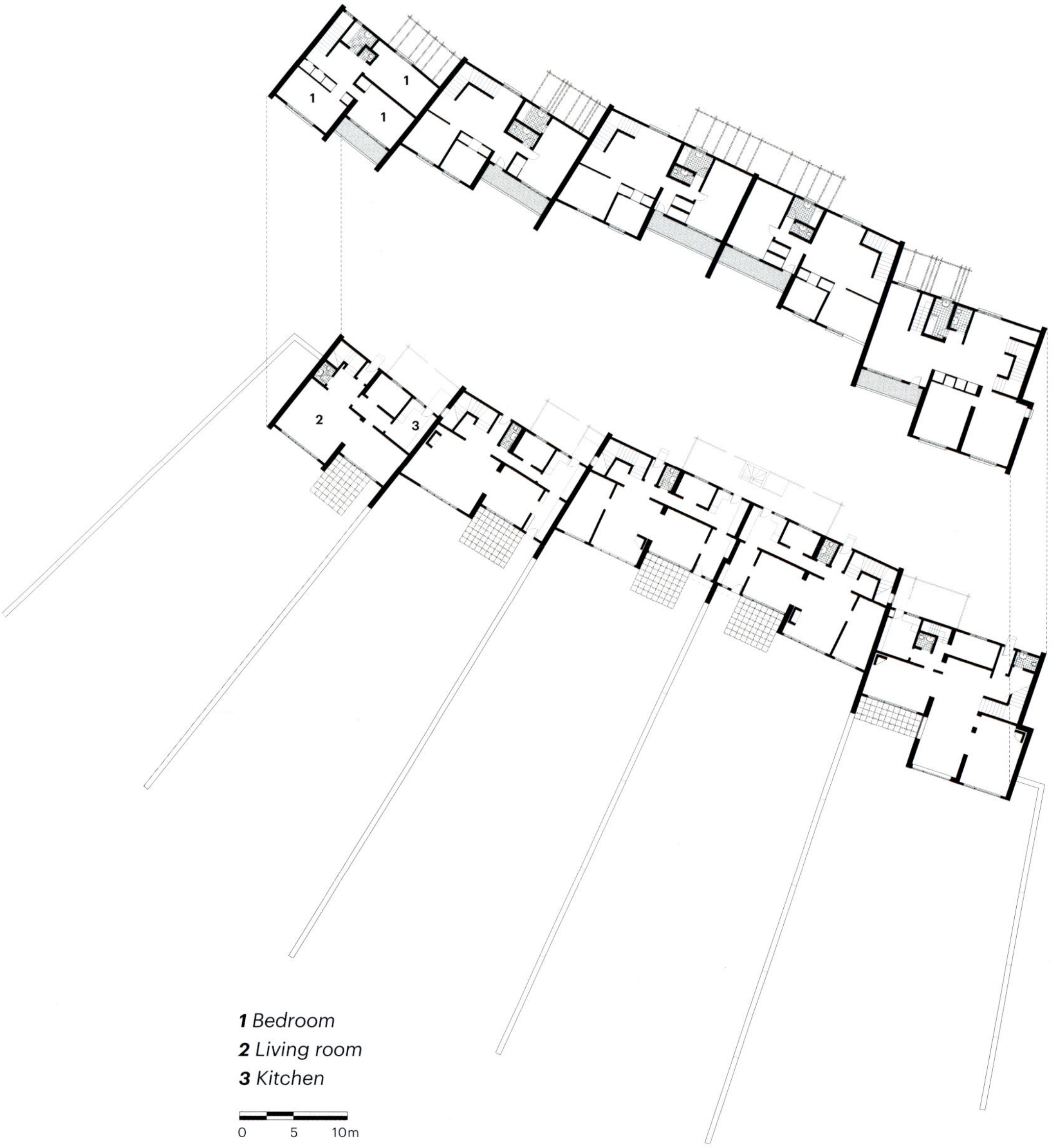

SECOND LEVEL

FIRST LEVEL

1 *Bedroom*
2 *Living room*
3 *Kitchen*

PRIMARY SOLAR PATHS AND CORRESPONDING SECTIONS

Kotka, Finland

60° North Latitude

SITE PLAN

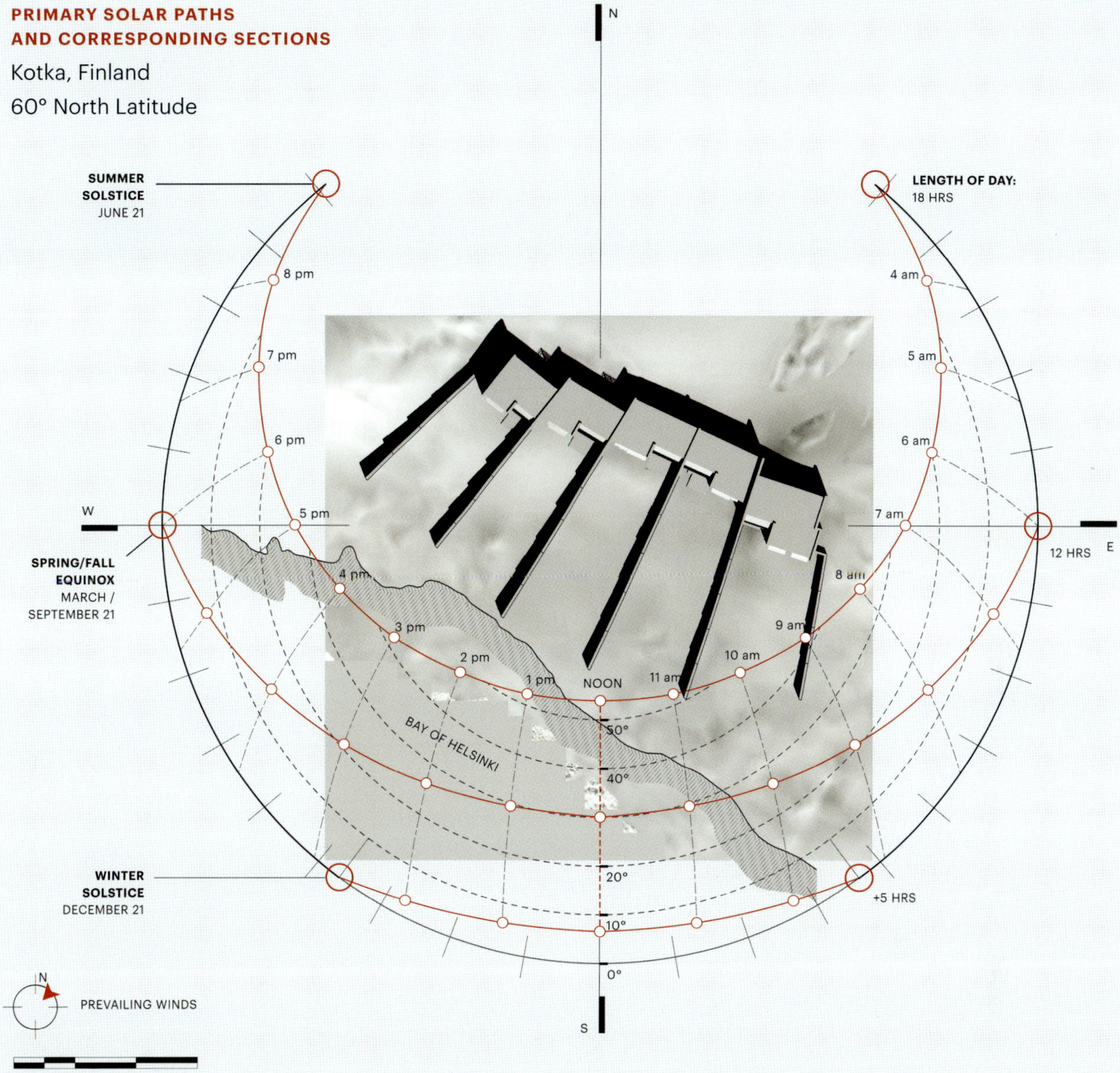

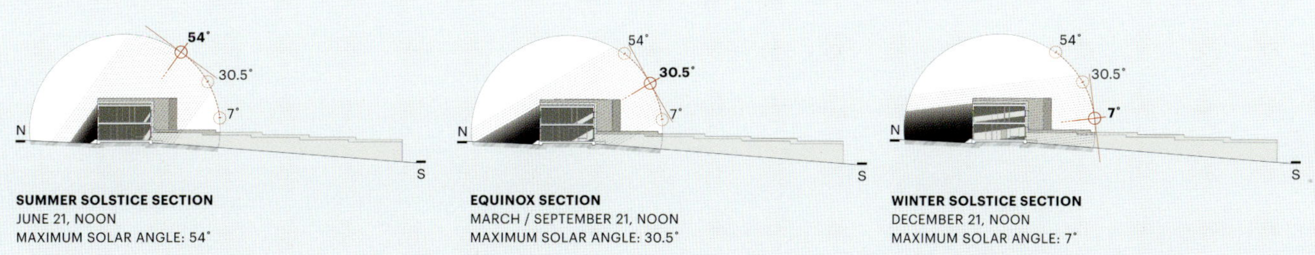

SUMMER SOLSTICE SECTION
JUNE 21, NOON
MAXIMUM SOLAR ANGLE: 54°

EQUINOX SECTION
MARCH / SEPTEMBER 21, NOON
MAXIMUM SOLAR ANGLE: 30.5°

WINTER SOLSTICE SECTION
DECEMBER 21, NOON
MAXIMUM SOLAR ANGLE: 7°

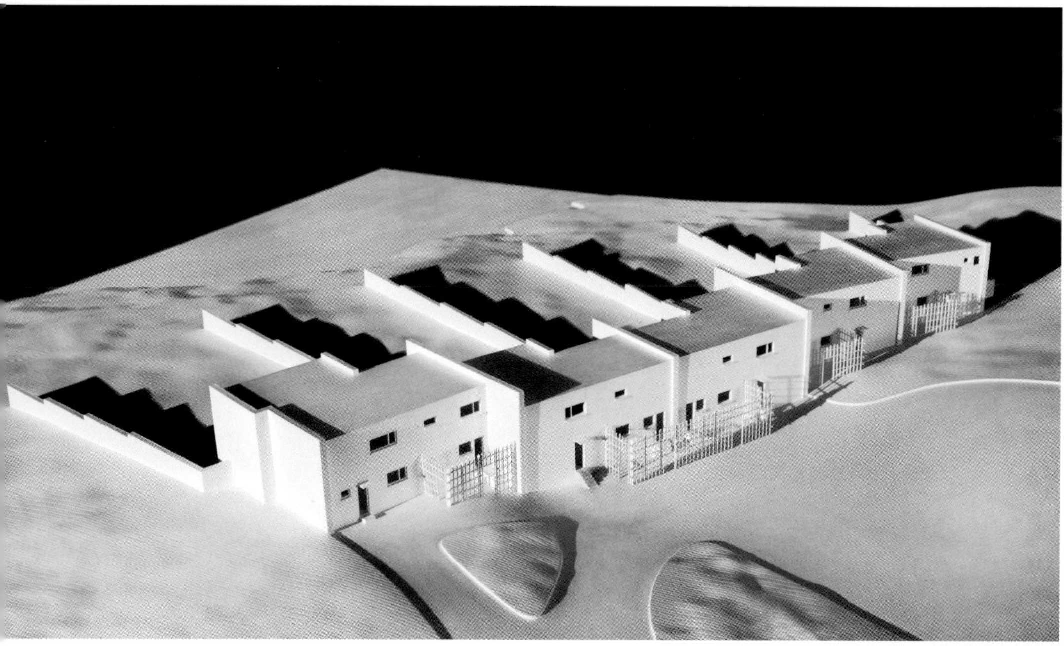

Jacobs House I
Frank Lloyd Wright

YEAR
1937

LOCATION
Madison, Wisconsin
43°3′30″N 89°26′29″W

CLIMATE ZONE
Temperate Continental

PROGRAM
Single-family
Residence

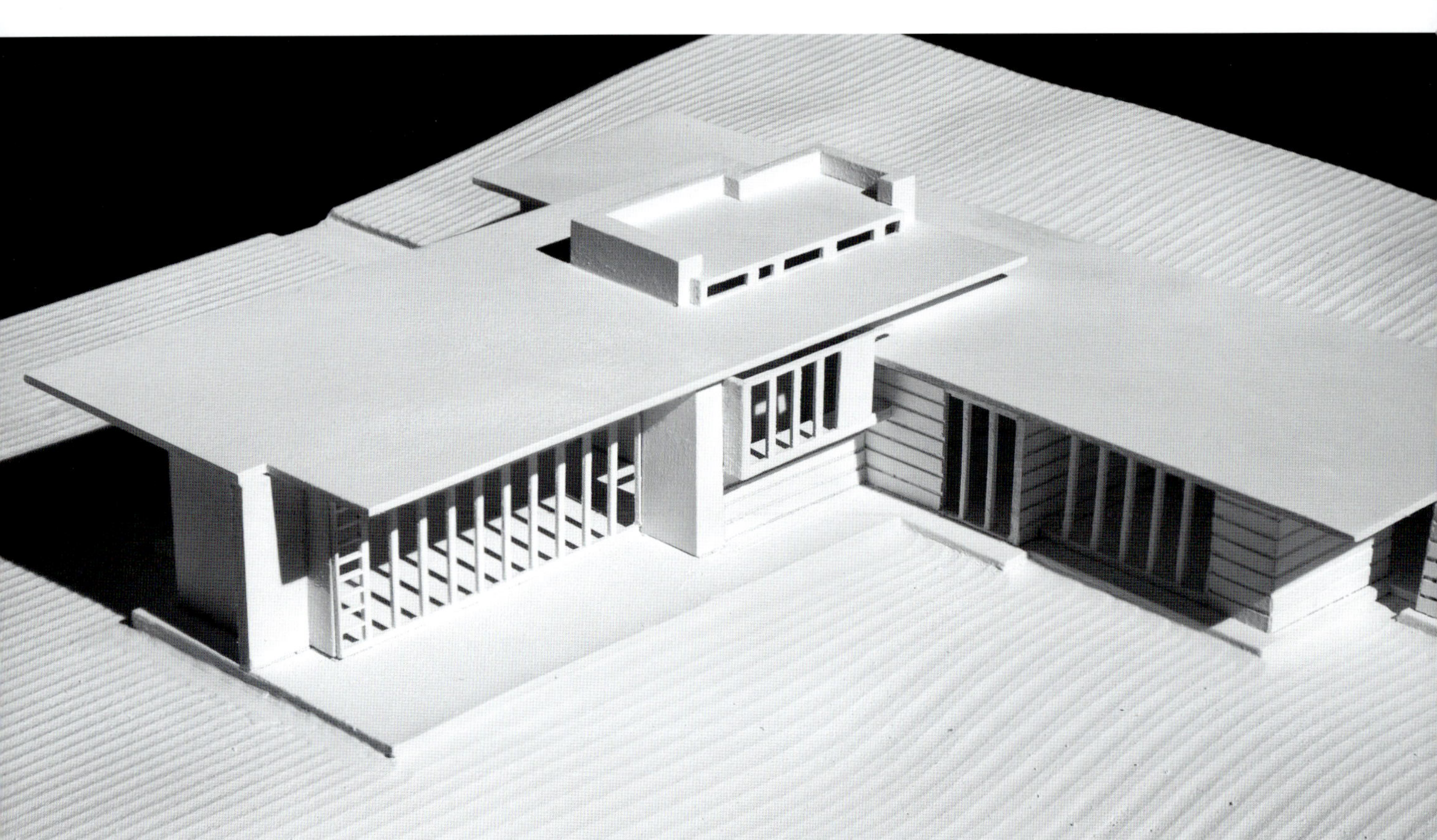

Jacobs House I, designed for Herbert and Catherine Jacobs, is Frank Lloyd Wright's first Usonian house. A modest 1,500 square feet, it was intended to reinvent the two-story Colonial Revival house typical of middle-class suburban construction of the 1930s. At this point in his career, Wright was concerned with what he called the problem of the "small house"[1] and he was striving to define an ethos for modern middle-class American living.

In his scheme for Jacobs House I, Wright discarded what he considered the unnecessary spaces and expensive construction techniques of the conventional home, eliminating the garage, dormered attic, basement, and decorative trim. Instead, he proposed a carport, flat roof, radiant floor heating, and a simple board and batten wood wall system. The relationship between man, structure, and nature was critical: "We can never make the living room big enough, the fireplace important enough, or the sense of relationship between exterior, interior and environment close enough . . . A Usonian house is always hungry for ground, lives by it, becoming an integral feature of it."[2]

Located on a corner lot and L-shaped in plan, the house is sited so that the protective enclosure of the "L" faces southeast, down a gently sloping hill. This protected "L" frames an outdoor terrace and garden, creating a microclimate that is sheltered from the wind and gathers and retains the warmth of the sun. The courtyard space is comfortable enough to use on the mild days of winter, and the garden, placed in this warmer pocket, enjoys an extended growing season. The southeastern walls of the "L" are almost fully glazed, allowing ample amounts of sunlight to enter during the winter months and for the absorption of solar warmth by the concrete floors. These glazed walls are protected from the high and intense summer sun by three-foot horizontal roof overhangs characteristic of Wright's prairie architecture. The north and western elevations of the home are mostly solid, punctured only by small clerestory windows.

Jacobs House I, now surrounded by a field of anonymous residential units, is a testament to Frank Lloyd Wright's conviction that even a humble, detached single-family house can be rich in architectural content and designed to optimize its relationship to the natural characteristics and seasonal forces of a given site.

1. Frank Lloyd Wright, "Frank Lloyd Wright," *Architectural Forum* 68, no. 1 (1938), 78.

2. Wright, "Frank Lloyd Wright," 82.

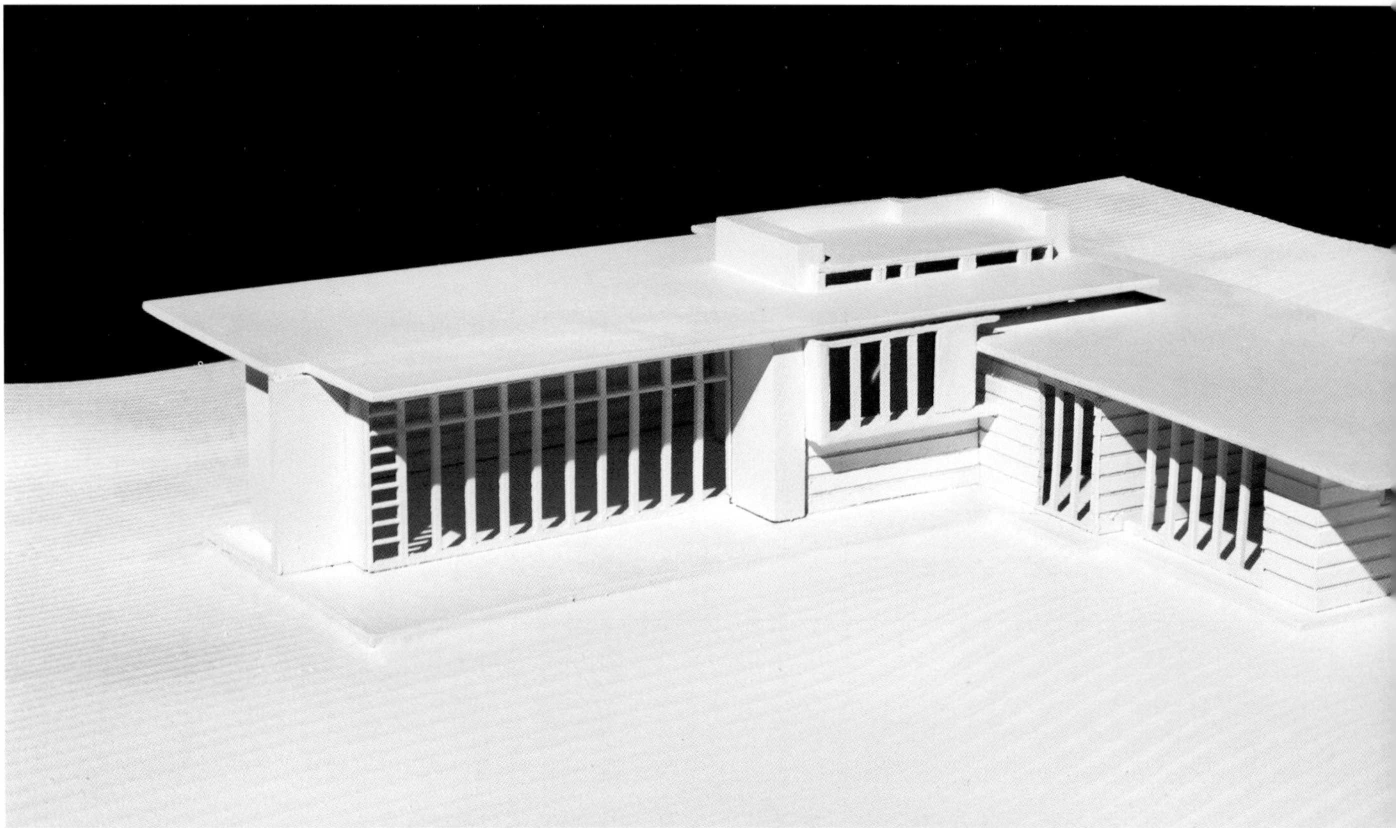

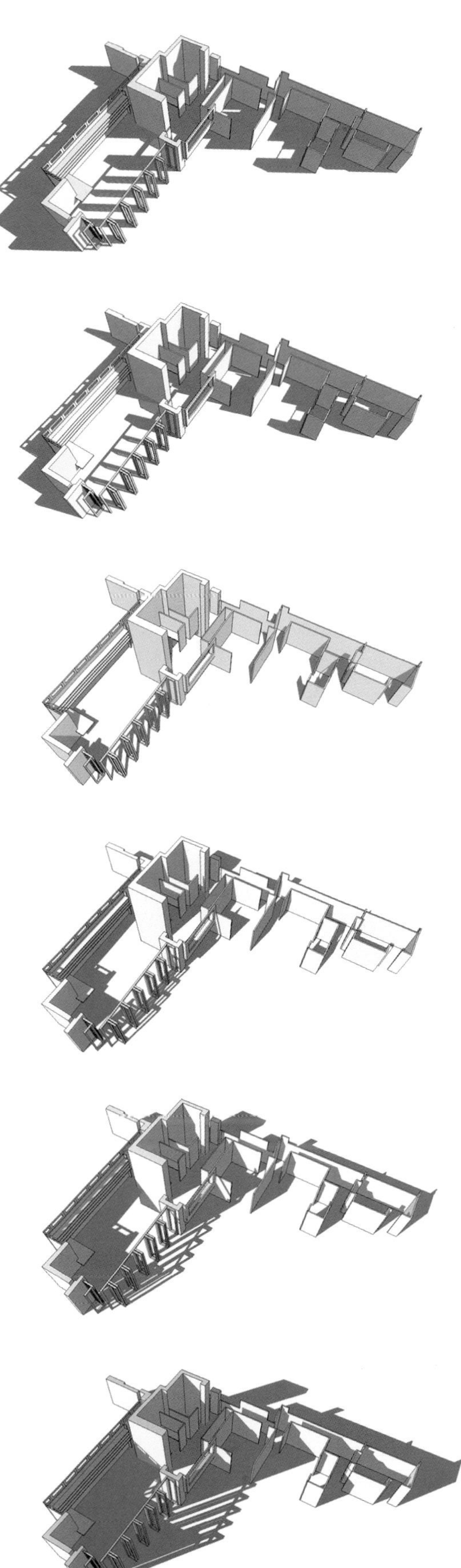

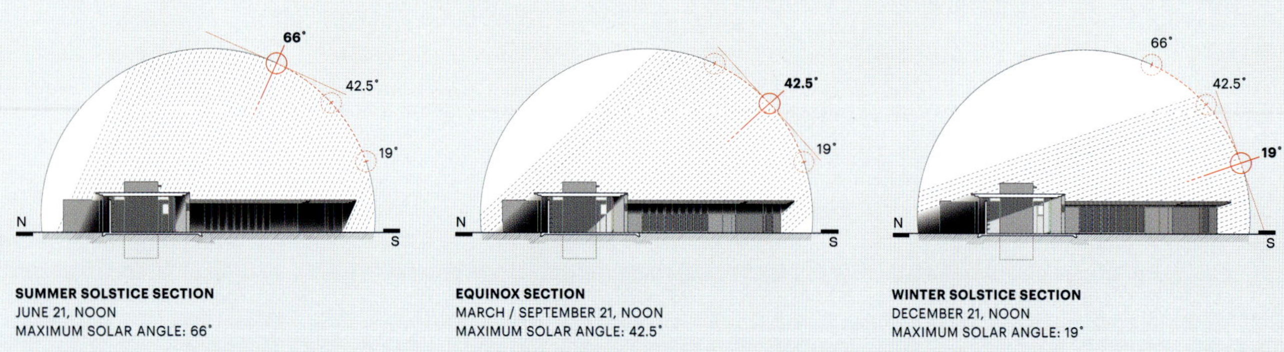

SITE PLAN

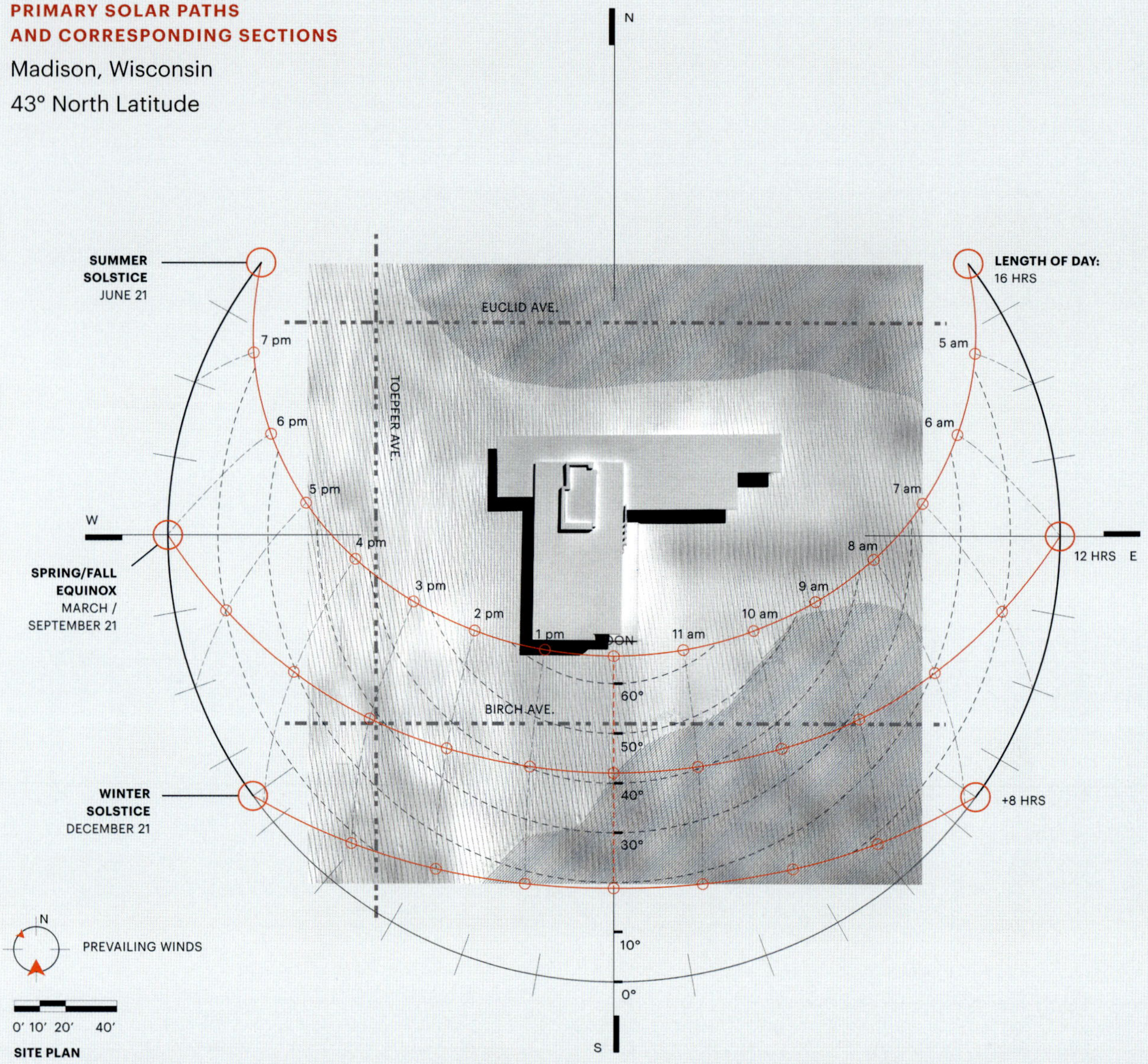

SUMMER SOLSTICE SECTION
JUNE 21, NOON
MAXIMUM SOLAR ANGLE: 66°

EQUINOX SECTION
MARCH / SEPTEMBER 21, NOON
MAXIMUM SOLAR ANGLE: 42.5°

WINTER SOLSTICE SECTION
DECEMBER 21, NOON
MAXIMUM SOLAR ANGLE: 19°

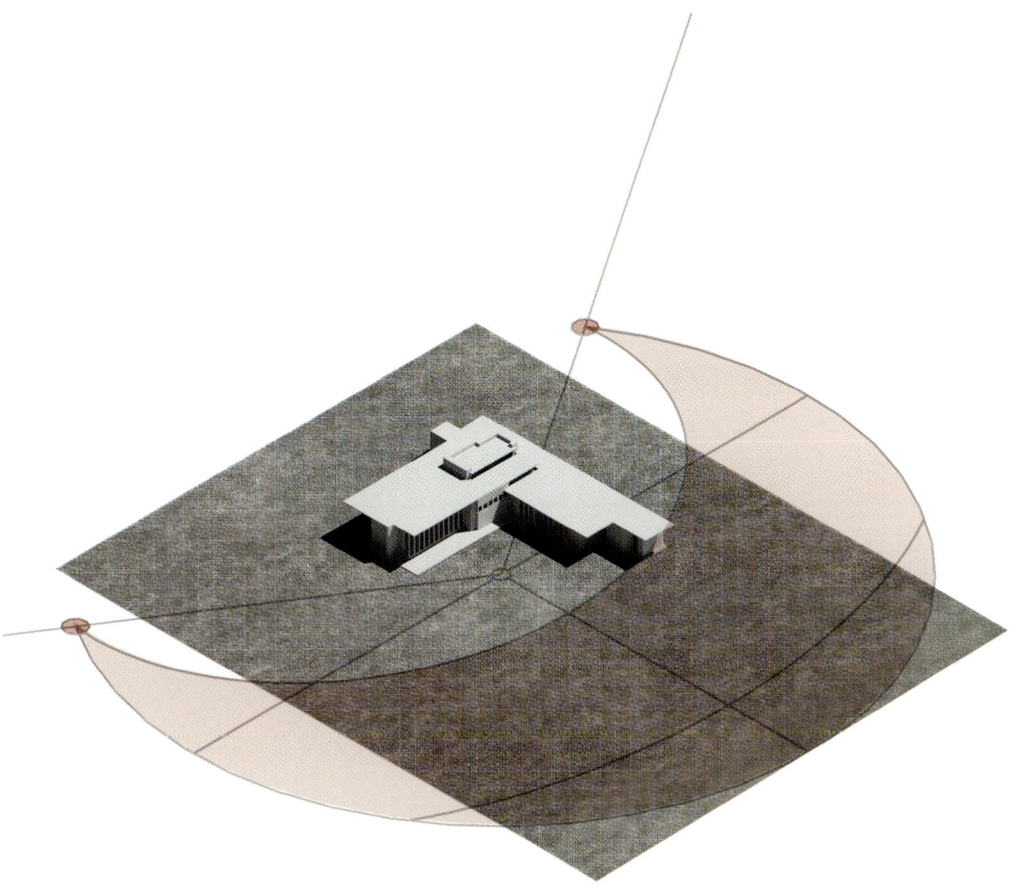

SUMMER SOLSTICE
JUNE 21, NOON

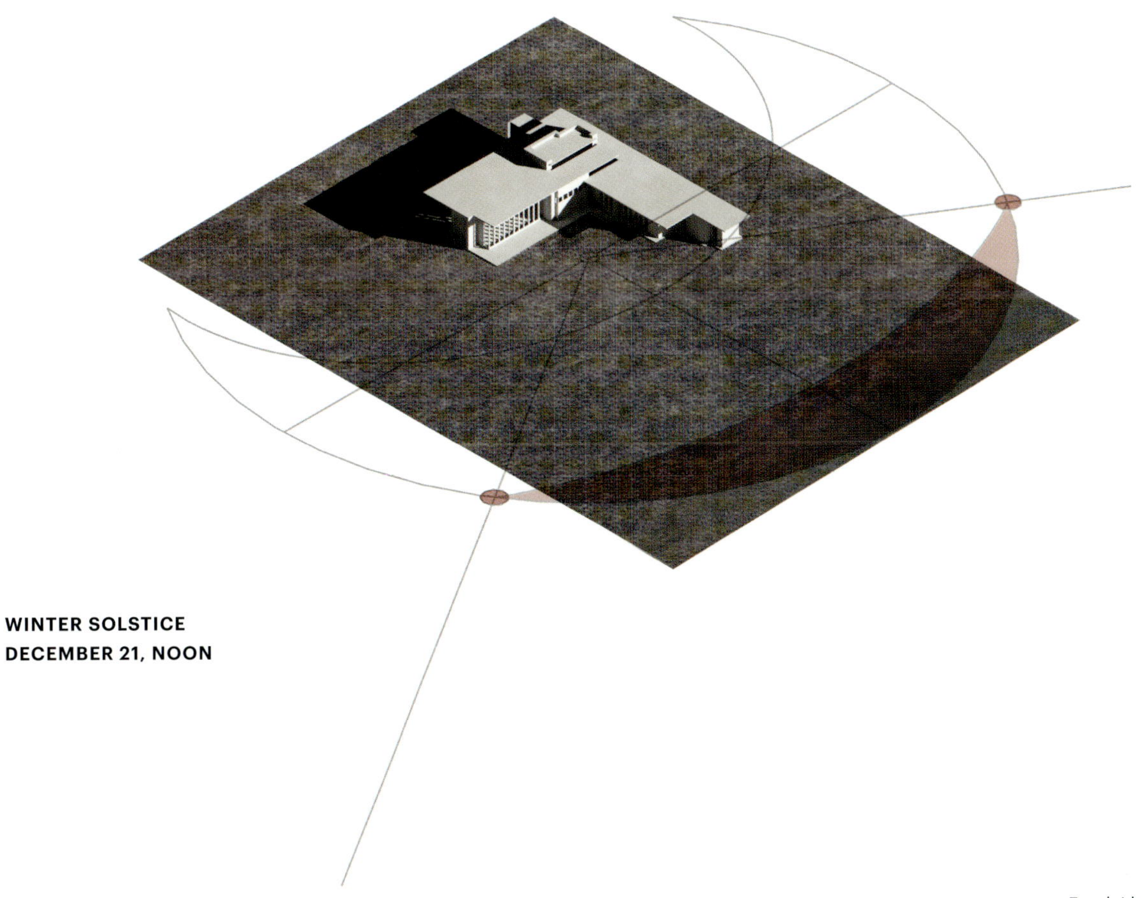

WINTER SOLSTICE
DECEMBER 21, NOON

Houses in Space
Amancio Williams

YEAR
1943

LOCATION
Buenos Aires,
Argentina (not built)
34°39.839'S 58°21.371'W

CLIMATE ZONE
Humid Subtropical

PROGRAM
Multifamily Housing

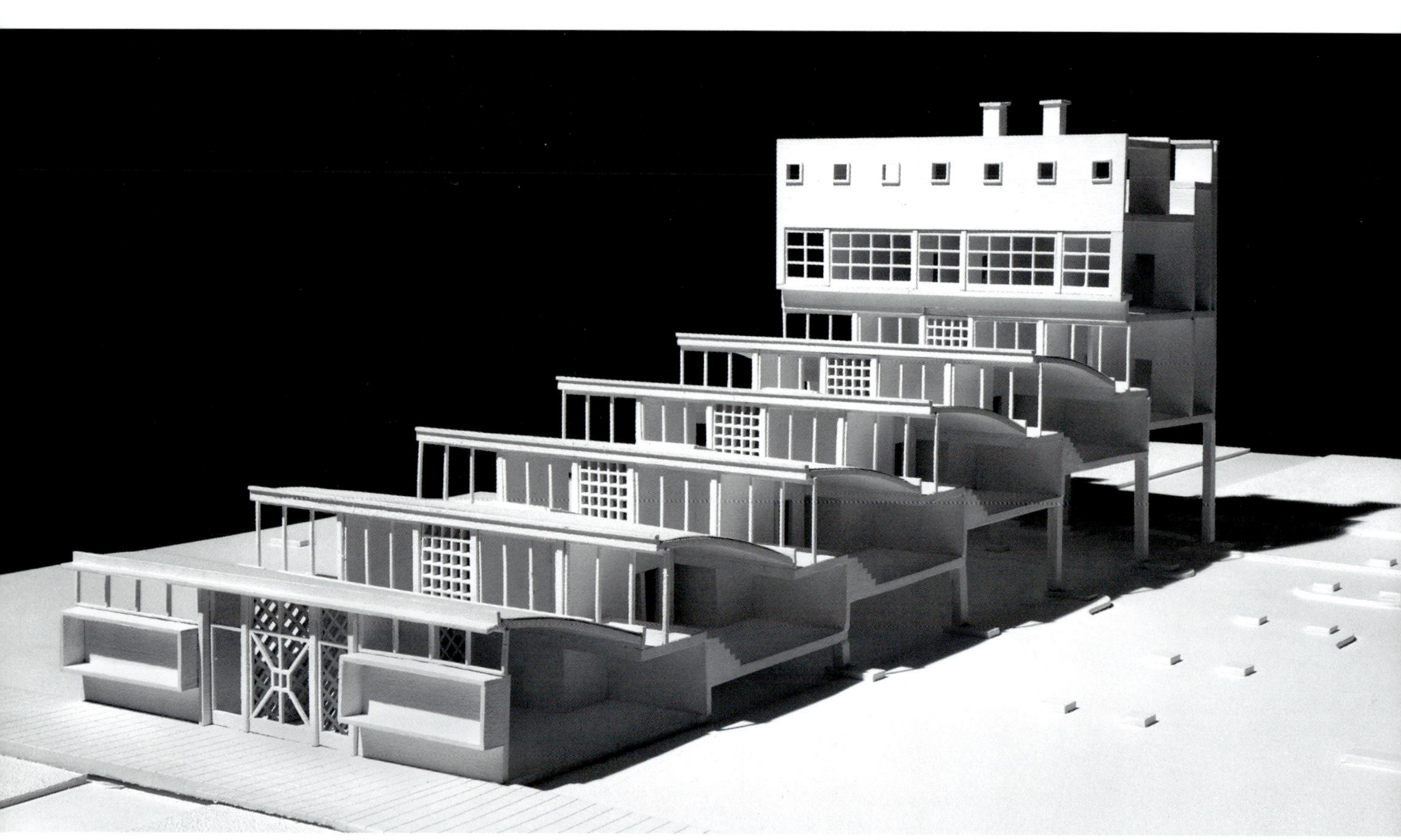

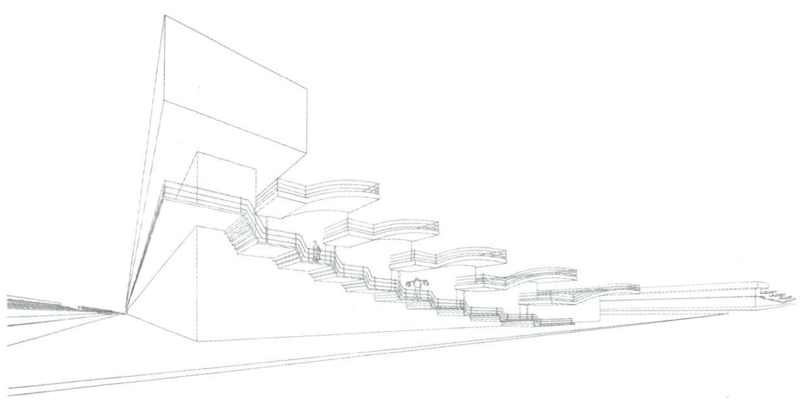

Amancio Wlliams' proposed Houses in Space addresses the architectural problem of stepped terraced housing on a flat or low sloping site. This unique building typology connects individual dwellings in a medium-density housing environment with outdoor living areas, views of garden space, and natural ventilation. The stepped building form, like Le Corbusier's proposed Domaine de Badjara housing project outside of Algiers, was a new strategy for housing that allowed all dwellings to face a landscaped terrace oriented towards the winter sun. In Corbusier's unbuilt project, the levels of the dwellings are stacked one on top of the other, and the roof of the lower level becomes the terrace of the unit above.

The proposed design by Williams resolves one of the limitations of the conventional stepped terrace model of housing. In more typical terraced housing, a full floor height separates each level of terraces and consequently, this model works best on relatively steep sites. In the unique cross-sectional design by Williams the different levels of the apartments are separated by only a few steps. Their curvilinear form exposes the north wall (the sunny side in the Southern hemisphere) of each apartment to the adjacent roof, which, from the vantage point of the apartment, offers a view of the hill-like landscaped surface. This spatial device establishes the main connection between the apartment and the exterior and allows winter sunlight to reach deep into the relatively flat section of the stepped form. Beneath the elevated, stepped forms, Williams suggested utility spaces, shops, driveways, and parking.

A central corridor ascends through the stepped structure with one apartment on each side at each level. The public corridor acts as a central ventilation device with a clerestory grill at each garden terrace. Connected to a stair tower to the south, the corridor allows warm air to move up and pulls a draft of cool air in from the garden levels. Each apartment contains small openings high on the interior walls that open onto the corridor and allow cross ventilation between the terrace windows and the corridor.

Williams later reimagined this original project and proposed a vast master plan with multiple rows of stepped forms spread out over a flat landscape. In this expanded vision the apartments were wider with more open glazing on the "hillside" of the curved roof.[1] This version of the project also remains unbuilt.

1. Jorge Silvetti, ed., *Amancio Williams* (New York: Rizzoli, 1987), 14.

PRIMARY SOLAR PATHS AND CORRESPONDING SECTIONS

Buenos Aires, Argentina

34° South Latitude

SITE PLAN

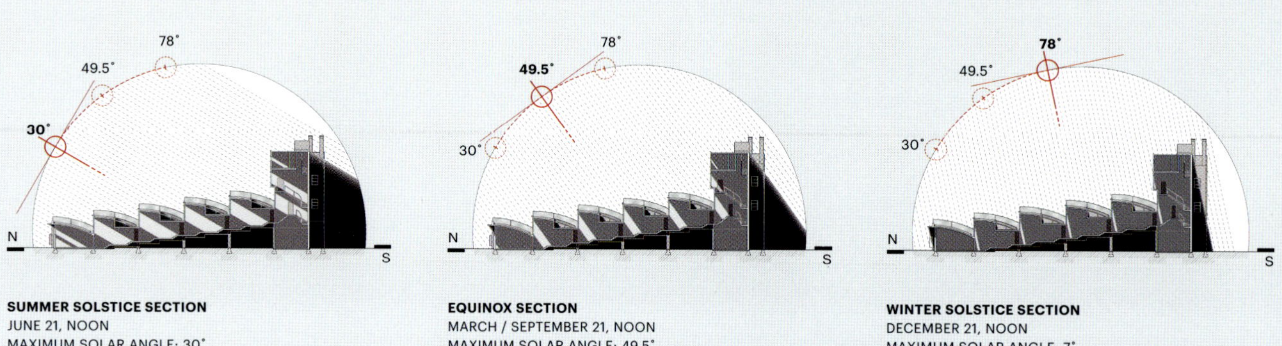

SUMMER SOLSTICE SECTION
JUNE 21, NOON
MAXIMUM SOLAR ANGLE: 30°

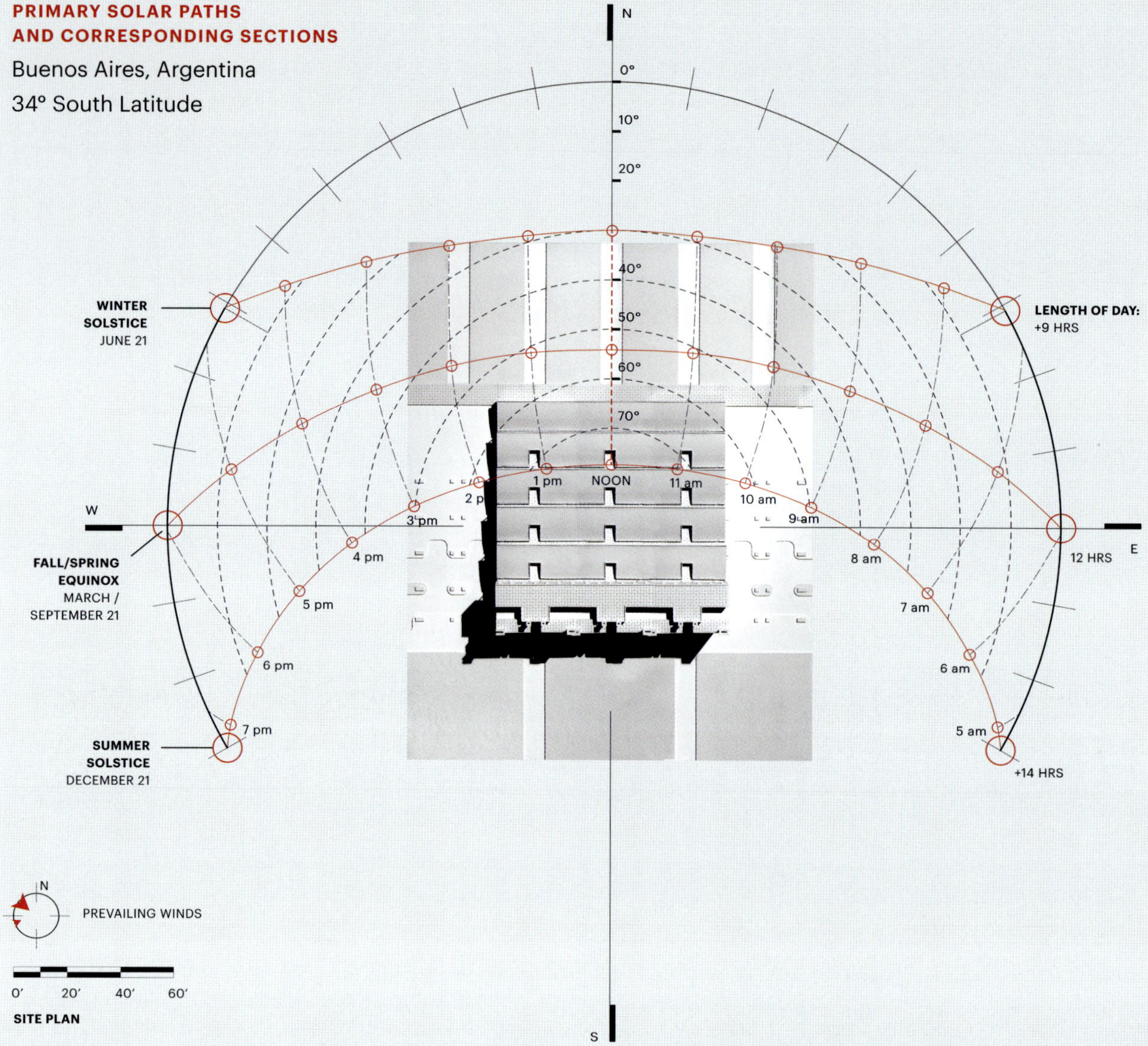

EQUINOX SECTION
MARCH / SEPTEMBER 21, NOON
MAXIMUM SOLAR ANGLE: 49.5°

WINTER SOLSTICE SECTION
DECEMBER 21, NOON
MAXIMUM SOLAR ANGLE: 7°

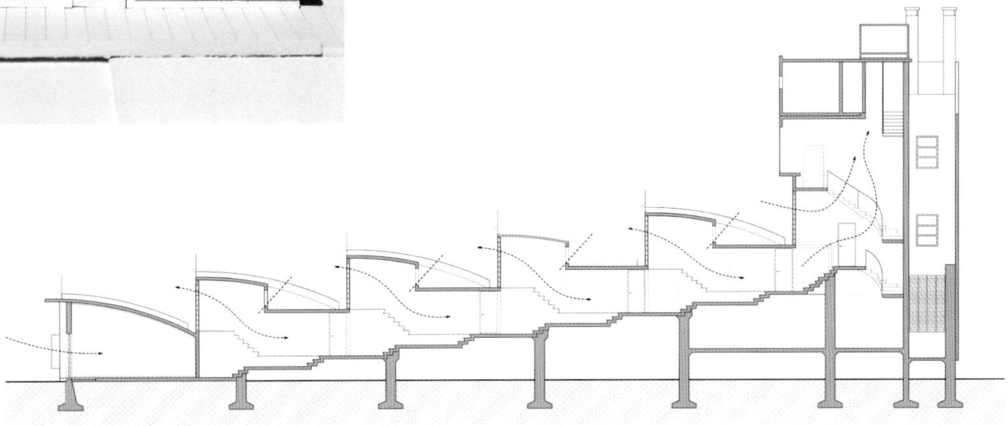

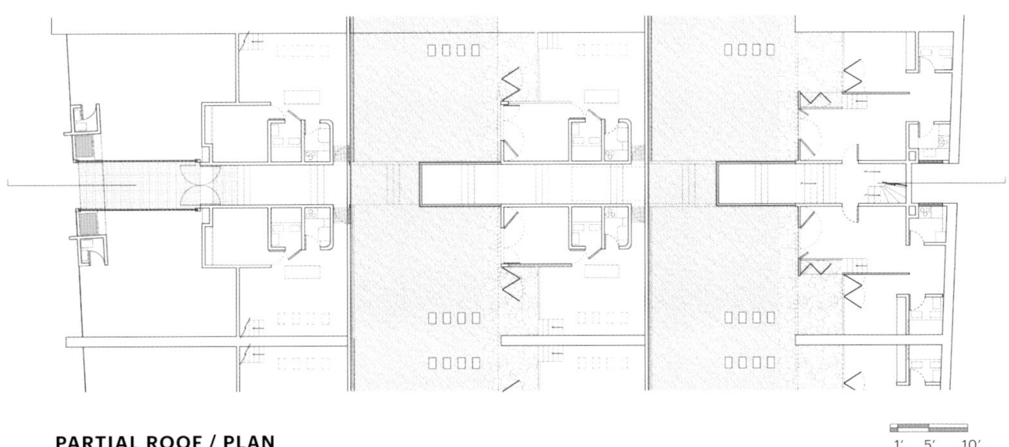

LONGITUDINAL SECTION

PARTIAL ROOF / PLAN

House Over the Brook
Amancio Williams

YEAR
1945

LOCATION
Mar Del Plata, Buenos
Aires, Argentina
38°0'31"S 57°34'247"W

CLIMATE ZONE
Humid Subtropical

PROGRAM
Single-family
Residence

Today, the muscular relationship of this project to the natural features of the site can be seen as the antithesis of what environmental design aspires to be. Now the prevailing wisdom would be to separate the building from the watercourse in order to protect the drainage and stream course habitats from the pressure of construction and human use. The House over the Brook is sited squarely in the most sensitive part of the landscape, but still, despite this location, the house is profoundly respectful of the natural conditions. The project steps over the stream, the most delicate part of the natural landscape, suggesting a site strategy that could be equally useful to the evolution of environmentally sustainable design: a close, careful integration of the built work and natural landscape features.

The embankments, placed away from the creek side, support the foundation buttresses, allowing the primary structure of the house, the arch, to spring across, leaving the brook undisturbed. The house itself, a volume floating on the arch and elevated within the canopy of trees, addresses, through visual connects, the space of the ravine, both upstream and down, as an extension of the living spaces. The architecture both celebrates the brook and protects the biological community along its banks.

Like other architectural propositions by Amancio Williams, the building volume is suspended in space, with the aim of freeing the ground. To formulate architecture in space is to propose a metaphysical project for humanity, leaving the ground untouched and preserved, separating man and nature. In Williams's words, "I insist that the order of Nature is different from the one of Man, meaning not to eliminate but rather integrate Nature in a different manner, keeping its beauty in the forms that it manifests itself."[1]

1. Amancio Williams, "The Force of a Creative Thought," *Crisis Magazine,* no. 39 (1976), 22–27.

PRIMARY SOLAR PATHS AND CORRESPONDING SECTIONS

Mar Del Plata, Buenos Aires, Argentina
38° South Latitude

SITE PLAN

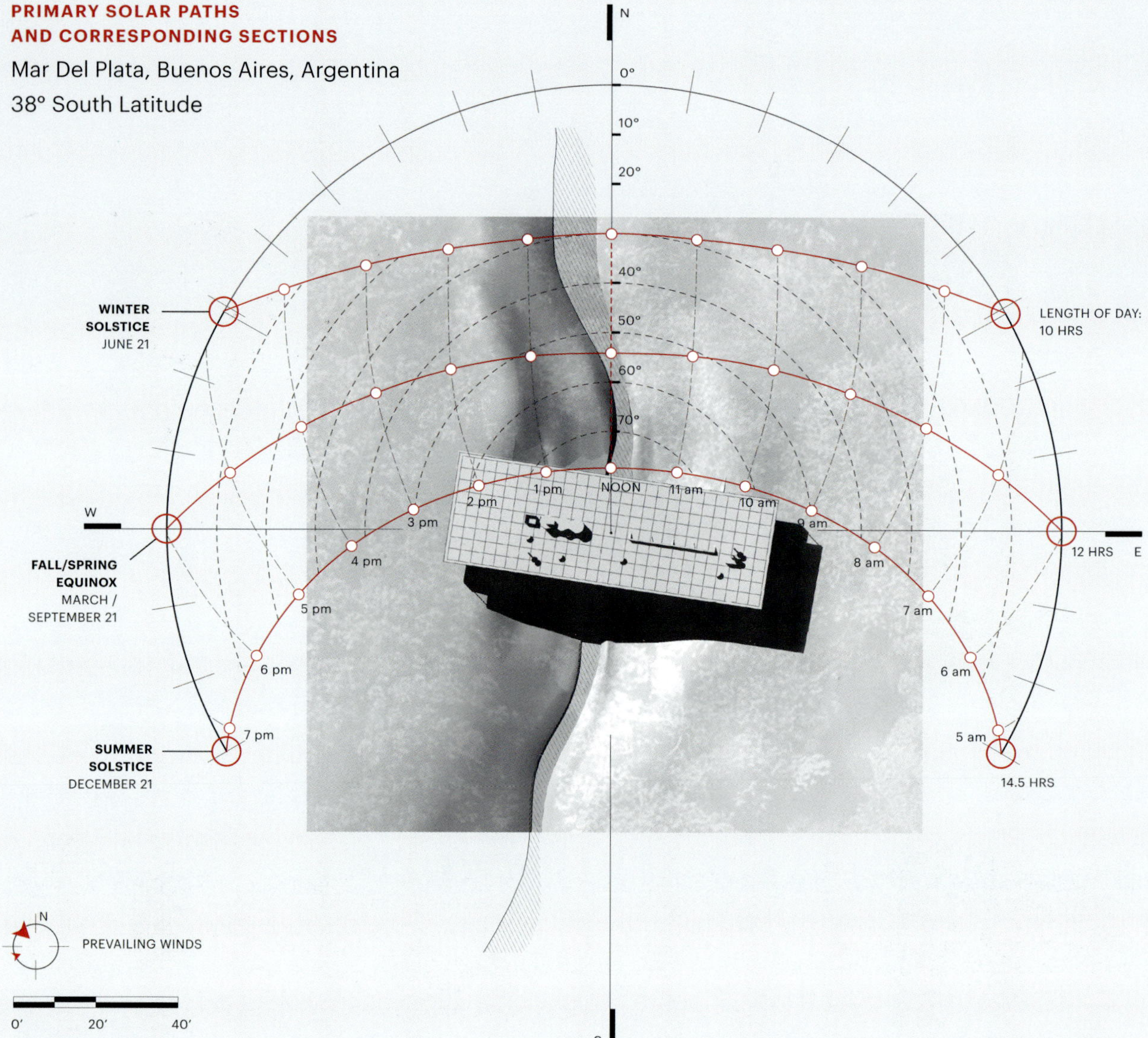

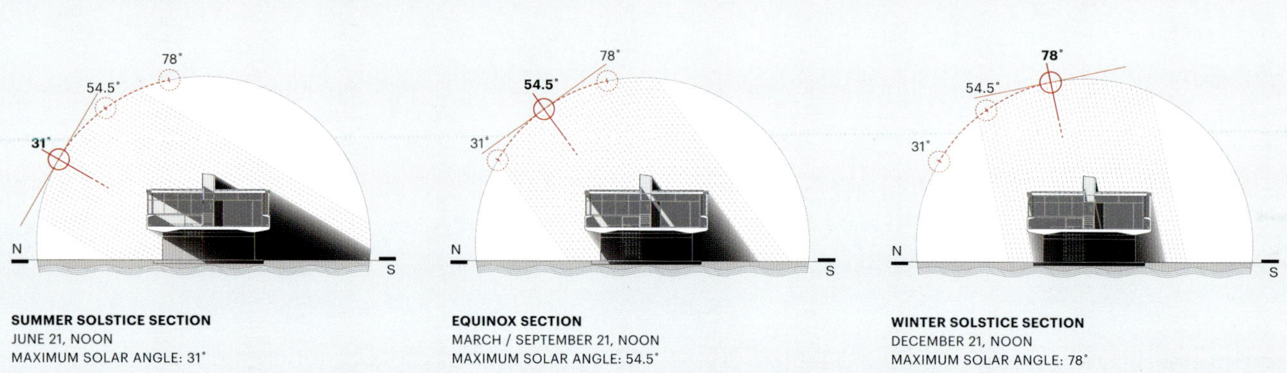

SUMMER SOLSTICE SECTION
JUNE 21, NOON
MAXIMUM SOLAR ANGLE: 31°

EQUINOX SECTION
MARCH / SEPTEMBER 21, NOON
MAXIMUM SOLAR ANGLE: 54.5°

WINTER SOLSTICE SECTION
DECEMBER 21, NOON
MAXIMUM SOLAR ANGLE: 78°

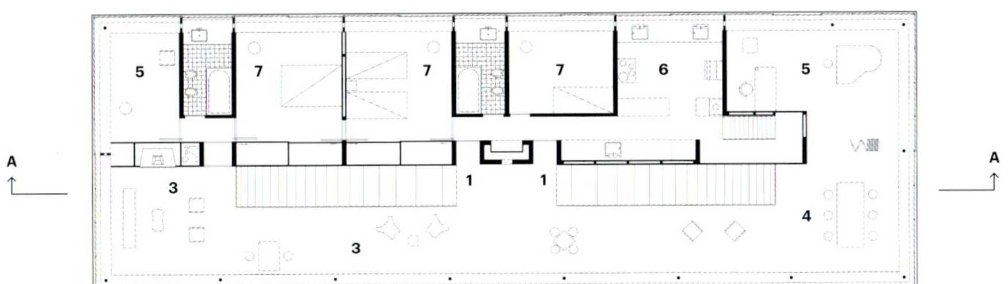

MAIN LEVEL

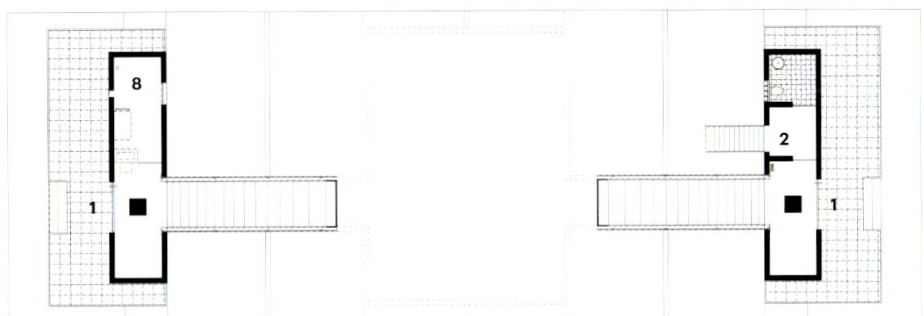

GROUND LEVEL

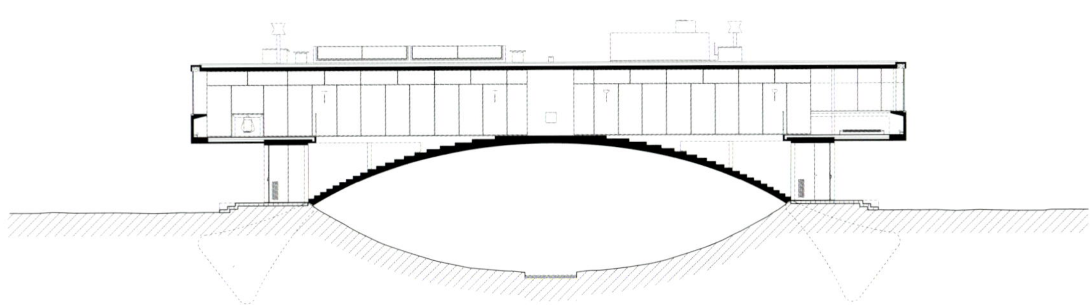

SECTION A – A

1 *Entrance*
2 *Service stairway*
3 *Living area*
4 *Dining area*
5 *Study*
6 *Kitchen*
7 *Bedroom*
8 *Mechanical room*

Jacobs House II
Frank Lloyd Wright

YEAR
1948

LOCATION
Middleton, Wisconsin
43°4'25"N 89°32'6"W

CLIMATE ZONE
Temperate Continental

PROGRAM
Single-family
Residence

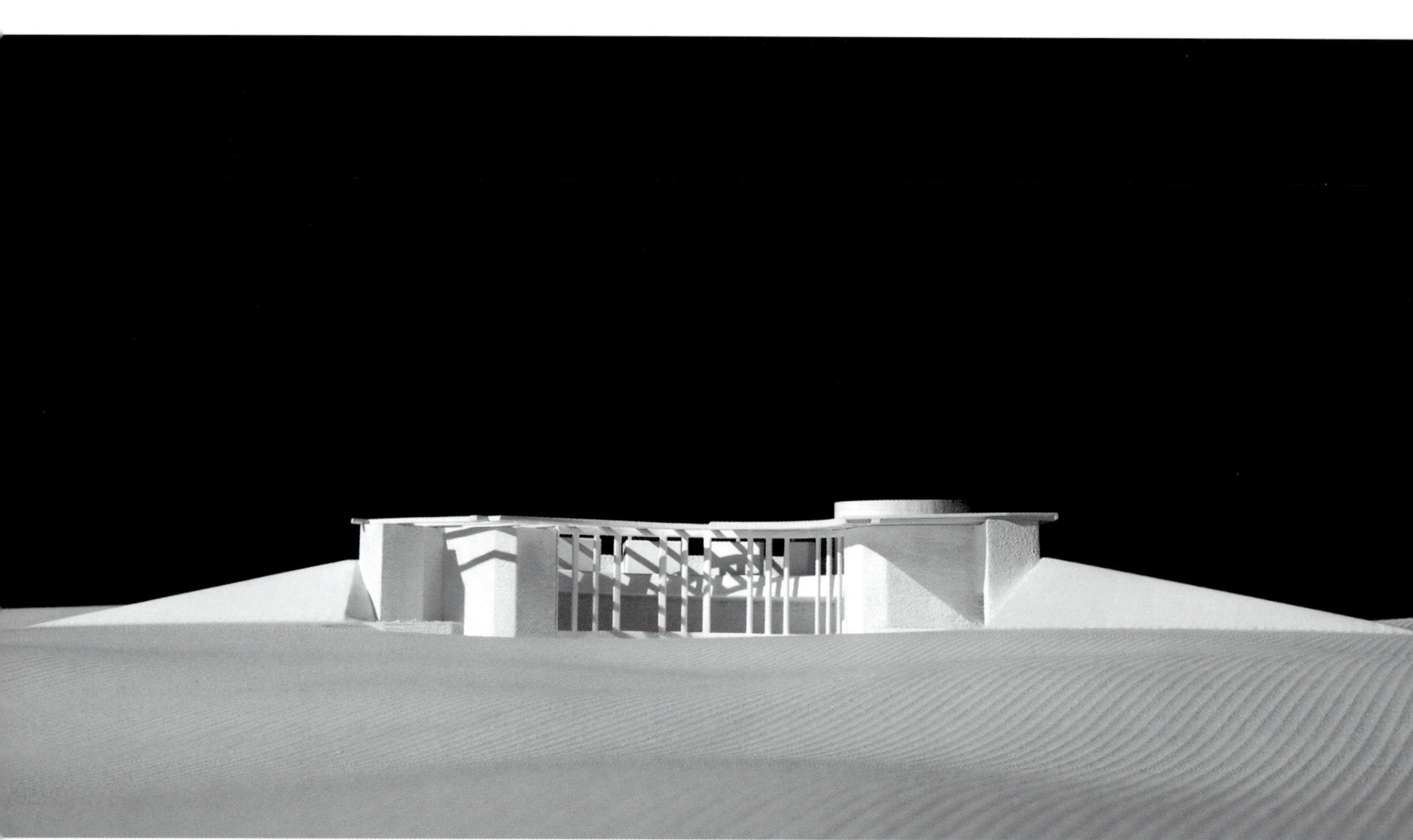

Also known as the Solar Hemicycle, the Jacobs II house is a continuation of Wright's exploration of small-scale house design and a precursor of the 1970s passive solar movement. Unlike the rectilinear Jacobs I, Jacobs II is a crescent in form, slightly embedded into the earth along its northern edge, and completely open to the south. The first level of the house was designed as a single, curved room measuring 17 feet wide by 80 feet long. The bedrooms are on a second-level mezzanine. The house is protected and insulated from the prevailing north winds of the Wisconsin prairie by a sculpted earth berm that surrounds its northern wall.[1]

Wright maximized the solar potential of the site. The curved plan is designed around the primary vectors of the sun path (at 43 degrees north latitude) where the house is located. On the shortest day of the year, the solar angle hits the eastern edge of the building at sunrise and the western edge at sunset. In order to take full advantage of natural daylight and heating in the winter, Wright established a low, circular sunken garden on the south side of the house. This outdoor space creates a warm microclimate similar to that of Jacobs I. To insure sufficient heat and air circulation, Wright cantilevered the second-floor bedrooms over the northern berm wall. This sectional shift creates a four-foot setback in the interior, pulls the mezzanine level away from the south-facing glazed wall, and allows the heat stored in the limestone floor of the lower level to radiate up to the mezzanine during winter nights. Heavy curtains can be closed to insulate the glass wall when necessary. Deep roof eaves and operable windows on the south side of the house protect the glass from the sun, decrease the heat gain from solar radiation and induce cross ventilation during the hot and humid summer months.

1. Frank Lloyd Wright, "Frank Lloyd Wright," *Architectural Forum* 94, no. 1 (1951), 91.

PRIMARY SOLAR PATHS
AND CORRESPONDING SECTIONS

Middleton, Wisconsin

43° North Latitude

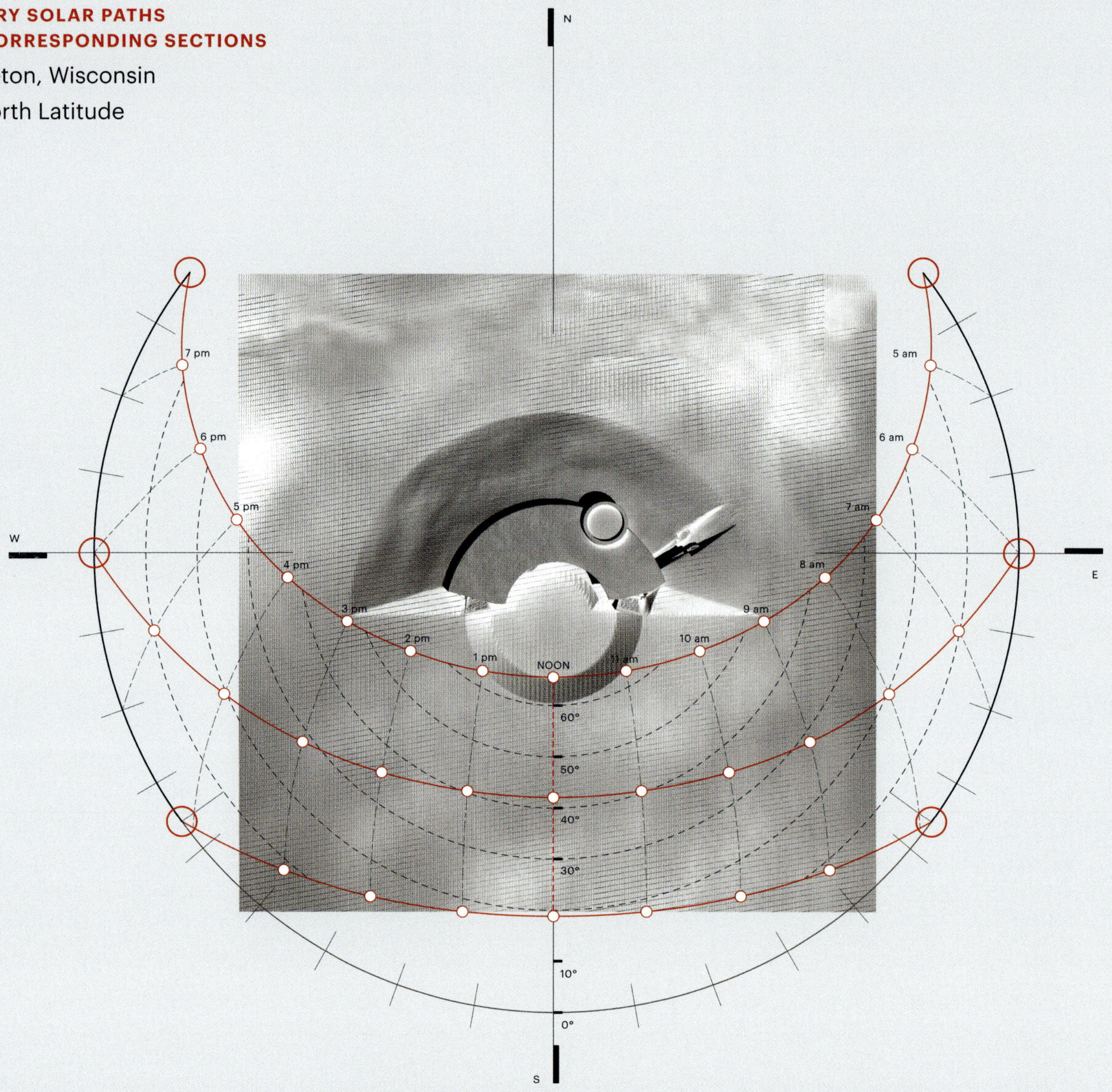

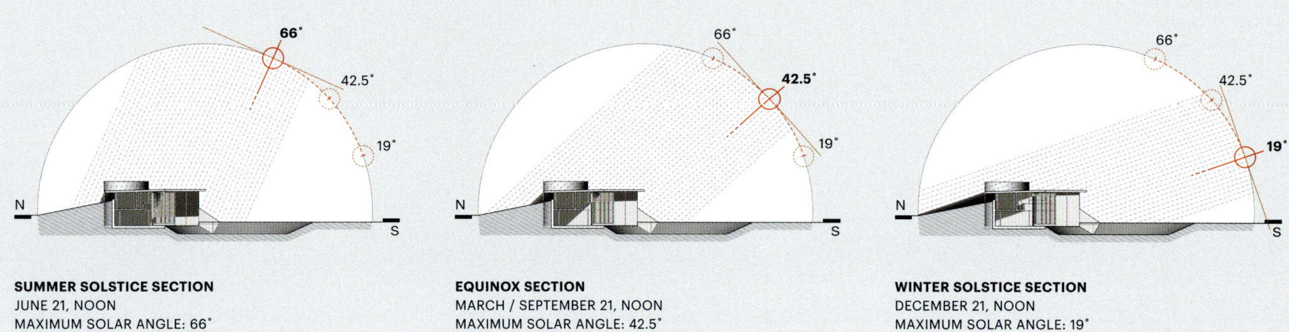

SUMMER SOLSTICE SECTION
JUNE 21, NOON
MAXIMUM SOLAR ANGLE: 66°

EQUINOX SECTION
MARCH / SEPTEMBER 21, NOON
MAXIMUM SOLAR ANGLE: 42.5°

WINTER SOLSTICE SECTION
DECEMBER 21, NOON
MAXIMUM SOLAR ANGLE: 19°

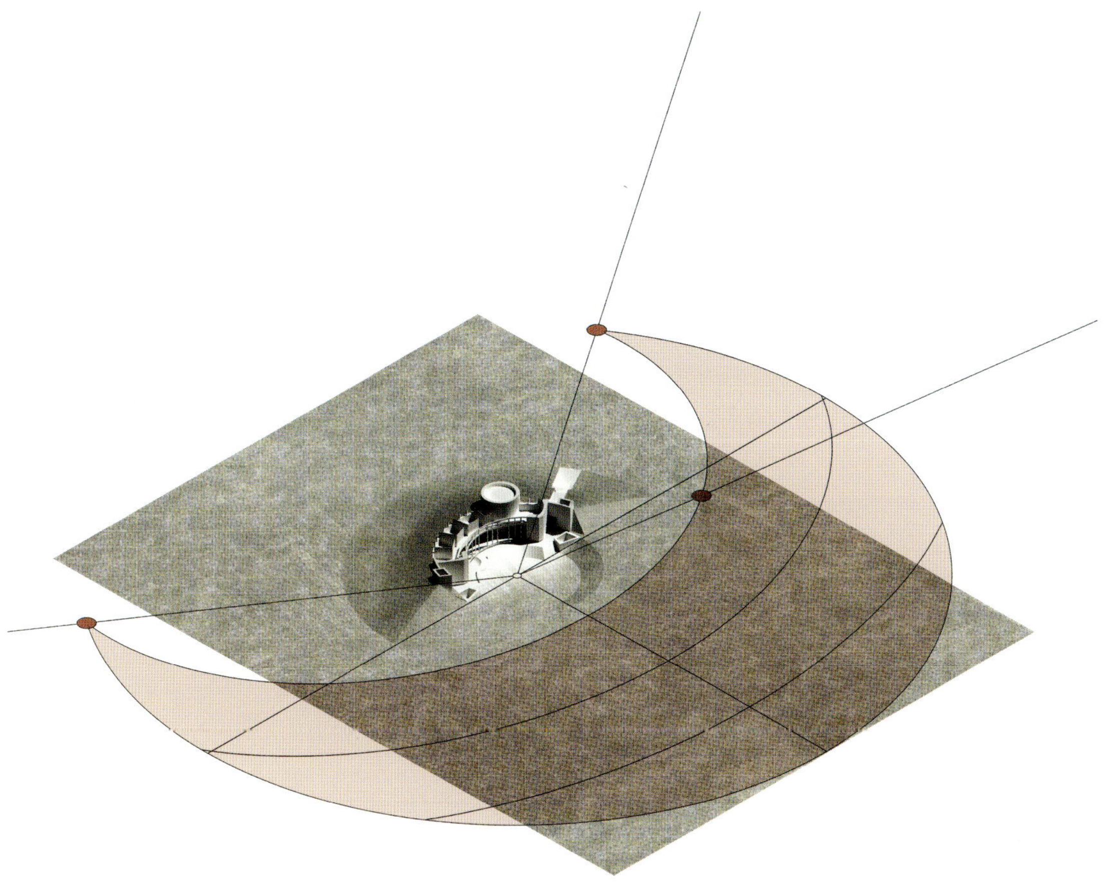

SUMMER SOLSTICE
JUNE 21, NOON

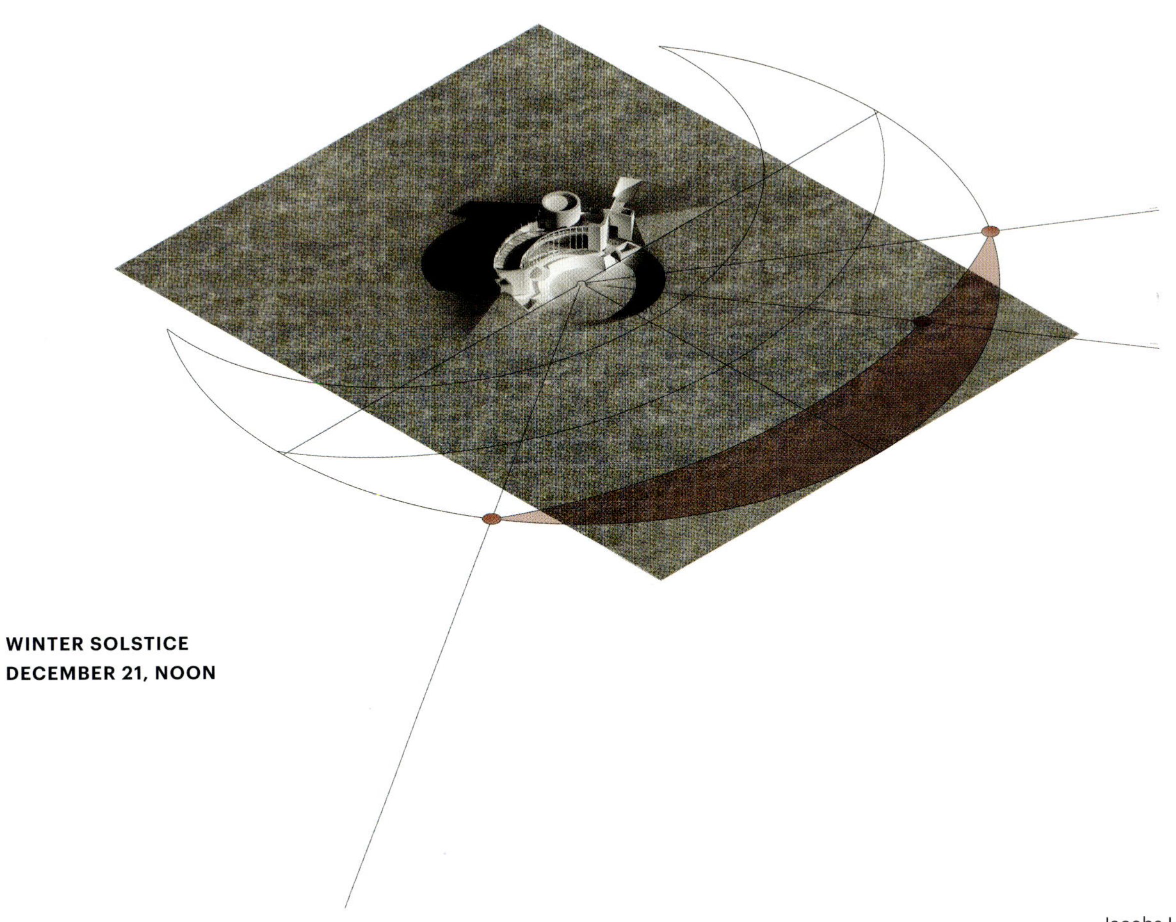

WINTER SOLSTICE
DECEMBER 21, NOON

Building for the Emprezas Gráficas o Cruzeiro
Oscar Niemeyer

<table>
<tr><td>YEAR
1949</td><td>LOCATION
Rio de Janeiro, Brazil
22°53'S 43°11'W</td><td>CLIMATE ZONE
Tropical Savannah</td><td>PROGRAM
Printing Facility and Offices</td></tr>
</table>

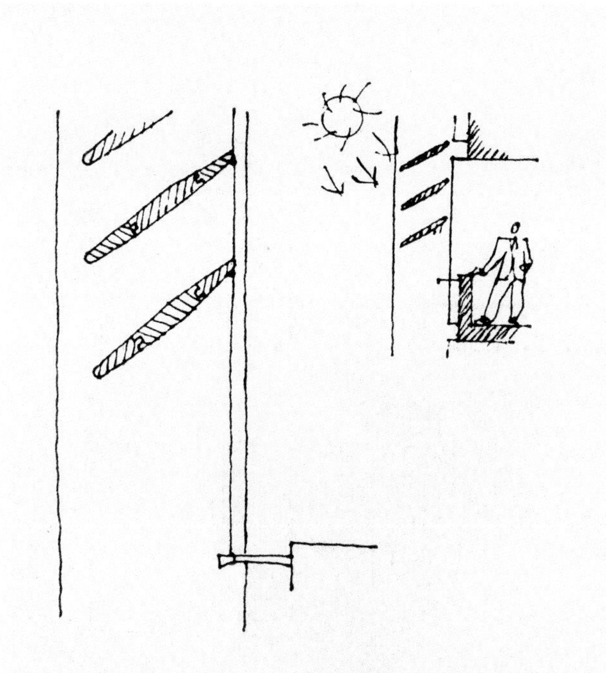

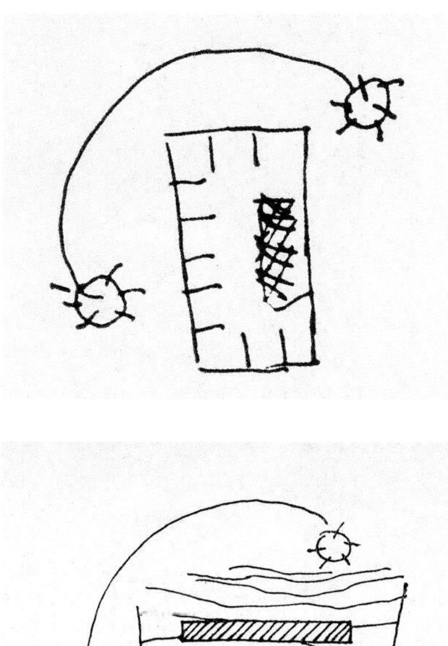

Oscar Niemeyer's first significant project was the 1937 Obra do Berço Day Nursery, a Rio de Janeiro facility that provided medical care to infants and mothers in need. Niemeyer used moveable vertical sunshades that resulted in a richly layered facade, creating a sculpturally powerful but minimal architectural assemblage. Twelve years later, Niemeyer designed a large-scale printing and publishing house for the Emprezas Gráficas o Cruzeiro in the industrial waterfront neighborhood of Gamboa. The building faced the same constraints as the day nursery: a very tight budget, a desire to overcome the aesthetic limitations of industrial buildings, and difficult environmental conditions.

In the ten-story composition, the north facade is an assemblage of three primary elements: oversized louvers, smaller scaled louvers, and rectangular voids cut into the field of sunshades. With these simple forms, Niemeyer produced a beautiful array of light and shadow in a complex composition. The north facade is raised off the ground to expose a colonnade structure. At the sixth floor, large voids in the field of louvers reveal a horizontal band of recessed windows; the industrial processes of printing, packaging, and shipping all generate heat but are most efficient when the heat is controlled. The louvers filter the sun, protect workspaces and windows from radiant heat gain, and allow the breezes from the Atlantic Ocean to pass through and cool the building. The east facade is a dense field of precast masonry units that establish a tight grid to filter the early morning sunlight.[1] The public spaces of the business are located at grade and entered through the colonnade.

The main access street on the north serves as both the route for trucks servicing the building and the street level presence for the public operations of the business. To resolve this cross circulation, Niemeyer took advantage of the topographic properties of the site. The building backs onto one of Rio's many hills, and the east facade is cut away on a steep diagonal where the structure pushes into the hillside. Niemeyer provided for truck circulation and loading dock requirements on the second level, while freeing up the ground floor level for public operations. Large-scale freight elevators connect interior loading docks with production facilities on the second, third, fourth, and fifth floors. The entire top floor was designed for staff facilities and included shaded, outdoor terraces on the north and east elevations.

1. Stamo Papadaki, *The Work of Oscar Niemeyer* (New York: Reinhold, 1950), 200.

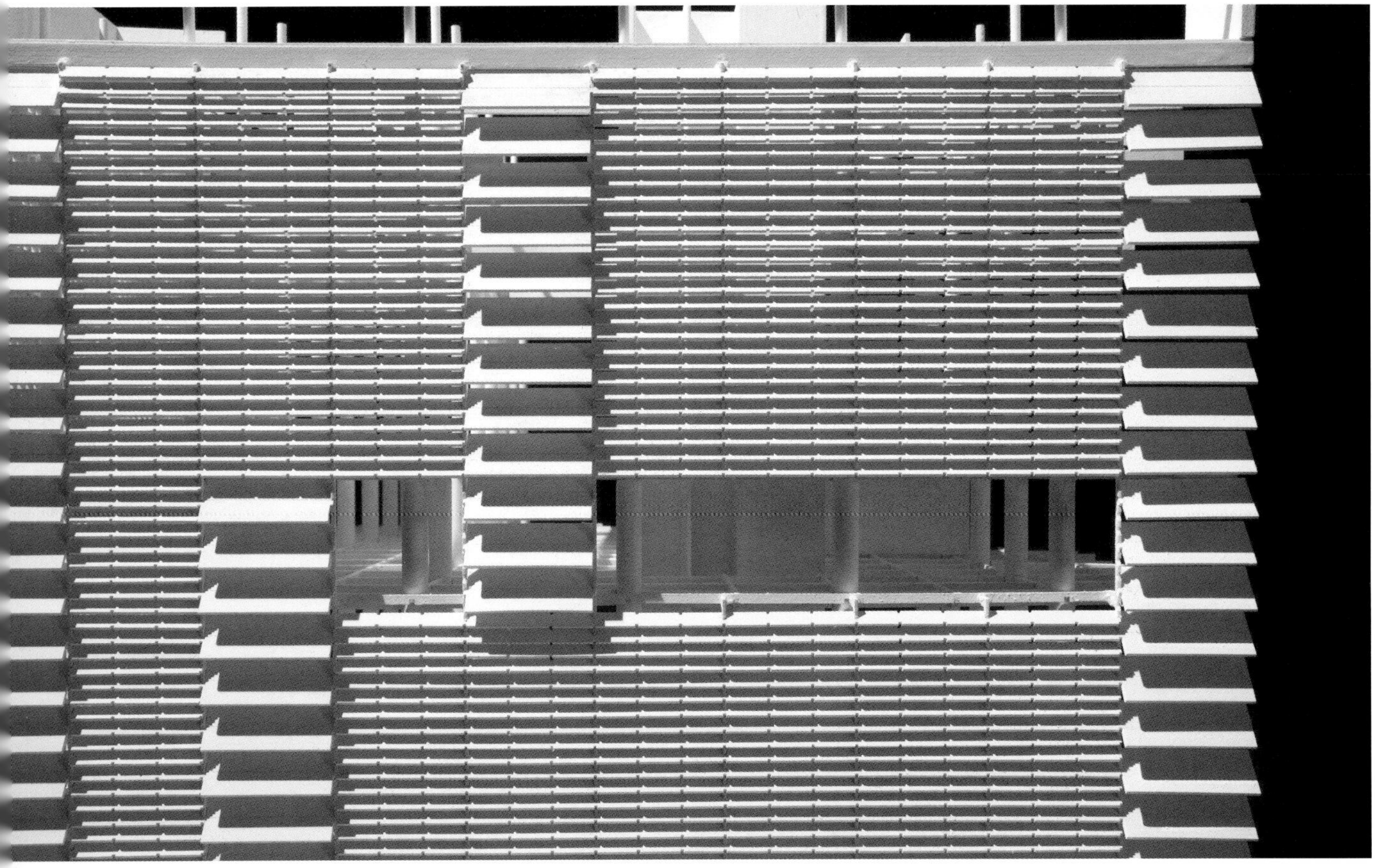

PRIMARY SOLAR PATHS AND CORRESPONDING SECTIONS

Rio De Janeiro, Brazil

22° South Latitude

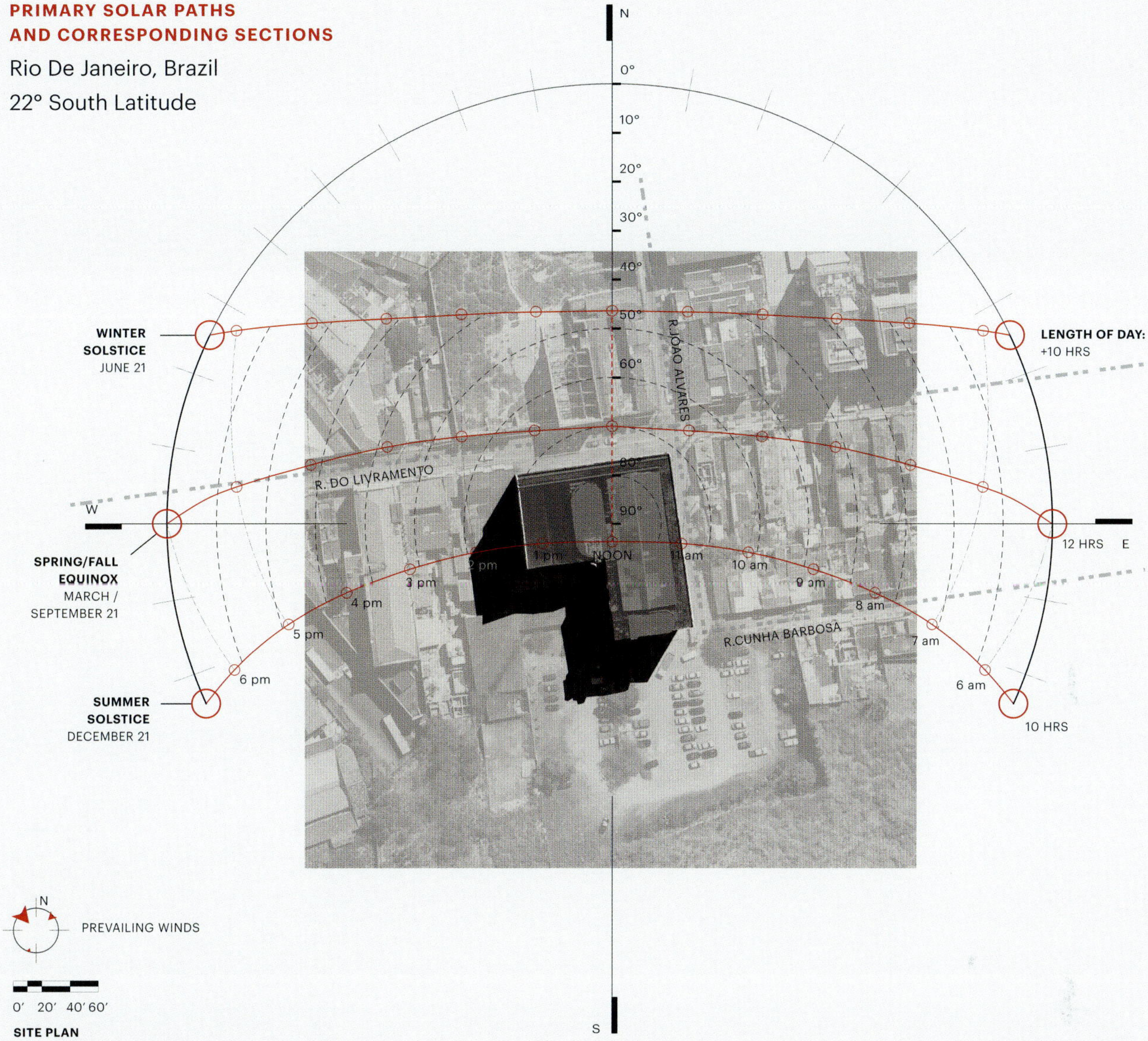

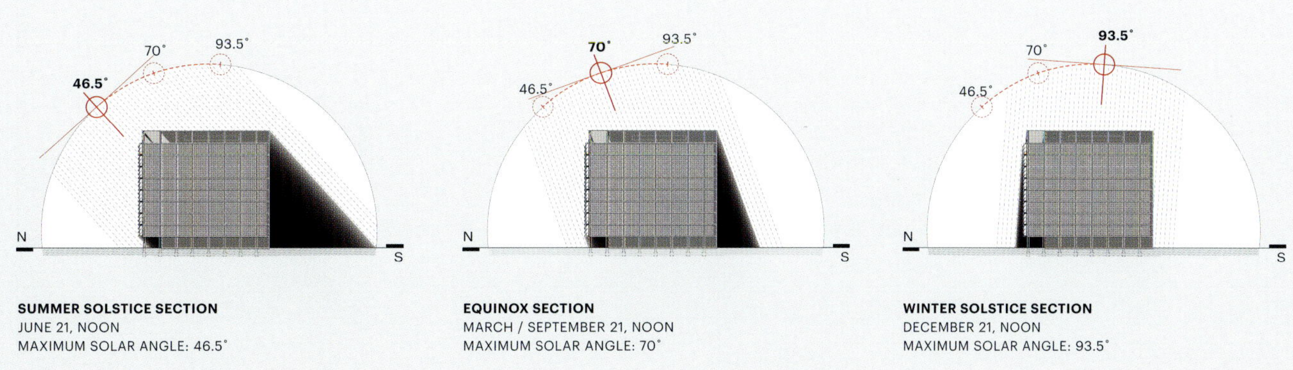

SUMMER SOLSTICE SECTION
JUNE 21, NOON
MAXIMUM SOLAR ANGLE: 46.5°

EQUINOX SECTION
MARCH / SEPTEMBER 21, NOON
MAXIMUM SOLAR ANGLE: 70°

WINTER SOLSTICE SECTION
DECEMBER 21, NOON
MAXIMUM SOLAR ANGLE: 93.5°

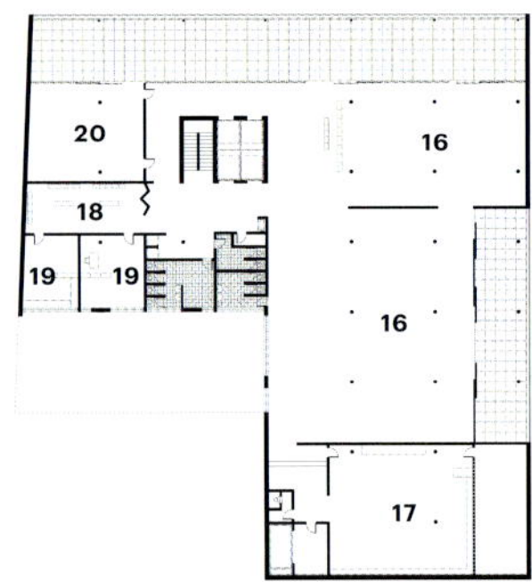

EIGHTH LEVEL

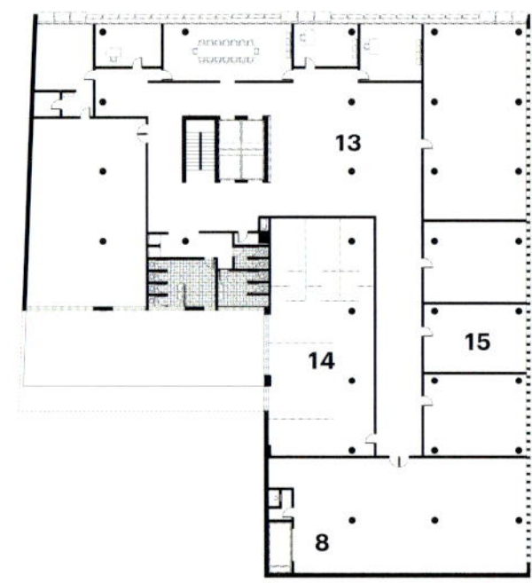

SEVENTH LEVEL

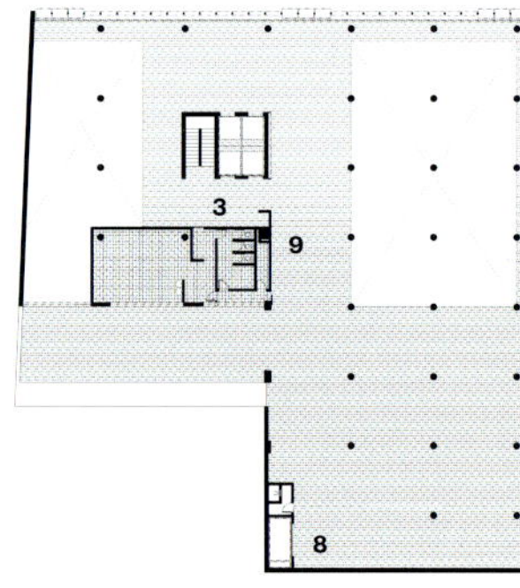

SIXTH LEVEL

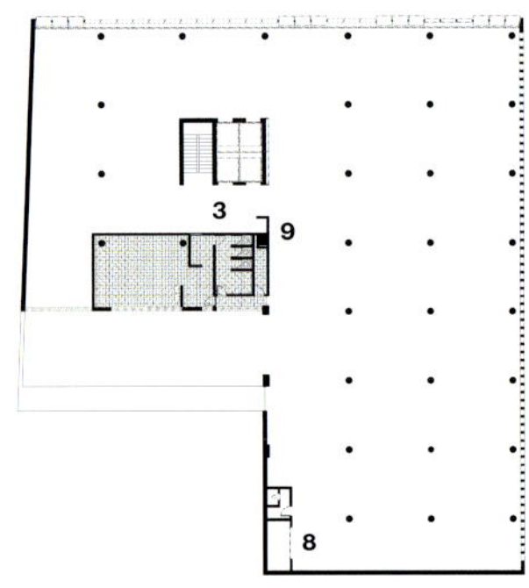

LEVELS 3–5

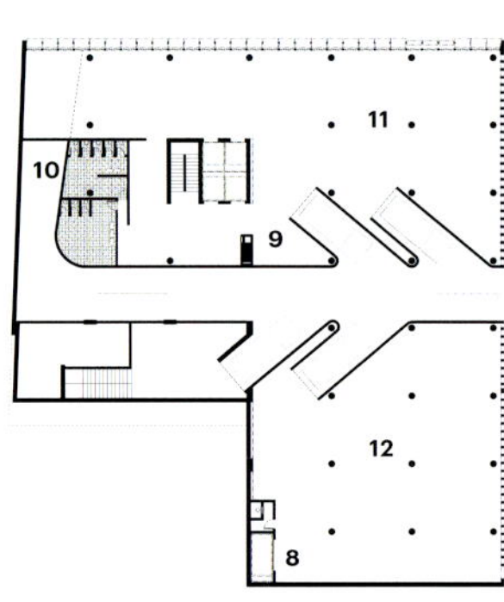

SECOND LEVEL

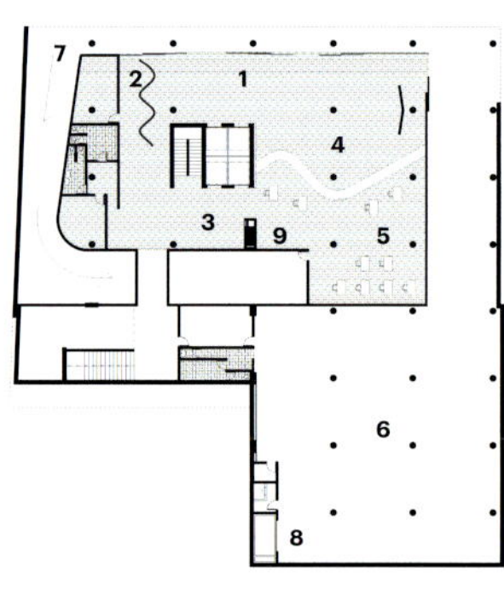

FIRST LEVEL

1 Public entrance
2 Personnel entrance
3 Personnel hall
4 Public hall
5 Information
6 Garage
7 Delivery
8 Service elevator
9 Paper elevator
10 Ramp

11 Shipping
12 Paper storage
13 Information
14 Editorial offices
15 General offices
16 Restaurant
17 Kitchen
18 Waiting room
19 Medical services
20 Lecture room

0 2 5 10m

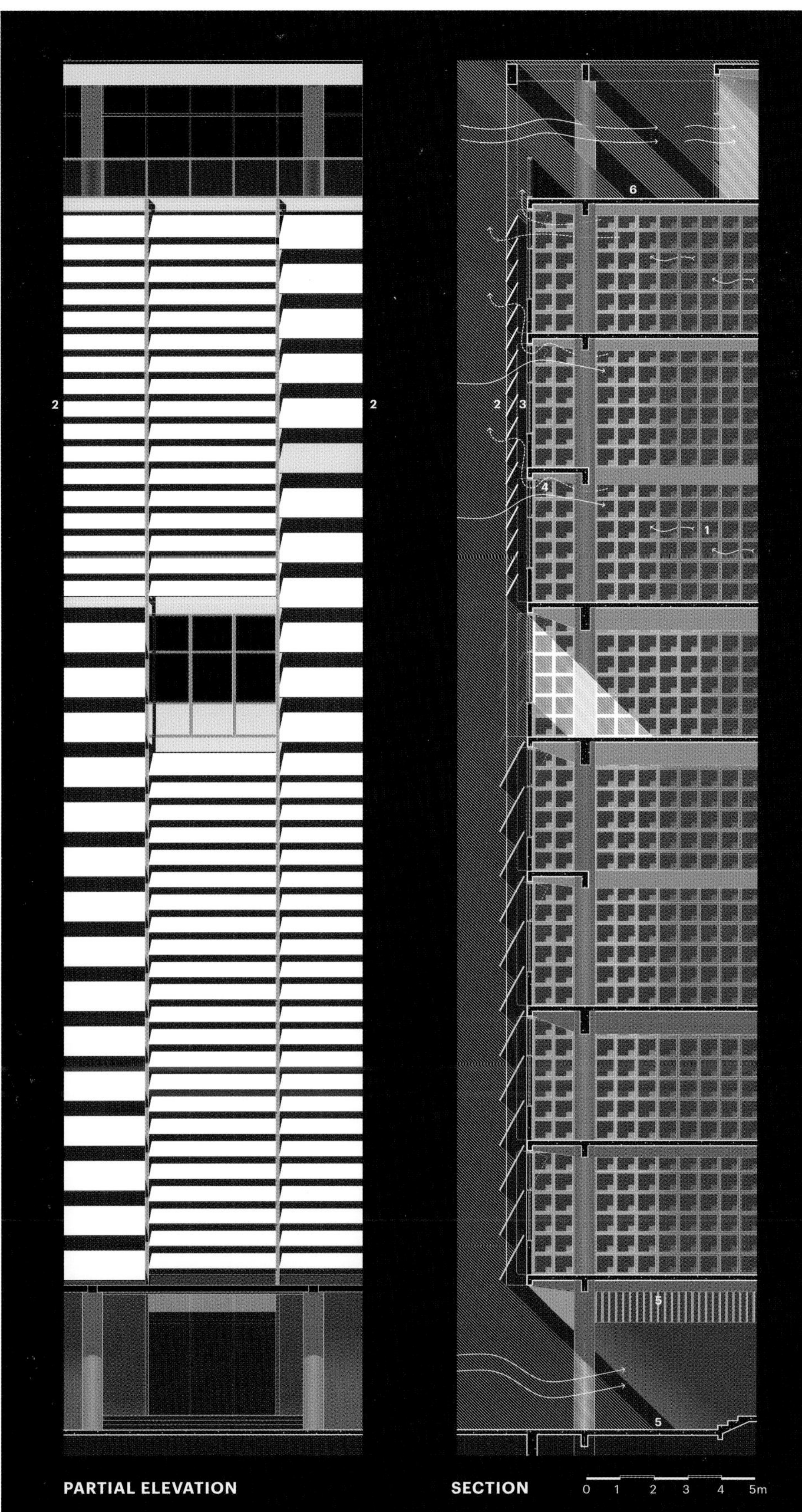

1 Solar and
ventilation screen
2 Solar and ventilation
louver
3 Natural light reflector
4 Operable hopper
window ventilation
5 Open ground floor
ventilation
6 Roof terrace

Maison Tropicale
Jean Prouvé Workshops

YEAR
1949

LOCATION
Niamey, Niger and Brazzaville, Republic of Congo
13°30'N 2°6'E; 4°15'S 15°16'E

CLIMATE ZONE
Semiarid and Tropical Savannah

PROGRAM
Prototype Housing Unit

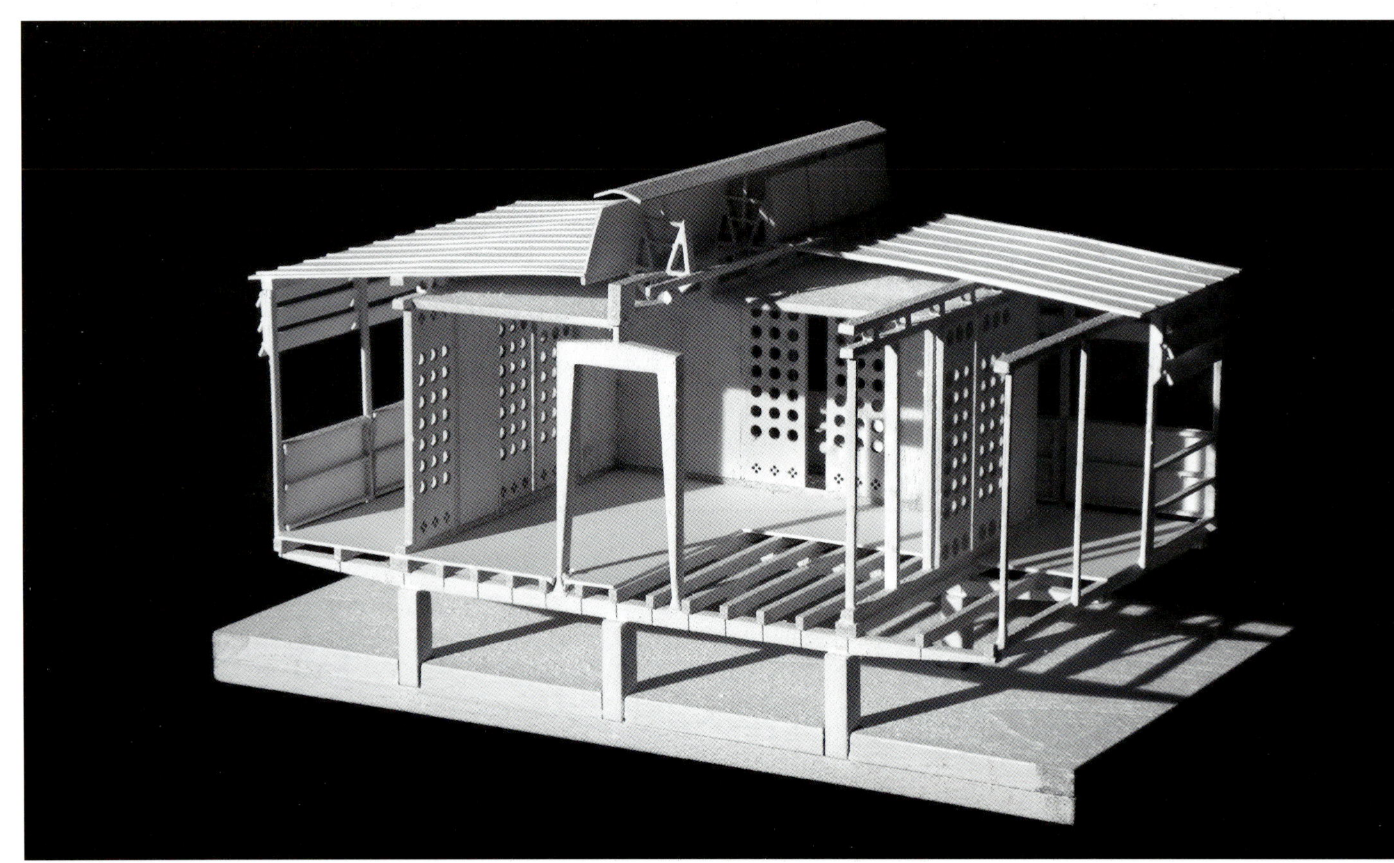

Jean Prouvé founded his fabrication workshops in Maxéville, France, in the early stages of postwar reconstruction and the international retooling of industrial war production facilities. In 1949, soon after receiving a contract from the French Ministry of Reconstruction and Urbanism for the design of prefabricated houses in Meudon, Prouvé was approached to develop a tropical variant of his finely detailed, precisely engineered building system for the French colonies in Africa. His solution was the Maison Tropicale.

Aluminum was the modern industrial material of the time: lightweight, easily machined, lustrous, and non-rusting. Prouvé's workshop conducted numerous experiments examining the potential of aluminum construction, and the metal would ultimately be used for all but the largest structural members of the Maison Tropicale. (L'Aluminium Français, an international mining company, would come to own 17 percent of Prouvé Workshops, a relationship that would last from 1944 to 1954, and act as a significant driving force behind Prouvé's use of aluminum in his designs.)[1] To facilitate shipping and ease of fabrication, the components of the house were designed to be as flat as possible, no longer than 13 feet,

and no heavier than 220 pounds, corresponding to the fabrication capacity and the interior dimensions of cargo planes. The houses could be erected by local labor without heavy machinery.[2]

The interior of the 1,500 square-foot house is contained within a complete and separate shade-envelope consisting of a double roof and walls. The walls are composed of operable reflective aluminum louvers at the roofline. Sliding perforated panels make up the balustrade. A perimeter porch separates the outer sunshade from the interior enclosure, providing a cooler zone and buffering the inner house from the outside heat. To aid in this heat transfer, the roof is vented along the ridgeline, inducing the passage of heat away from this protective zone. The inner enclosure is defined by alternating fixed panels and sliding doors. The doors are gridded in a pattern of blue glass portholes and round ventilation registers at the top and bottom. These perforations permit the user to control the ventilation.[3]

Only three Maison Tropicale prototypes were built. In 1949, as a promotional strategy, the first house was assembled on the banks of the Seine before being shipped to Niamey, Niger, a semiarid region. It was constructed on a concrete plinth with hollow airflow channels running through it.[4] The most well-known iterations of the house were two units later built as a residence and offices for the director of L'Aluminium Français in the humid tropical environments of Brazzaville, Congo.

The Maison Tropical, made primarily of aluminum, a material that is both energy intensive to produce and often destructive to the environment at the point of resource extraction, is easy to dismiss when considering environmentally appropriate architectural solutions for the tropical world. However, the design does offer insights into highly articulated passive climate control that are useful: the double roof, the deep shading, the flexibility of the wall system, and the accommodation of natural ventilation in all aspects of the assembly. All of these strategies could be applied using other construction methods and more appropriate materials.

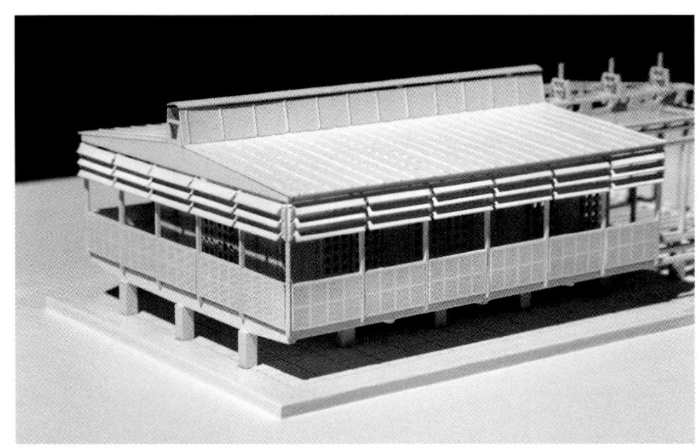

1. Peter Sulzer, *Jean Prouvé: Complete Works,* Volume 3: 1944–1954 (Berlin: Birkhauser–Publishers for Architecture, 2005), 19.

2. Robert Rubin, "Preserving and Presenting Prefab: Jean Prouvé's Tropical House," *Future Anterior* 2, no. 1 (2005): 32–36.

3. Ibid.

4. Ibid.

PRIMARY SOLAR PATHS AND CORRESPONDING SECTIONS

Brazzaville, Congo

4° South Latitude

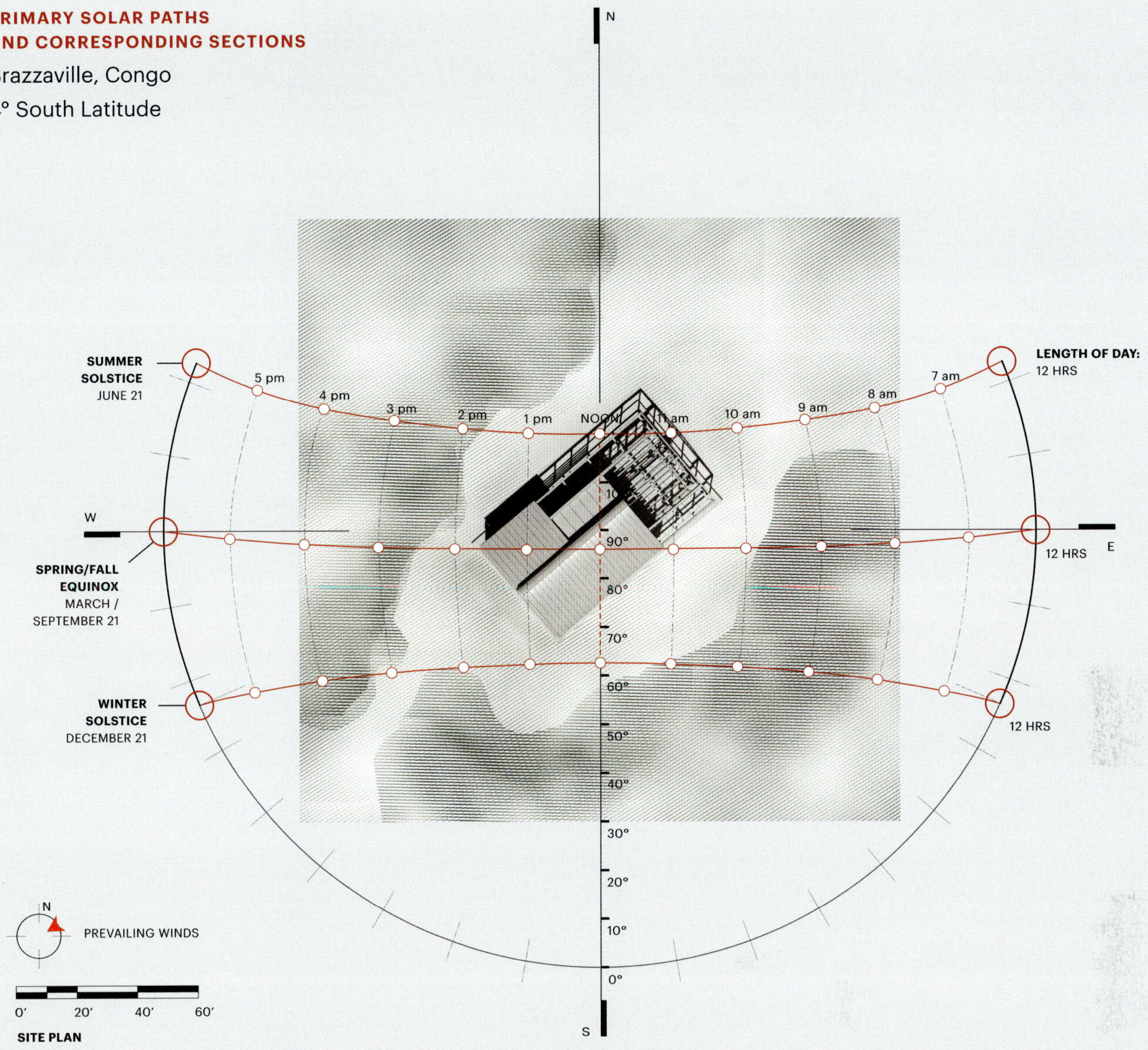

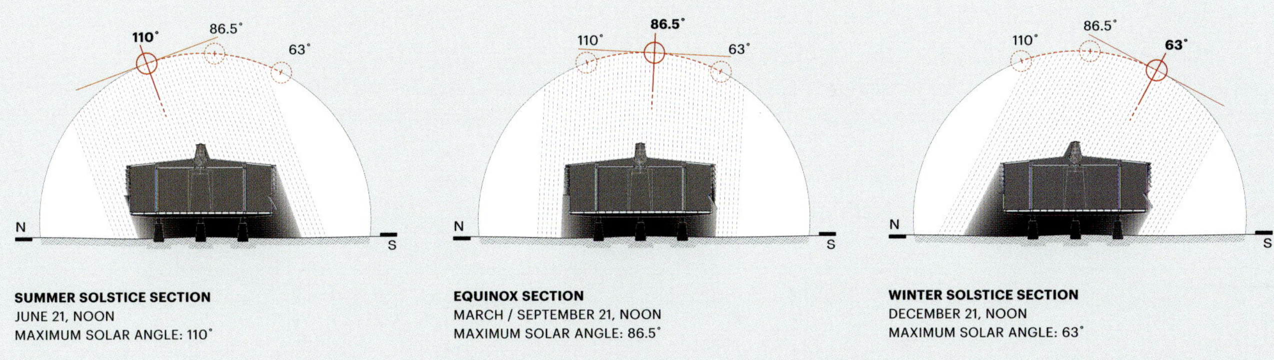

SUMMER SOLSTICE SECTION
JUNE 21, NOON
MAXIMUM SOLAR ANGLE: 110°

EQUINOX SECTION
MARCH / SEPTEMBER 21, NOON
MAXIMUM SOLAR ANGLE: 86.5°

WINTER SOLSTICE SECTION
DECEMBER 21, NOON
MAXIMUM SOLAR ANGLE: 63°

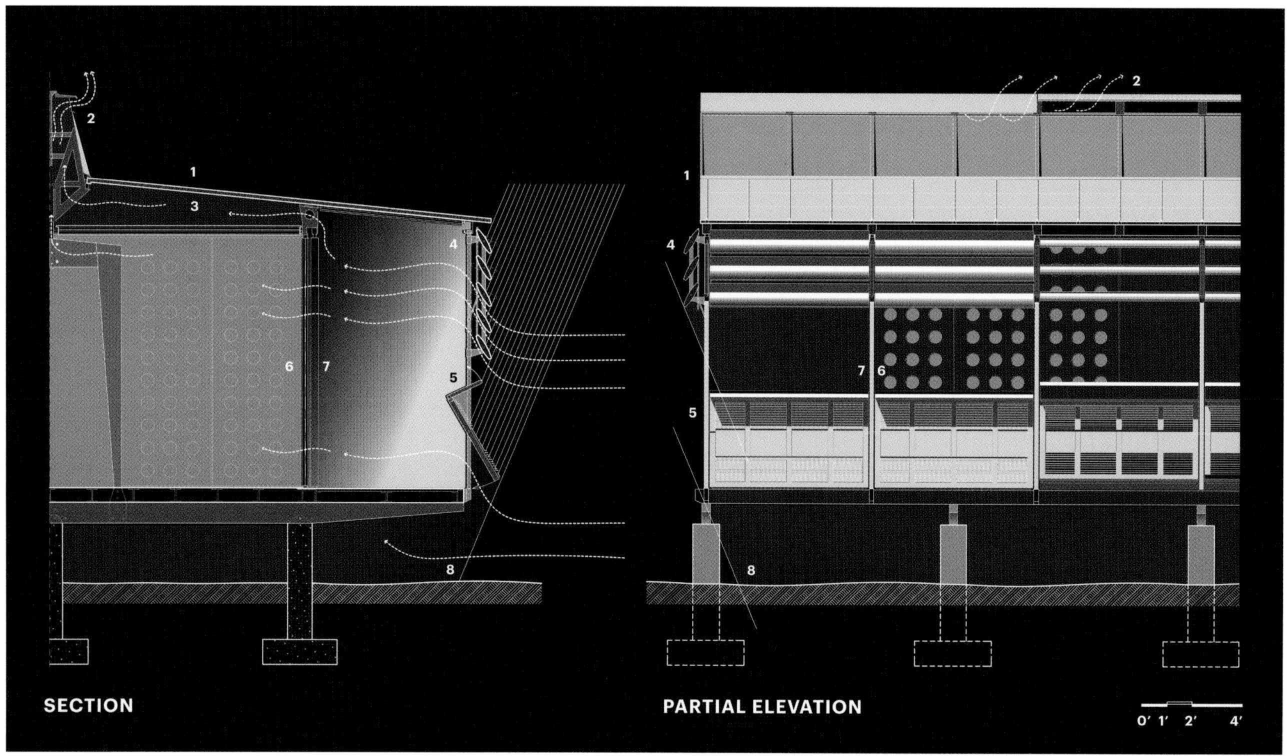

1 *Reflective roof*
2 *Operable roof ventilator*
3 *Induced roof cavity ventilation*
4 *Operable shading and ventilation louvers*

5 *Operable ventilation panels*
6 *Interior ventilated screens*
7 *Ventilated porch*
8 *Elevated building ventilation*

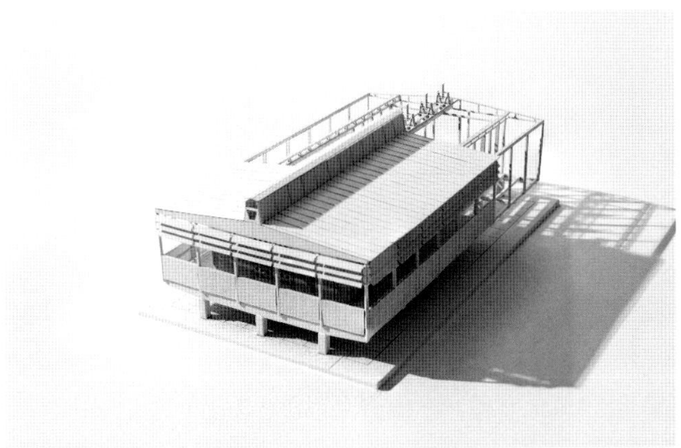

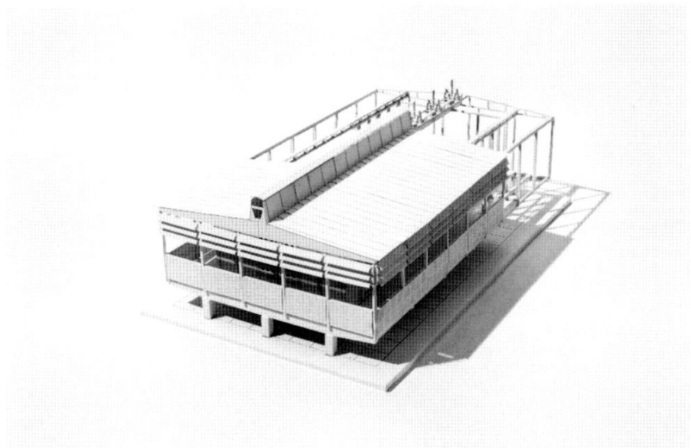

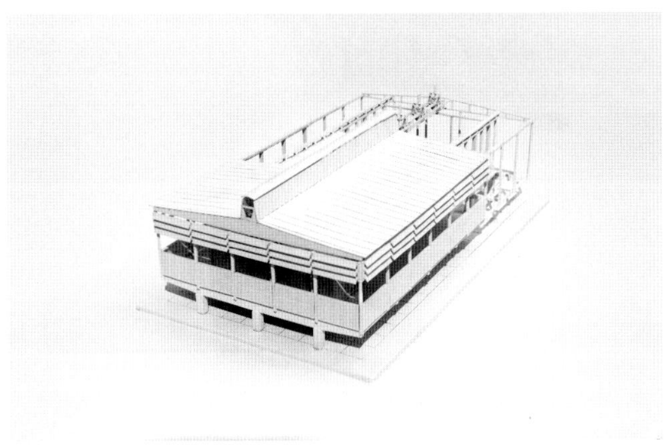

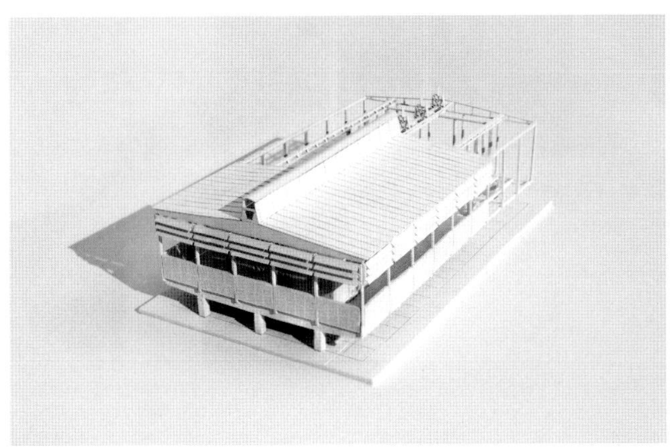

Soholm 1
Arne Jacobsen

YEAR
1950

LOCATION
Klampenborg, Denmark
55°46'28"N 12°35'27"E

CLIMATE ZONE
Temperate Oceanic

PROGRAM
Multifamily Housing

Designed by Arne Jacobsen, Soholm is one of the early postwar housing experiments in Denmark. The residential development, seven miles north of downtown Copenhagen, was built in three phases between 1946 and 1954, with each of the phases examining a different housing typology. Soholm I consists of five attached houses; Soholm II is nine terraced houses; and Soholm III is a group of four single-story houses. Jacobsen carefully considered the existing trees and plantings on the site as well as the interrelationship of the three groups of houses.[1] All are oriented toward the south to allow for maximum sunlight and views of the Bay of Bellevue in the Øresund Strait. The resultant site plan gave the building grouping the feeling of an open park.

Sited between the Strandvejen roadway and the Copenhagen S-train railway, Soholm I is a row of five interlocked two-story houses organized in a staggered manner, the strong simple forms making this project the most architecturally expressive of the group. Although the houses are the same shape and size, their volumetric composition allows each of them to remain distinct from the others. The houses are connected by an intermediary one-story building, which contains the kitchen of the house to the northeast and a bathroom of the house to the southwest. The entrance on the first level opens into a large dining room with a glass wall opening to the southwest garden terrace. The staggered plan of the houses defines an outdoor area that is walled on three sides, creating a courtyard-like space that is warmed by the low winter sun. [2] The first-level bedrooms also face the garden. The sloped roof of the house allows for a two-story dining room, with a staircase leading up to the living room and a balcony overlooking the space below. A horizontal strip of windows above the balcony allows northern light into the room, emphasizing the reliance on natural daylight where possible. The southwest-facing wall of the living room is glazed with a large window and a door leading to an exterior balcony and views of the Øresund Strait[3]

Jacobsen lived and worked in the southeasternmost house in the group. He would later add a two-story addition that expanded the basement office, created a meeting room on the first level, and added a studio on the second level. The construction methods of Solholm I, dictated by post war shortages of materials, and Jacobsen's Danish sensibilities that emphasized thrift, produced architectural works of spartan efficiency and clean simple detailing, ideas that Jacobsen would build on in his later works.

1. Carsten Thau and Kjeld Vindum, *Arne Jacobsen* (Copenhagen: The Danish Architectural Press, 1998), 340–47.

2. Ibid.

3. Peter Thule Kristensen, *Arne Jacobsen's Own House – Strandvejen 413* Odense (Denmark: Realadania Byg A/S, 2007), 6.

Bebyggelse ved Søholm
Arne Jacobsen d ¾. 47.

PRIMARY SOLAR PATHS AND CORRESPONDING SECTIONS

Klampenborg, Denmark
55° North Latitude

SITE PLAN

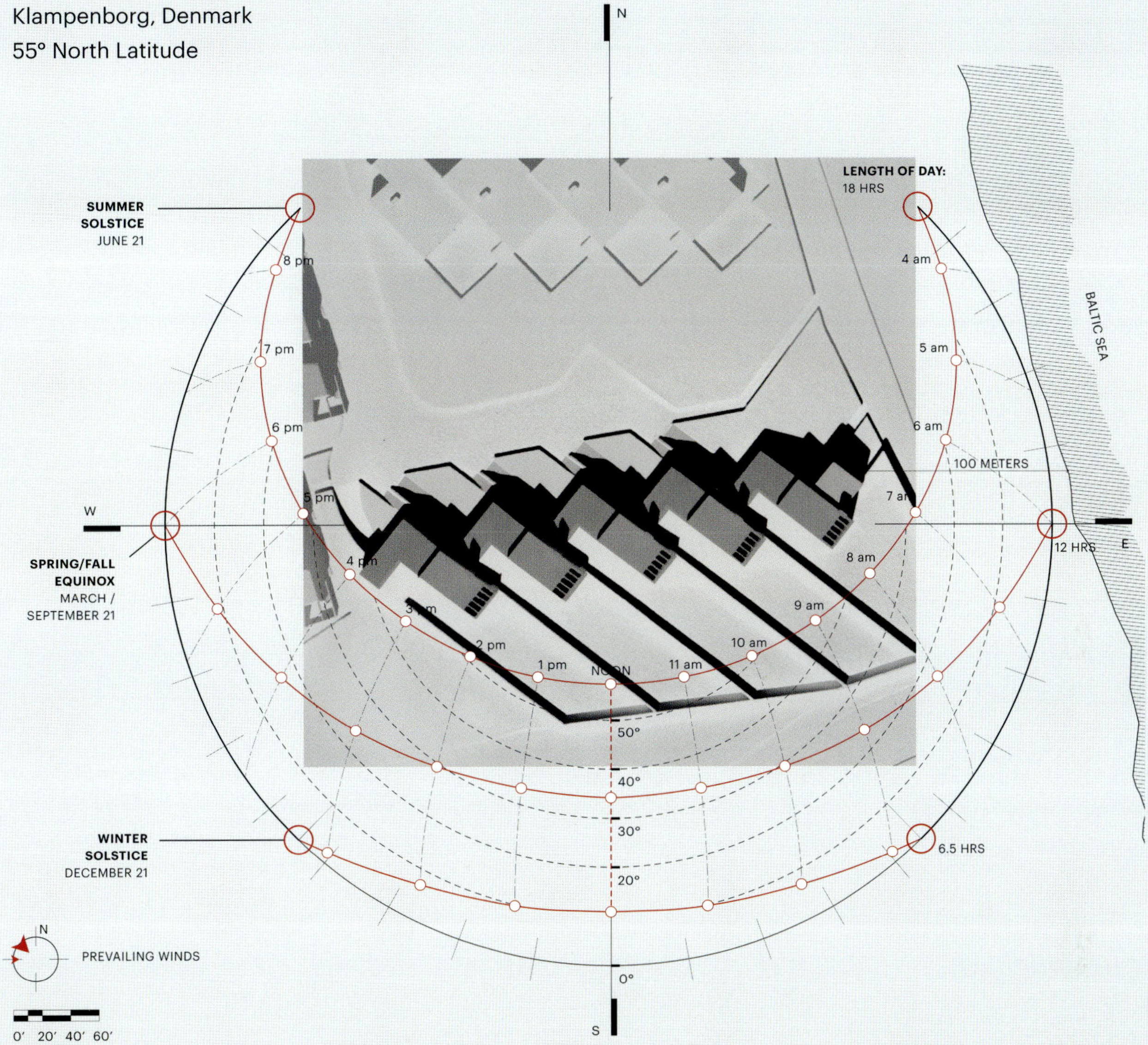

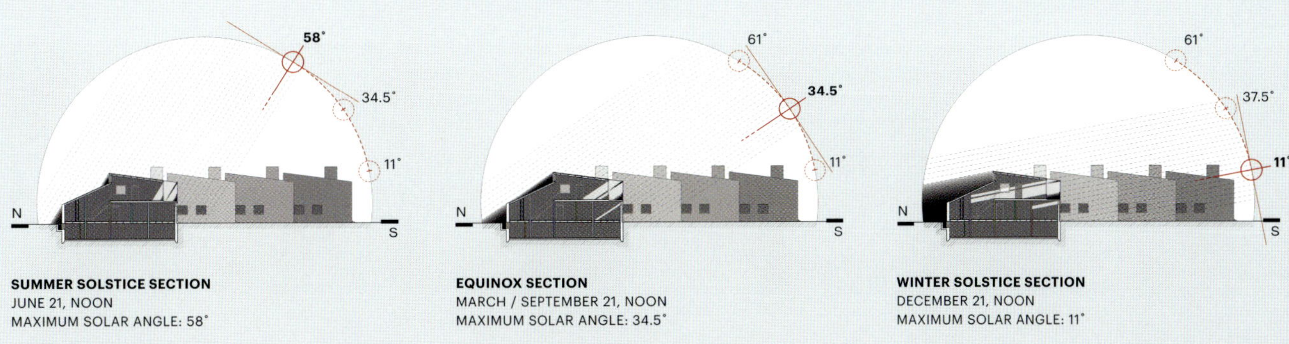

SUMMER SOLSTICE SECTION
JUNE 21, NOON
MAXIMUM SOLAR ANGLE: 58°

EQUINOX SECTION
MARCH / SEPTEMBER 21, NOON
MAXIMUM SOLAR ANGLE: 34.5°

WINTER SOLSTICE SECTION
DECEMBER 21, NOON
MAXIMUM SOLAR ANGLE: 11°

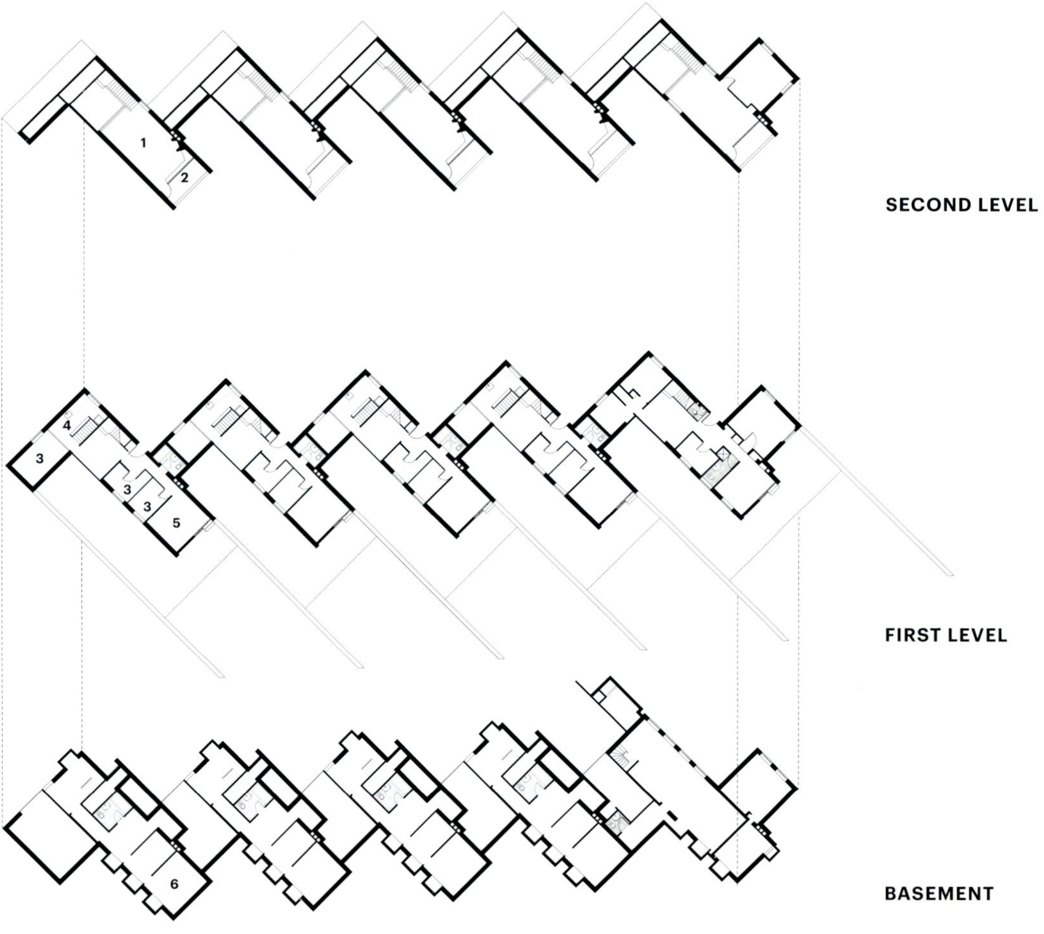

SECOND LEVEL

FIRST LEVEL

BASEMENT

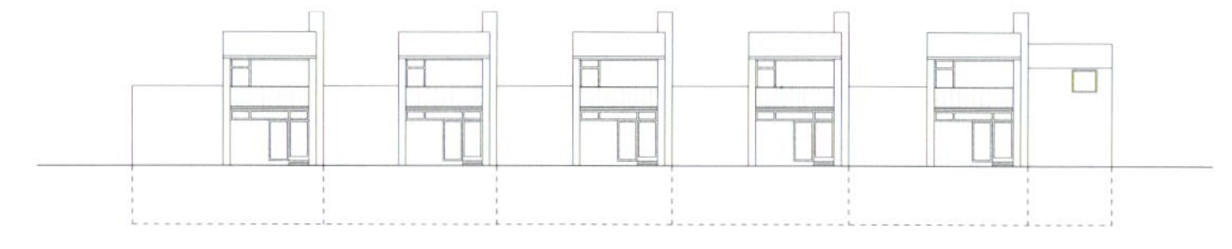

SOUTHEAST ELEVATION

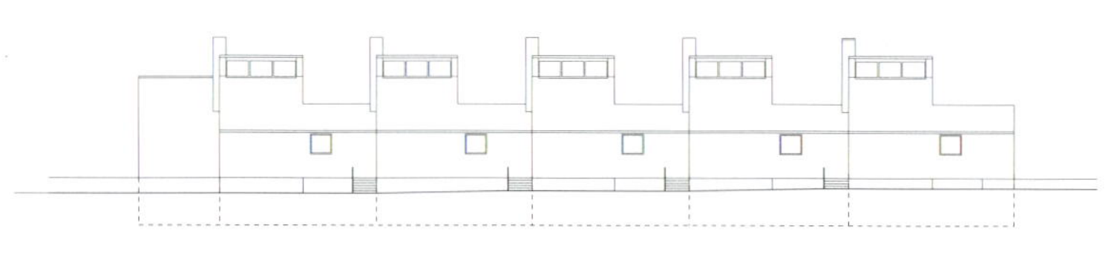

NORTHWEST ELEVATION

1 Living room
2 Balcony
3 Bedroom
4 Kitchen
5 Dining room
6 Boiler room

0   5   10m

Bachelor Flats
Bronek Katz + Reginald Vaughan

YEAR
c. 1950

LOCATION
Rufisque, Dakar, Senegal
14°43'N 7°16'W

CLIMATE ZONE
Semiarid

PROGRAM
Workers' Housing

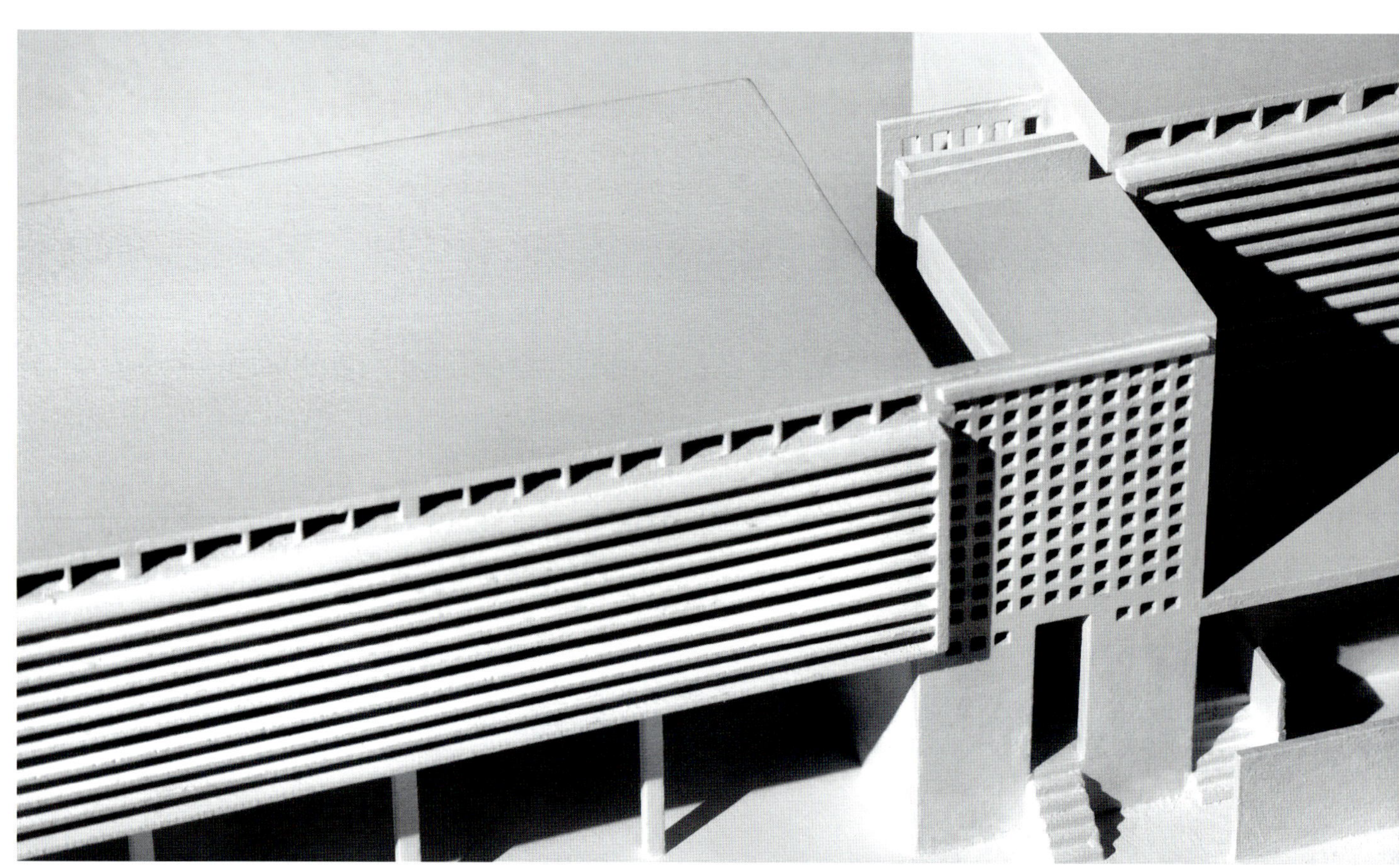

In 1936 Bronek Katz, a Polish-born architect, moved to England to work for Walter Gropius and Maxwell Fry designing exhibitions for the Ministry of Information. After the war, Katz and Reginald Vaughan, a former assistant to Fry, established a practice. They became the official architects for Bata Development, a Czech-based multinational retailer, manufacturer, and distributor of footwear. Katz and Vaughan designed housing for "Bata Cities," factory towns in what was then French West Africa.[1]

The bachelor flats (a term that Jane Drew and Maxwell Fry used to characterize the program of workers' housing), is located on a peninsula of land projecting off the west coast of Africa into the Atlantic Ocean. The building is a small-scale twelve unit project that demonstrates many of the core principals for designing in a semiarid tropical region, suggesting why this work was selected as representative of tropical housing in Drew and Fry's seminal work *Tropical Architecture*.

The linear building is sited 45 degrees off due north, taking advantage of the prevailing ocean breezes. Its diagonal orientation also limits heat gain in the early morning and late afternoon. Elevated above grade, the structure creates a shaded outdoor communal yard, which is adjacent to an enclosed lounge, kitchen, and dining room. The entire envelope of the building is articulated to limit solar gain. The double roof significantly reduces the transfer of heat to the interior residential spaces. The thin upper slab absorbs direct solar radiation while the gap between the slabs is open to facilitate the flow of air between the roofs, carrying away accumulated heat. The portion of the plan oriented to the southeast is used for the circulation corridors. Outdoor circulation space is protected by horizontal sun shades, each twelve inches deep and spaced twelve inches apart from floor to ceiling. A perforated masonry facade allows for natural ventilation and only the earliest morning sun can directly penetrate the corridor. During the rest of the day, the area is fully shaded, creating a cooler protective zone for the living spaces. The northwestern side of the building includes individual balconies within every unit. Relatively deep in plan, they are shaded by a high parapet wall and a gridded sunshade structure from above. The exterior walls of the actual living space receive little direct sun.

The cross section shows that every aspect of the building was designed to allow the natural flow of air

PRIMARY SOLAR PATHS AND CORRESPONDING SECTIONS

Rufisque, Dakar, Senegal

14° North Latitude

SITE PLAN

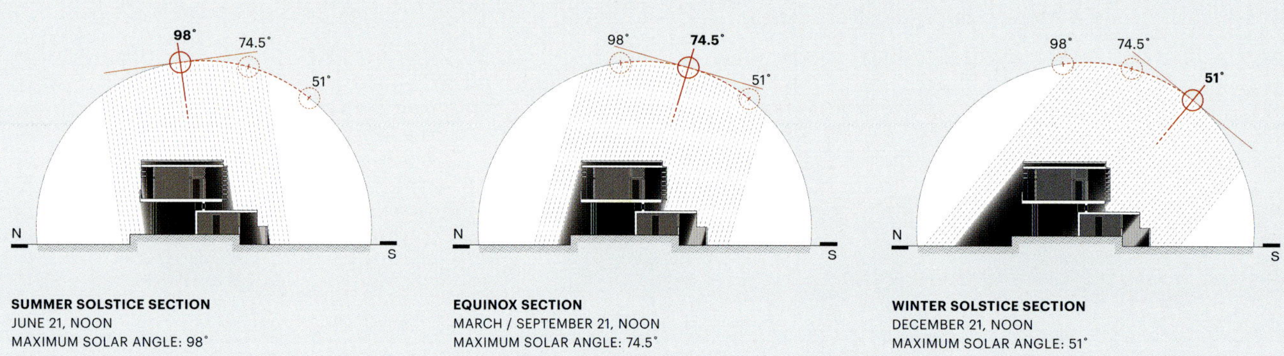

SUMMER SOLSTICE SECTION
JUNE 21, NOON
MAXIMUM SOLAR ANGLE: 98°

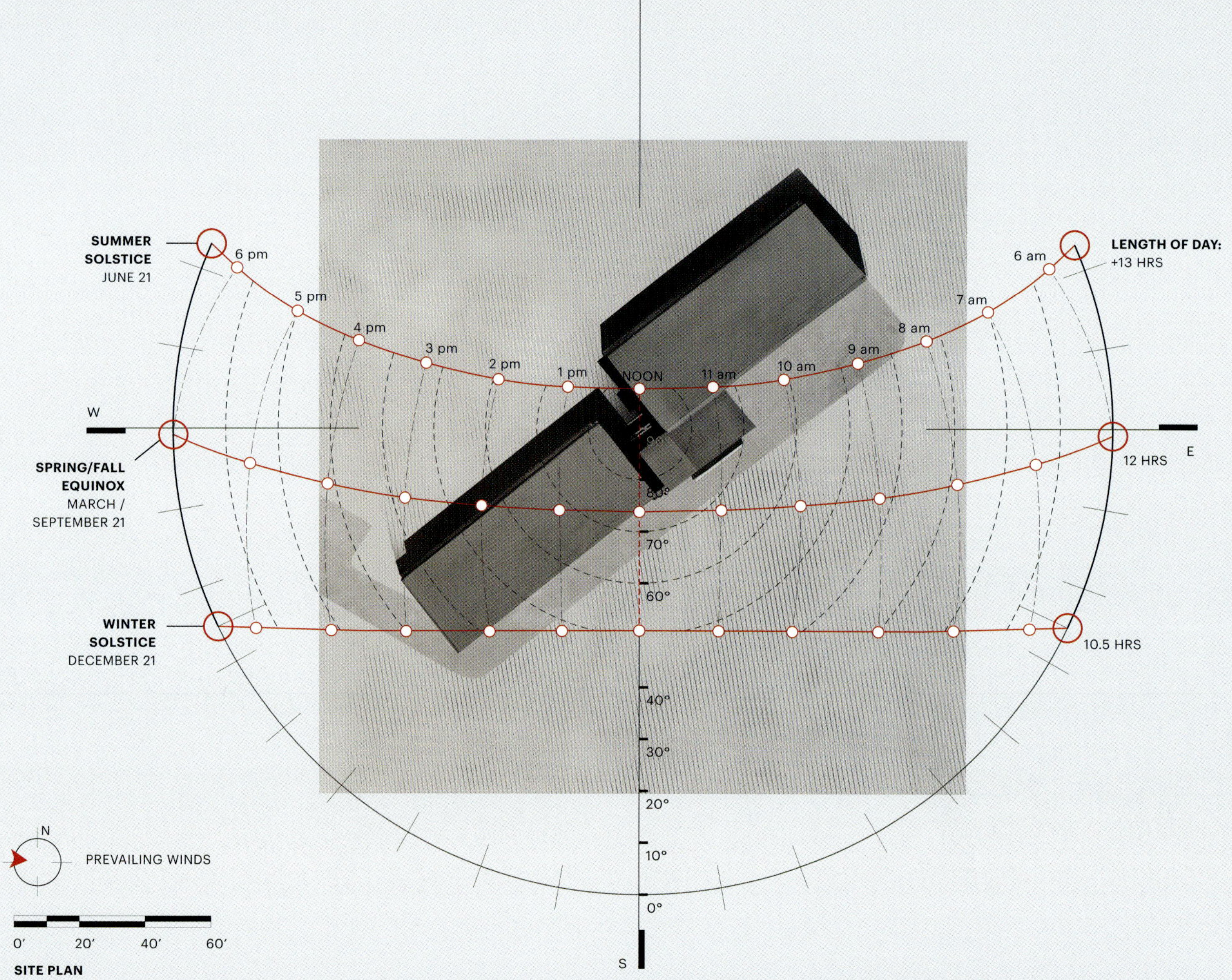

EQUINOX SECTION
MARCH / SEPTEMBER 21, NOON
MAXIMUM SOLAR ANGLE: 74.5°

WINTER SOLSTICE SECTION
DECEMBER 21, NOON
MAXIMUM SOLAR ANGLE: 51°

from the coastal breezes to pass through the dwelling areas, unrestricted by the louvered transoms, windows, and doors. This small building employs many of the tools of passive climate control required in hot semiarid tropical climates; the shaded roofs, walls, and outdoor spaces, and the cross sectional emphasis on natural ventilation make this a fine example of how these basic design strategies can be combined.

1. Maxwell Fry, "Bronek Katz," *Journal of the Royal Institute of British Architects,* (May 1960): 248–49.

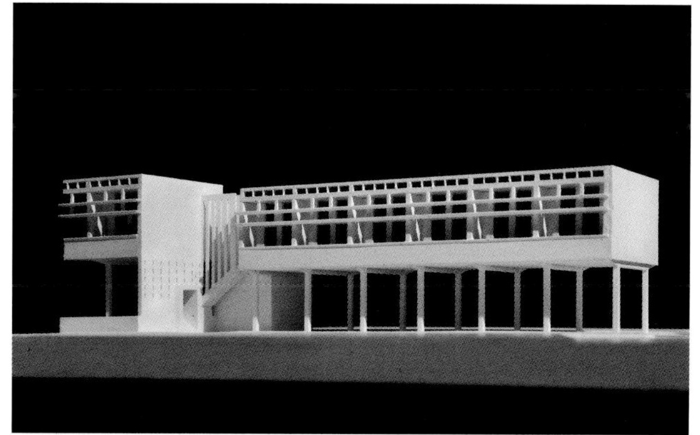

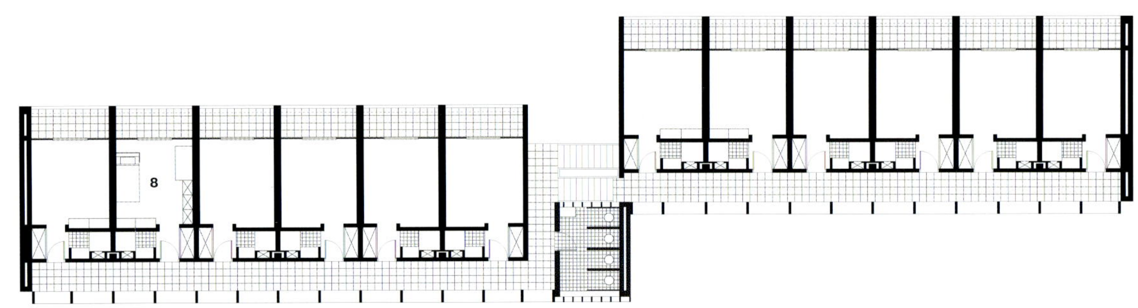

SECOND LEVEL

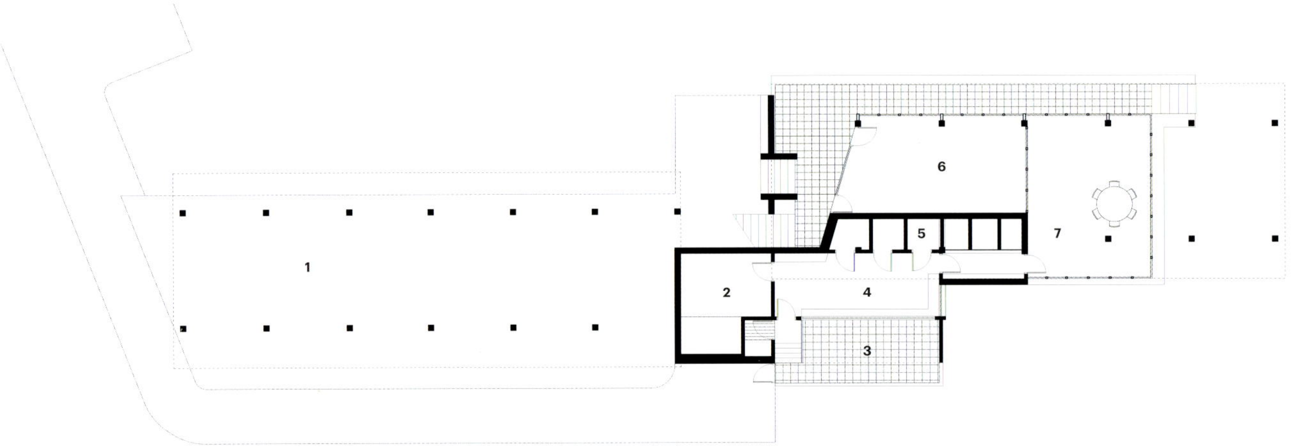

GROUND LEVEL

1 *Covered parking*
2 *Laundry*
3 *Kitchen yard*
4 *Kitchen*

5 *Storage*
6 *Lounge*
7 *Dining room*
8 *Typical flat*

0 1 2   5m

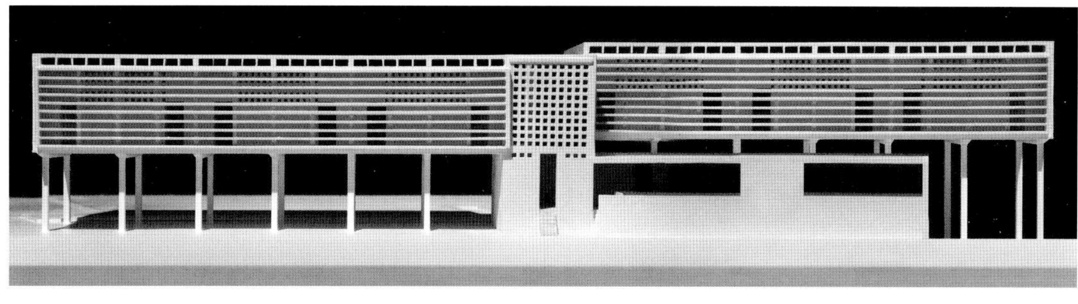

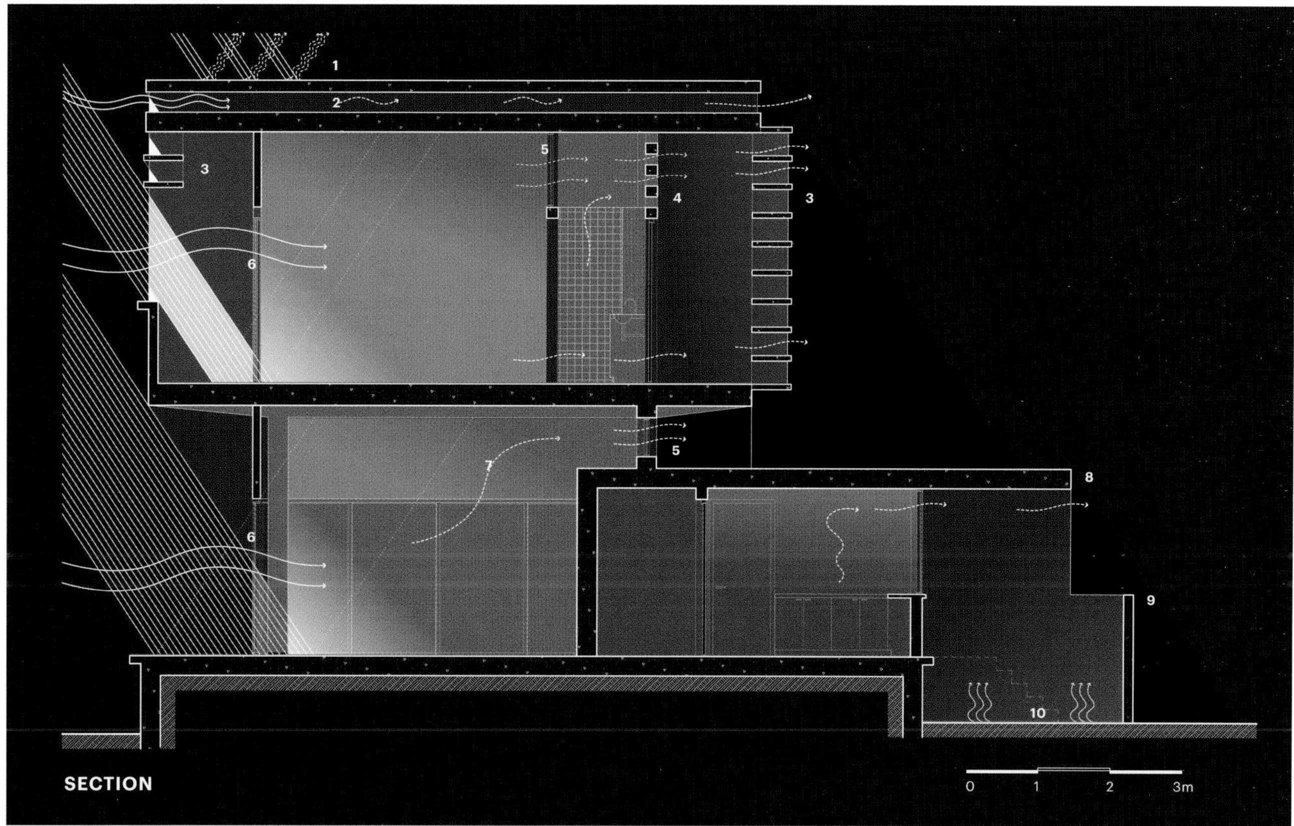

1 Reflective roof
2 Roof ventilation
3 Shading louver/light reflector
4 Interior ventilation grill
5 Operable window
6 Operable sliding door
7 Induced cross ventilation
8 Shading overhang
9 Wind-break wall
10 Sunken terrace evaporative cooling

Dexter M. Ferry Jr. Cooperative House
Marcel Breuer

YEAR
1951

LOCATION
Poughkeepsie, New York
41°41'9"N 73°53'39"W

CLIMATE ZONE
Temperate Continental

PROGRAM
Student Dormitory

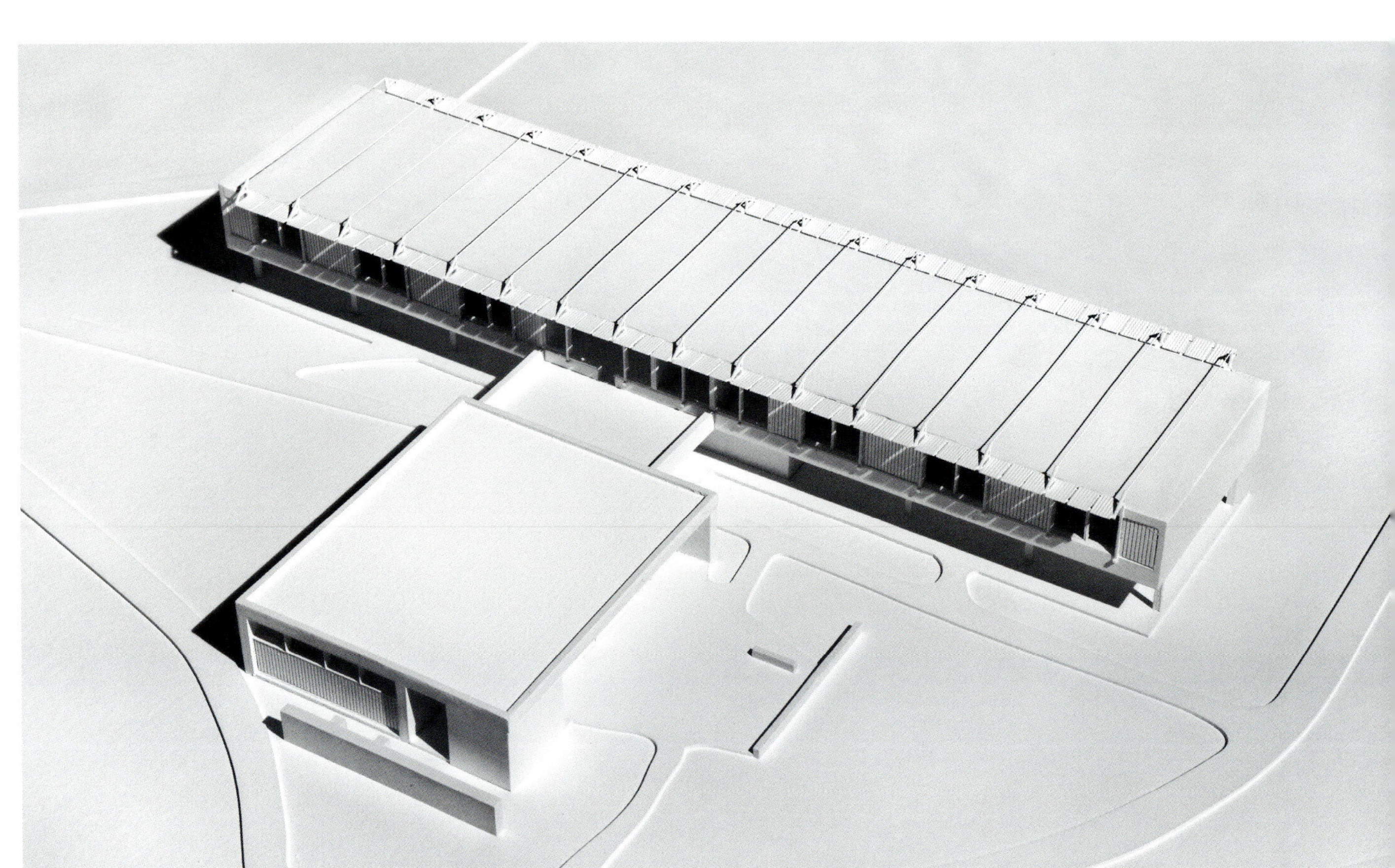

Marcel Breuer once stated: "The real impact of any work is the extent to which it unifies contrasting notions."[1] His scheme for a dormitory at Vassar College in Poughkeepsie, New York, utilizes the contrasting elements of sun and shadow to create a unified design that achieves optimal sun shading and cooling.

The building consists of an elevated dormitory wing supported by steel columns and oriented perpendicular to a lower-level communal area consisting of living, dining, and kitchen areas. The thick stone walls of the ground floor absorb heat and serve as a thermal mass for heating during colder months. In contrast, the elevation of the dormitory allows for cross ventilation through the upper floor. Operable windows provide further air circulation within the twenty-seven units. The shaded exterior space below the wing provides a covered area for outdoor recreation and bicycle storage while the roof of the communal area serves as a sun deck.[2]

The windows of the east and west elevations are protected by a sunshade supported by a steel frame and tensioned cables suspended across the roof. This balanced structure holds sections of corrugated asbestos cement placed at regular intervals, permitting strips of light to penetrate the sunshade and punctuating the east and west walls.[3] The pattern of sun and shadow across the surface visually represents the program's unified design and its naturally balanced climatic condition.

Ferry House was the first modernist building at Vassar College. The design was controversial and stood in sharp contrast to the heavy masonry architecture of the Victorian campus. But in addition to being an experiment in architectural possibilities, the Ferry House was also an expression of Vassar's continuing experiment in cooperative housing. Cooperative living began at the college as a response to the financial stress of the Great Depression. Students, all female at that time, determined to stay in school despite the hardships, were given the opportunity to share in meal preparation, serving, dish washing, and general housekeeping in return for financial assistance. Students would meet once a week to discuss the division of responsibilities and house policies. Later in the college's history, the term "cooperative" also came to mean co-educational. The college's progressive housing plan, in combination with Breuer's redistribution of programming, created an economical, egalitarian living environment, that one Vassar trustee called "a living demonstration of democracy in action."

1. Marcel Breuer, Sun and Shadow, *The Philosophy of an Architect* (New York: Dodd, Mead, 1955), 32.

2. Breuer, 181.

3. Aladar Olgyay and Victor Olgyay, *Solor Control & Shading Devices* (Princeton: Princeton University Press, 1957), 109.

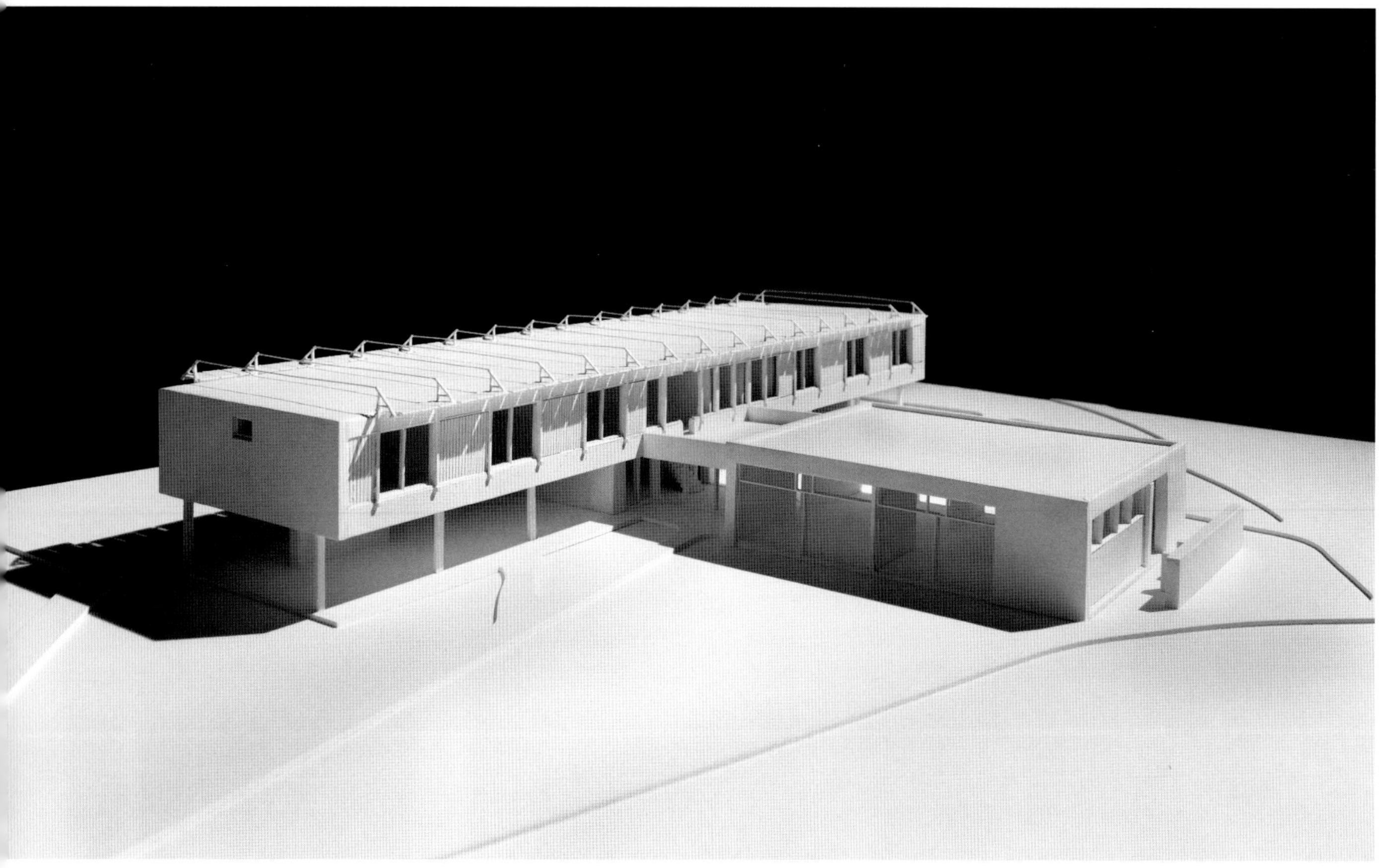

114   Dexter M. Ferry Jr. Cooperative House

PRIMARY SOLAR PATHS AND CORRESPONDING SECTIONS

Poughkeepsie, New York

41° North Latitude

SITE PLAN

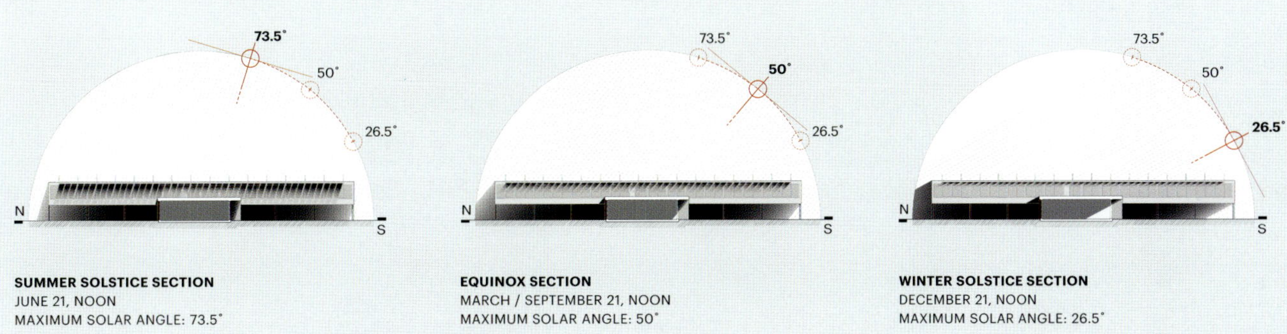

SUMMER SOLSTICE SECTION
JUNE 21, NOON
MAXIMUM SOLAR ANGLE: 73.5°

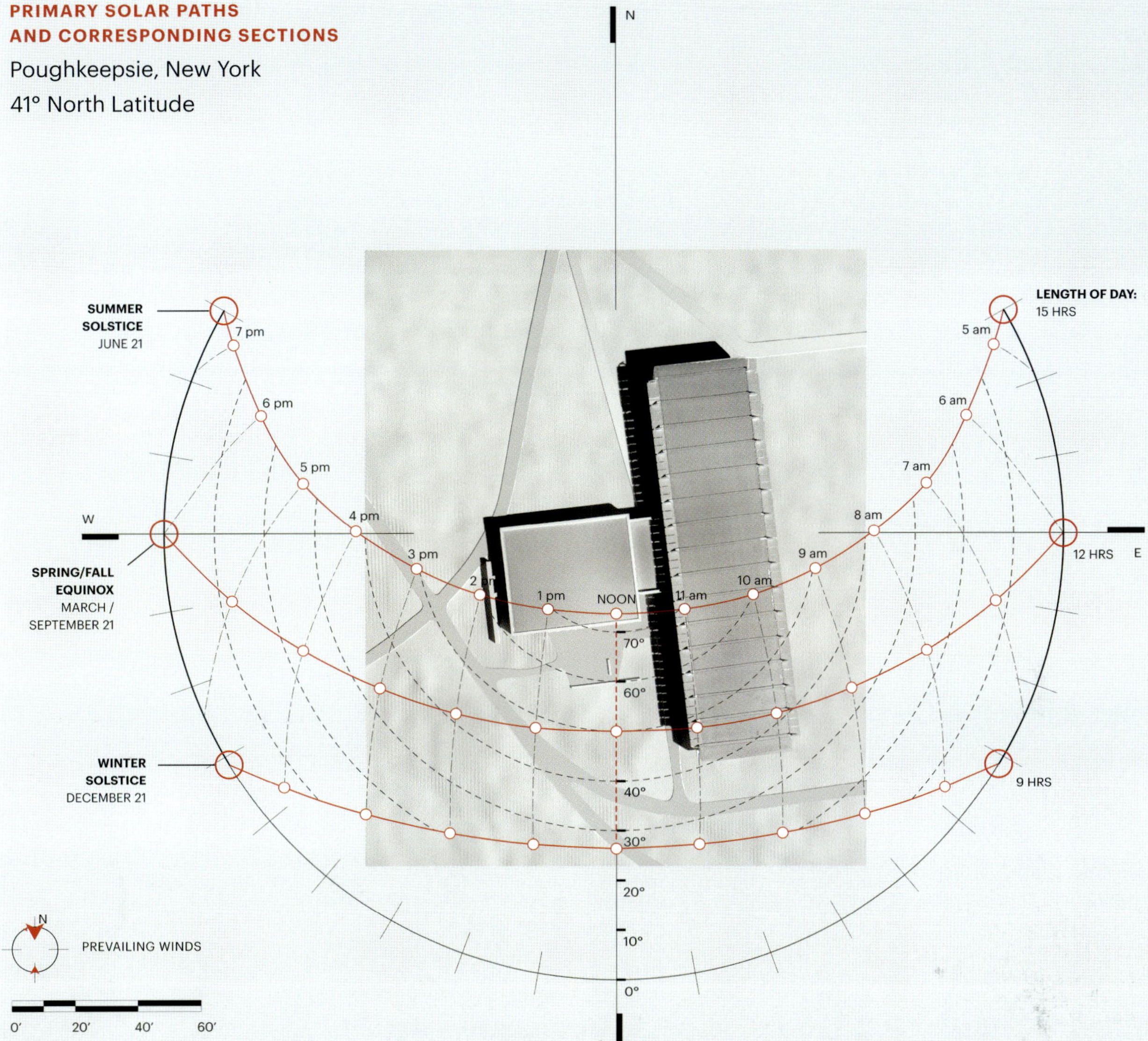

EQUINOX SECTION
MARCH / SEPTEMBER 21, NOON
MAXIMUM SOLAR ANGLE: 50°

WINTER SOLSTICE SECTION
DECEMBER 21, NOON
MAXIMUM SOLAR ANGLE: 26.5°

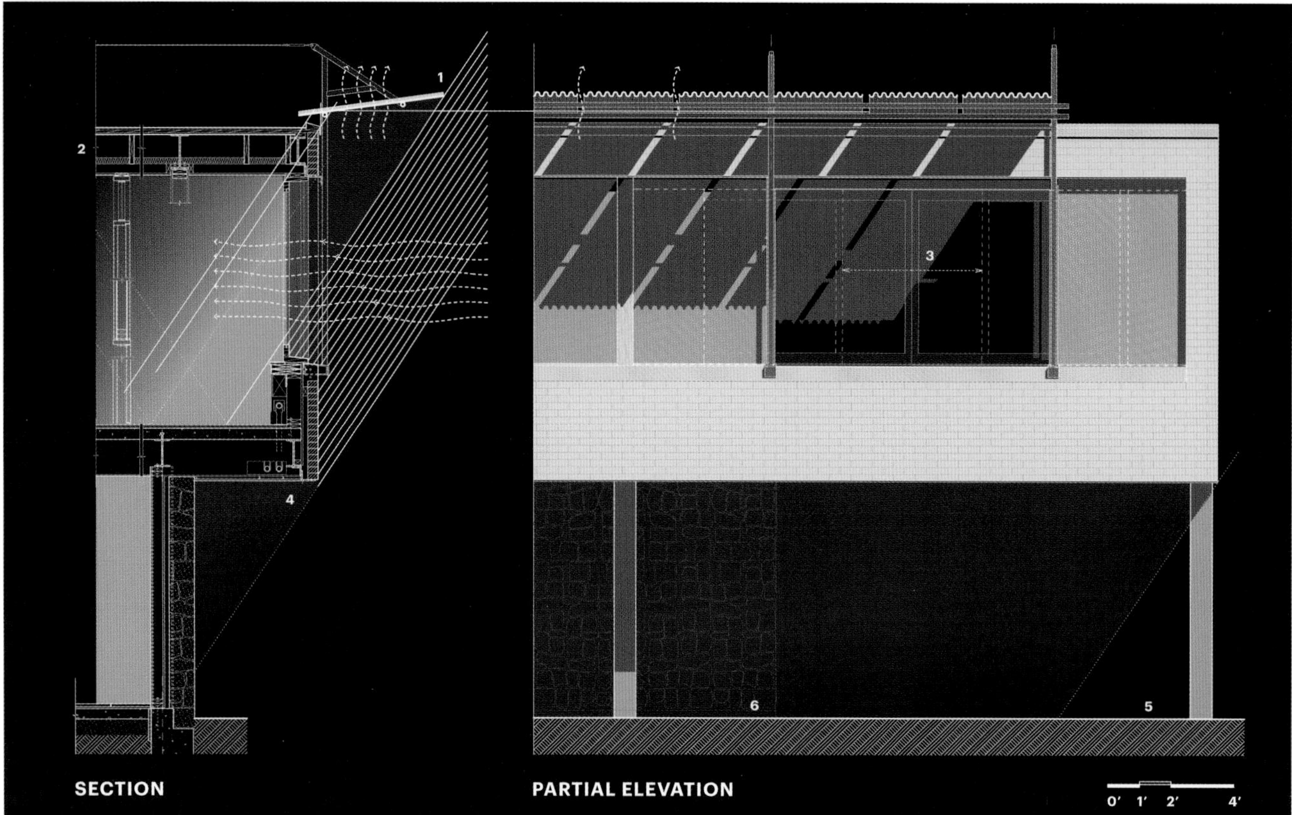

1 *Shading awning*
2 *Insulated roof*
3 *Operable sliding window*
4 *Shading overhang*
5 *Open ground floor ventilation*
6 *Outdoor recreation area*

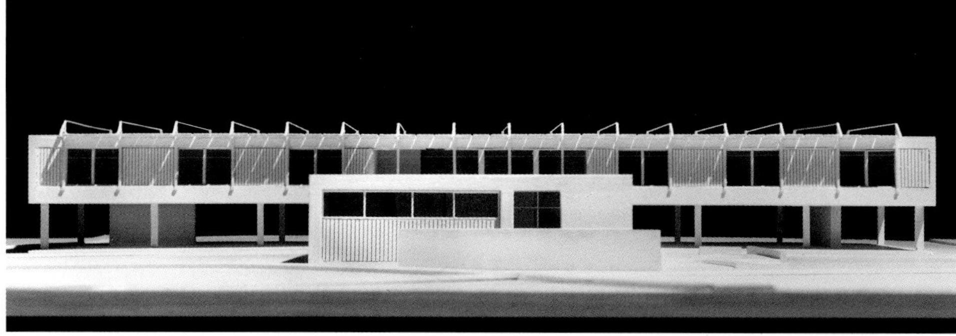

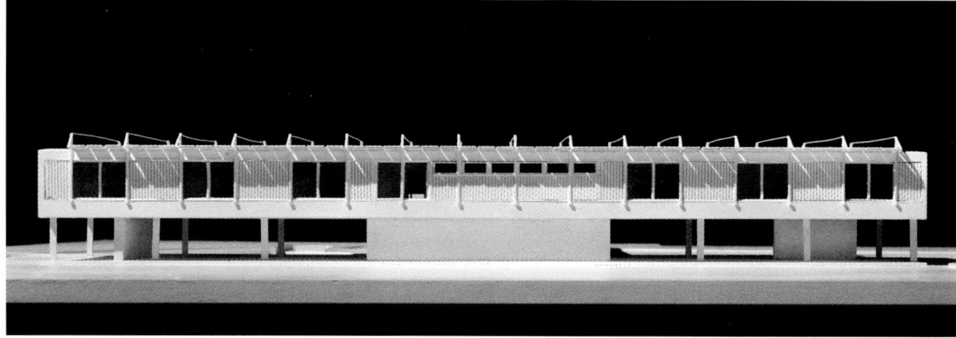

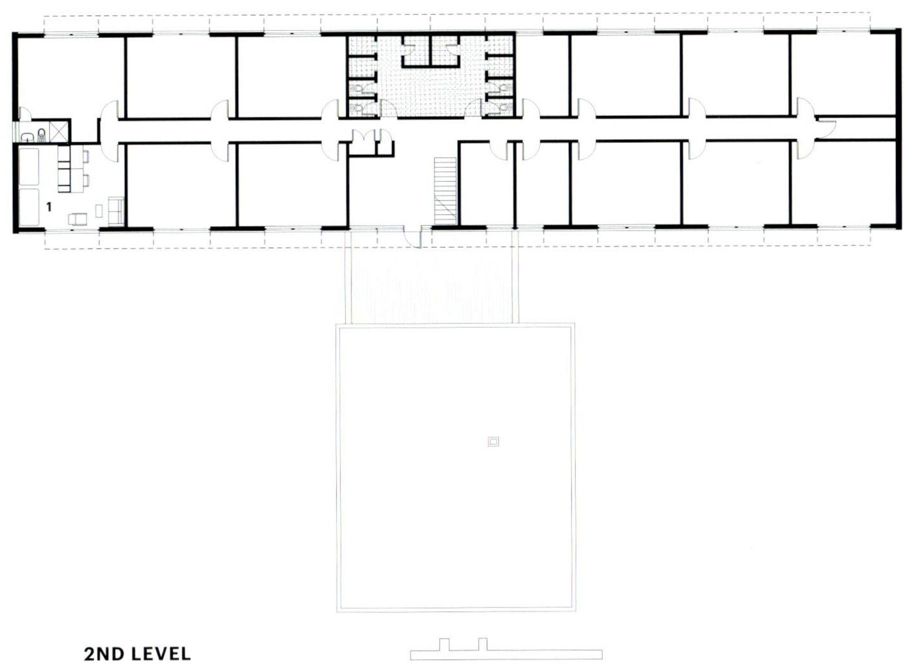

2ND LEVEL
1

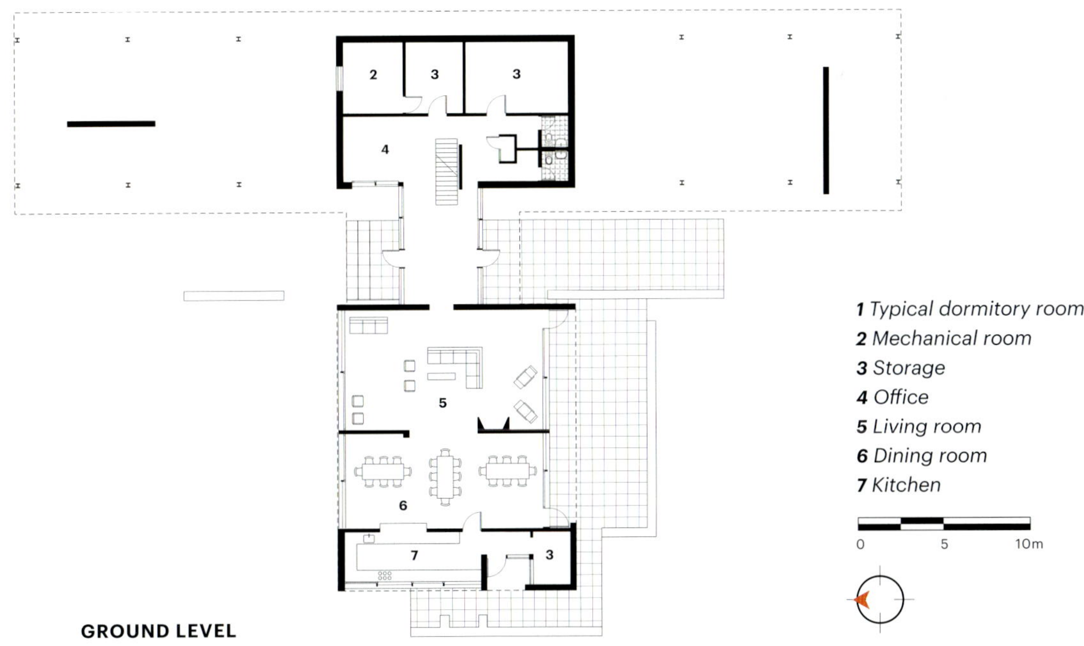

2
3
3
4
5
6
7
3
GROUND LEVEL
1 Typical dormitory room
2 Mechanical room
3 Storage
4 Office
5 Living room
6 Dining room
7 Kitchen
0
5
10m

Walker Beach House
Paul Rudolph

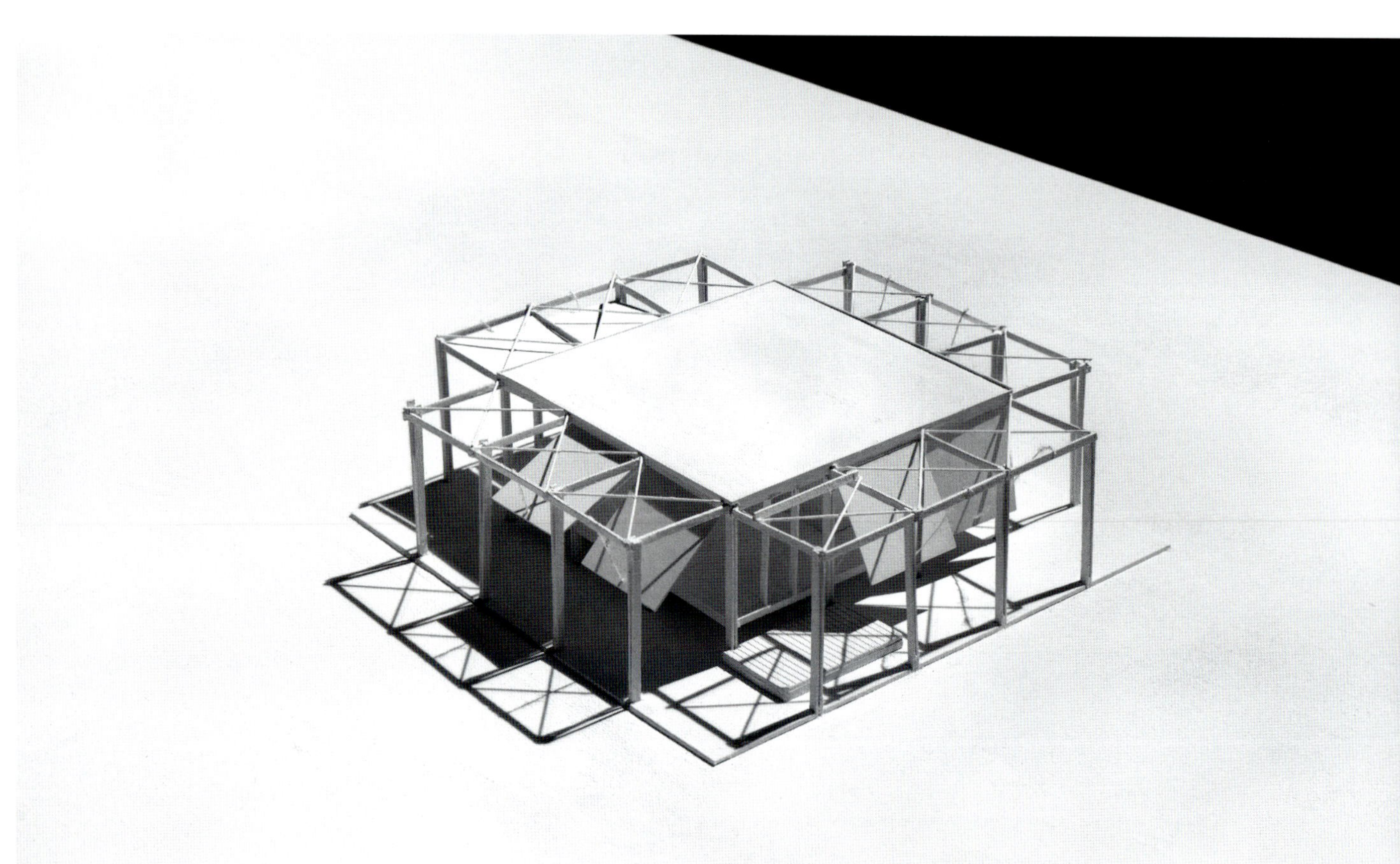

The Walker beach house is constructed of a simple, painted wooden framework that rests on modest concrete footings. The one-story structure is slightly elevated above the ground, allowing airflow to cool the interior from below. An open box frame extends from each elevation and, like the facades, is divided into three square bays. Two bays on each elevation are enclosed by full-height hinged panels, operable through the use of marine hardware, ropes, and counterweights.[1] The openings behind the hinged panels are covered with full height screens. The third bay is glazed. The center bay of each elevation is stiffened with cable cross-bracing on the exterior. The entrance is on the north facade.

The panels can be raised to various angles to provide controlled shading and ventilation. When fully raised, the panels extend to the full depth of the open frames around the perimeter of the house, providing maximum shading and extensive views of the ocean and surrounding beachfront landscape. The panels also define the space of exterior porches on each side of the structure. Alternately, the panels can be fully closed for privacy or to reduce airflow through the house on cooler nights and to protect the interior during storms. Interior curtains on the glazed bays visually seal the home from the exterior altogether.[2] Square in plan, the interior is divided into an open living and dining area, a bedroom, kitchen, and bathroom.

Rudolph's design for the Walker beach house is an inventive and modestly elegant approach to the seaside cottage, and allows for a diversity of spatial configurations while providing for the control of airflow, shading, and privacy around the structure.

1. Christopher Domin and Joseph King, *Paul Rudolph: The Florida Houses* (New York: Princeton Architectural Press, 2005), 157.

2. Aladar Olgyay and Victor Olgyay, *Solor Control & Shading Devices* (Princeton: Princeton University Press, 1957), 121.

PRIMARY SOLAR PATHS AND CORRESPONDING SECTIONS

Sanibel Island, Florida

26° North Latitude

SITE PLAN

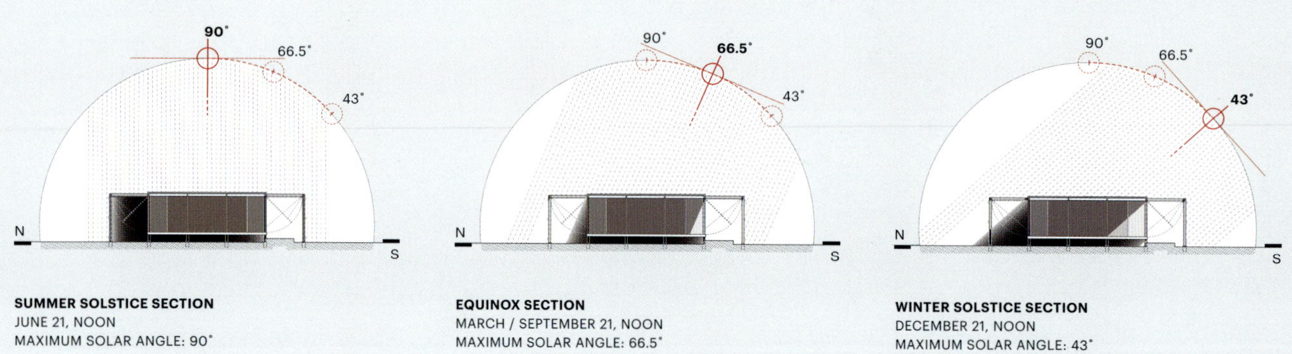

SUMMER SOLSTICE SECTION
JUNE 21, NOON
MAXIMUM SOLAR ANGLE: 90°

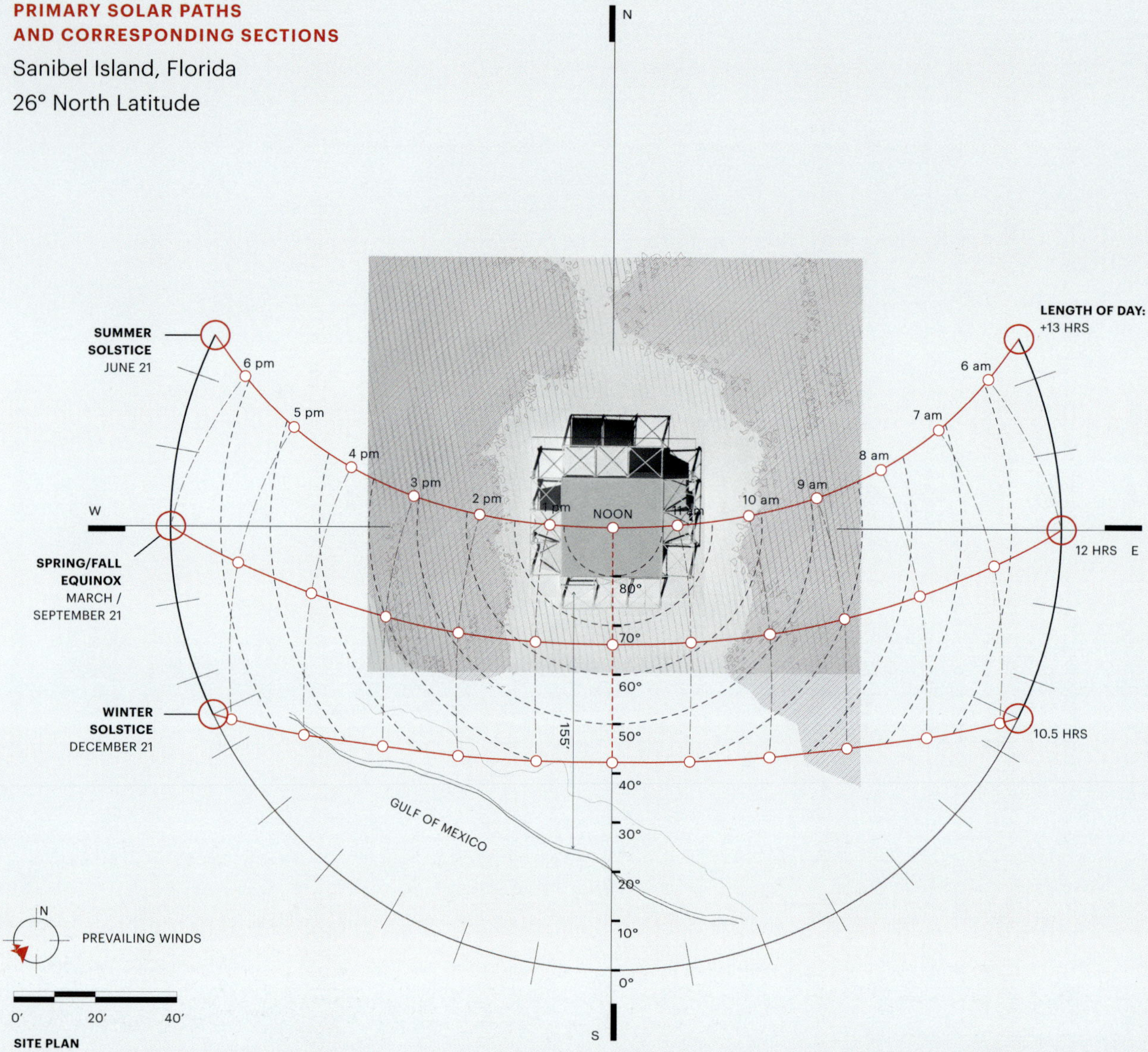

EQUINOX SECTION
MARCH / SEPTEMBER 21, NOON
MAXIMUM SOLAR ANGLE: 66.5°

WINTER SOLSTICE SECTION
DECEMBER 21, NOON
MAXIMUM SOLAR ANGLE: 43°

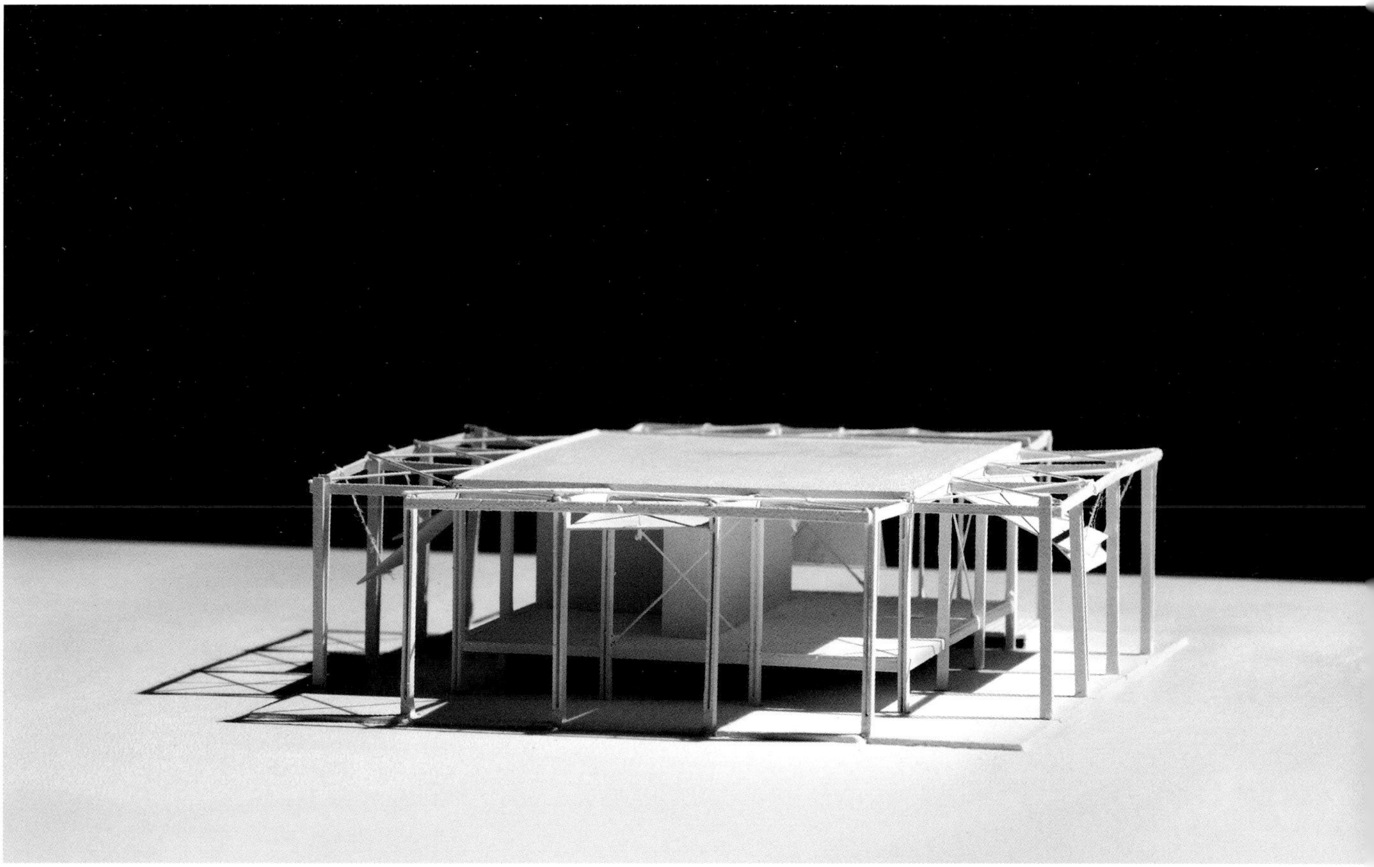

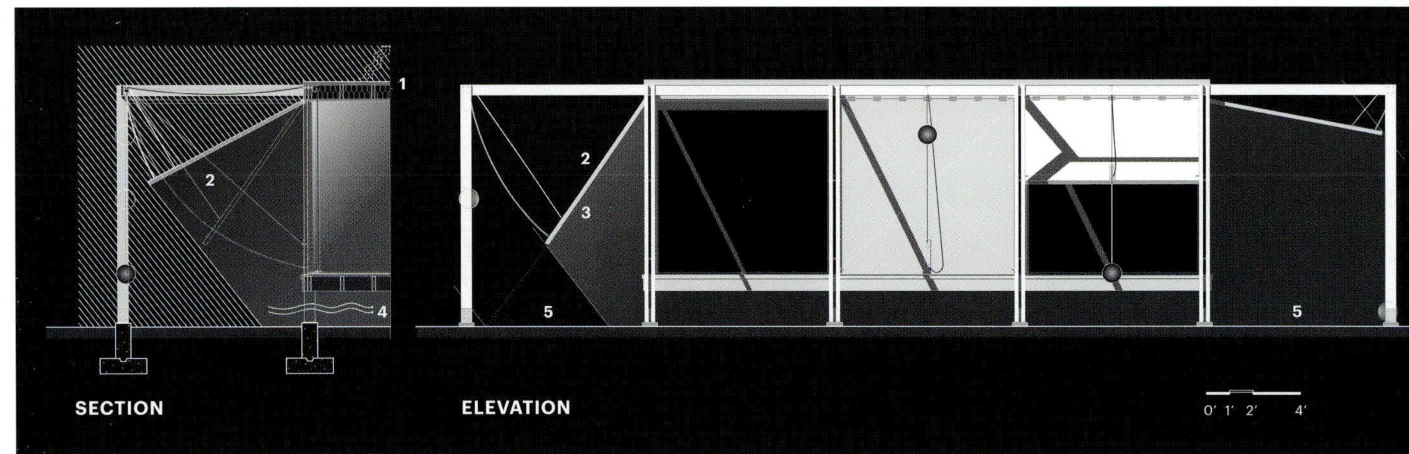

*1 Insulated roof with reflective
surface*
*2 Counter-balanced operable
panels*
3 Natural light shading
4 Elevated building ventilation
5 Shaded outdoor living space

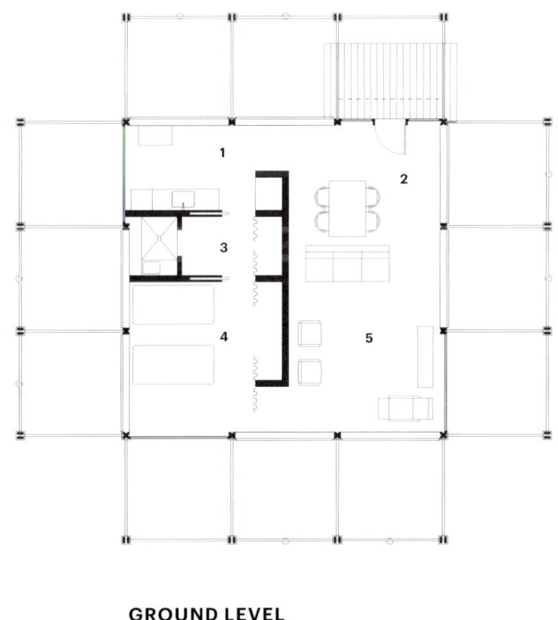

GROUND LEVEL

1 Kitchen
2 Dining area
3 Bathroom
4 Bedroom
5 Living area

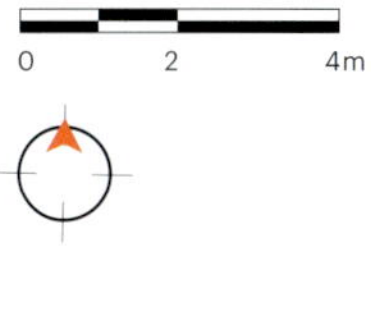

0   2   4m

Munkegaard Elementary School
Arne Jacobsen

YEAR
1956

LOCATION
Soborg, Denmark
55°44'6"N 12°31'19"E

CLIMATE ZONE
Temperate Oceanic

PROGRAM
Elementary School

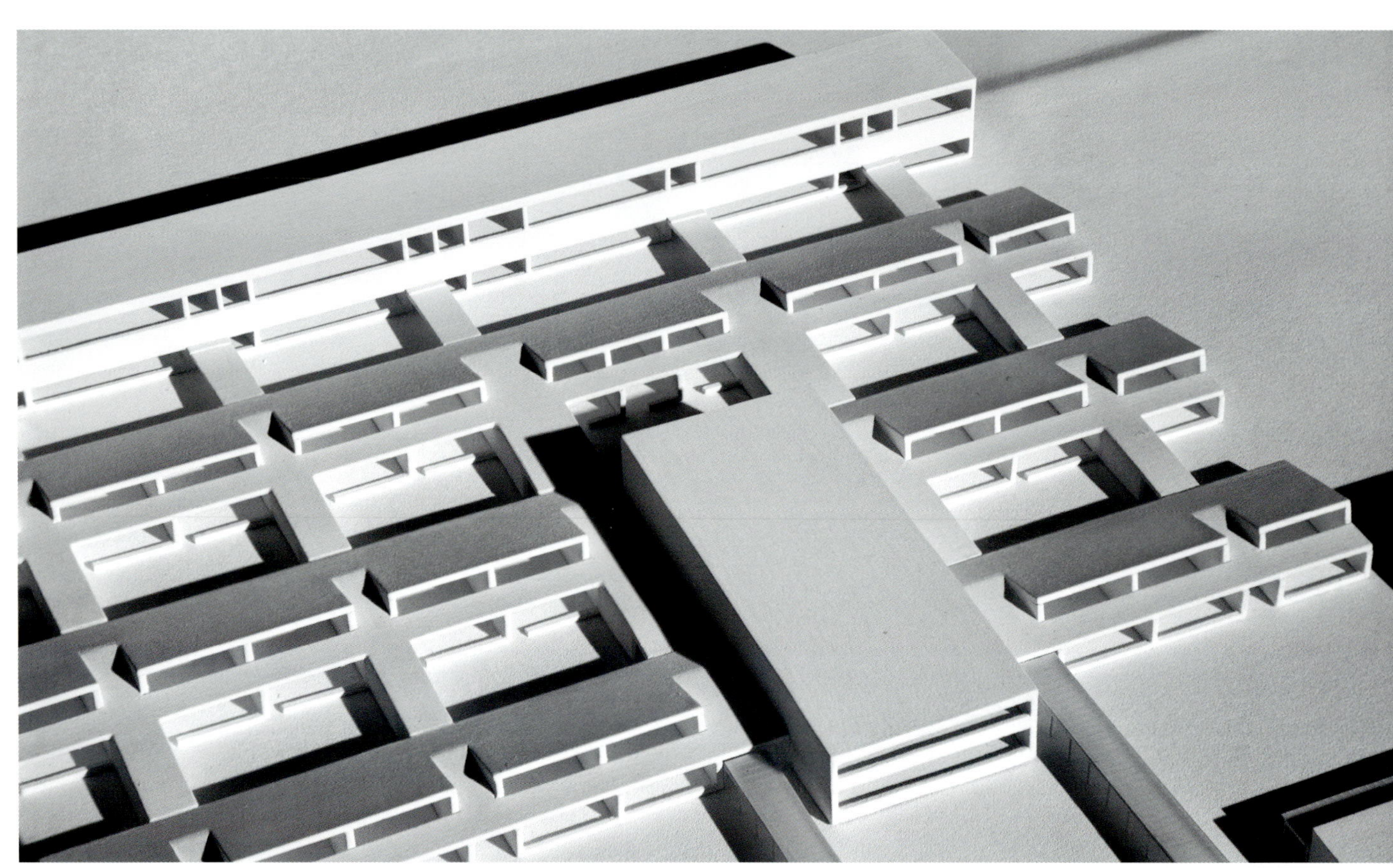

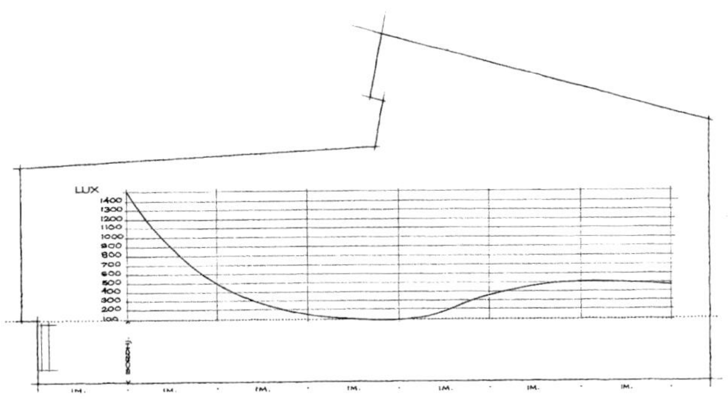

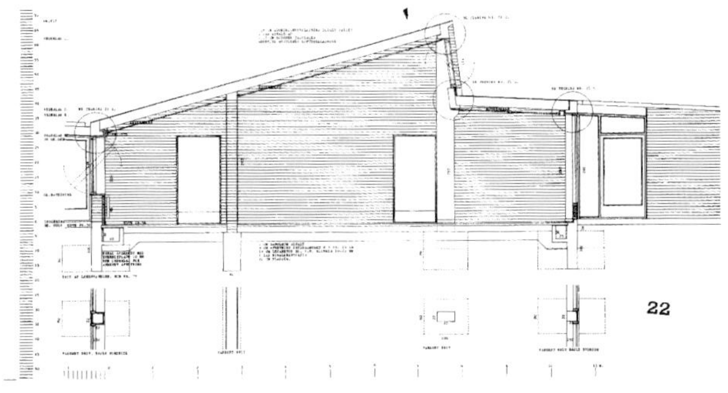

Munkegaard Elementary School responded to the postwar need for larger schools but at the same time it reflected a contemporary move away from monumentality in school design toward a scale more suitable for children.[1]

The site is primarily flat, with a slight westward slope. A path along its southern edge connects to two adjacent streets and leads to the main entrance. Bicycle storage sheds and gymnasium buildings frame the area outside the main entrance, forming a courtyard that provides a large area for recreation as well as individual outdoor spaces for the row of classrooms that crosses the site from east to west. Two covered passageways lead to the main entrance, where administrative offices, a large assembly hall, and a teachers' lounge are located.

The building is organized on a grid. Five enclosed passageways run parallel to the north-south axis and connect three rows of classrooms that are perpendicular to the passageways. The classrooms are grouped in pairs; each pair shares a courtyard that is used as outdoor classroom space during warmer months and becomes a warmer microclimate during cooler months. Jacobsen broke the uniformity of these courtyard spaces by varying both the paving and plantings in each.[2] The assembly hall, which measures the width of two classrooms, is nestled within the center of the entry structure.

Each of the twenty-four classrooms is divided into a south-facing main space and a smaller space for group work facing north. The ceilings slope up to the south creating a clerestory with operable windows that project above the roofs and maximize daylight and airflow. The south-facing lower level of each classroom is also fenestrated and provides courtyard access. Windows on the opposite side of the classrooms face the adjacent courtyard to the north. The smaller workspaces within each classroom allow for access to classrooms or passageways to the east and west; together these serve as cross-corridors that connect to the main auditorium and office spaces within the school. A two-story building along the north edge of the site is designated for multipurpose classrooms. Metal frame awnings for sun shading project from its southern facade above each level.

In his design for Munkegaard, Jacobsen incorporated simplicity of proportions and economy of materials while maximizing light and thermal gain provided by

the sun. Although the school is large enough to accommodate 850 students, the low-rise structure, with its alternating rhythm of solid and void, creates a feeling of intimacy and community.[3]

1. Kjeld Vindum, "Munkegaard Elementary School," in *Arne Jacobsen,* Carsten Thau, ed. (Copenhagen: The Danish Architectural Press, 1998), 369.

2. Felix Solaguren-Beascoa de Corral, *Arne Jacobsen: Obras y Proyectos* (Barcelona: G. Gili, 1997), 44.

3. Vindum, 371.

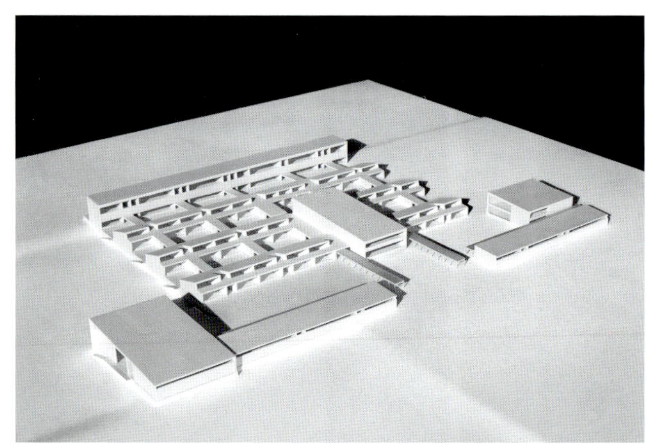

PRIMARY SOLAR PATHS AND CORRESPONDING SECTIONS

Soborg, Denmark

55° North Latitude

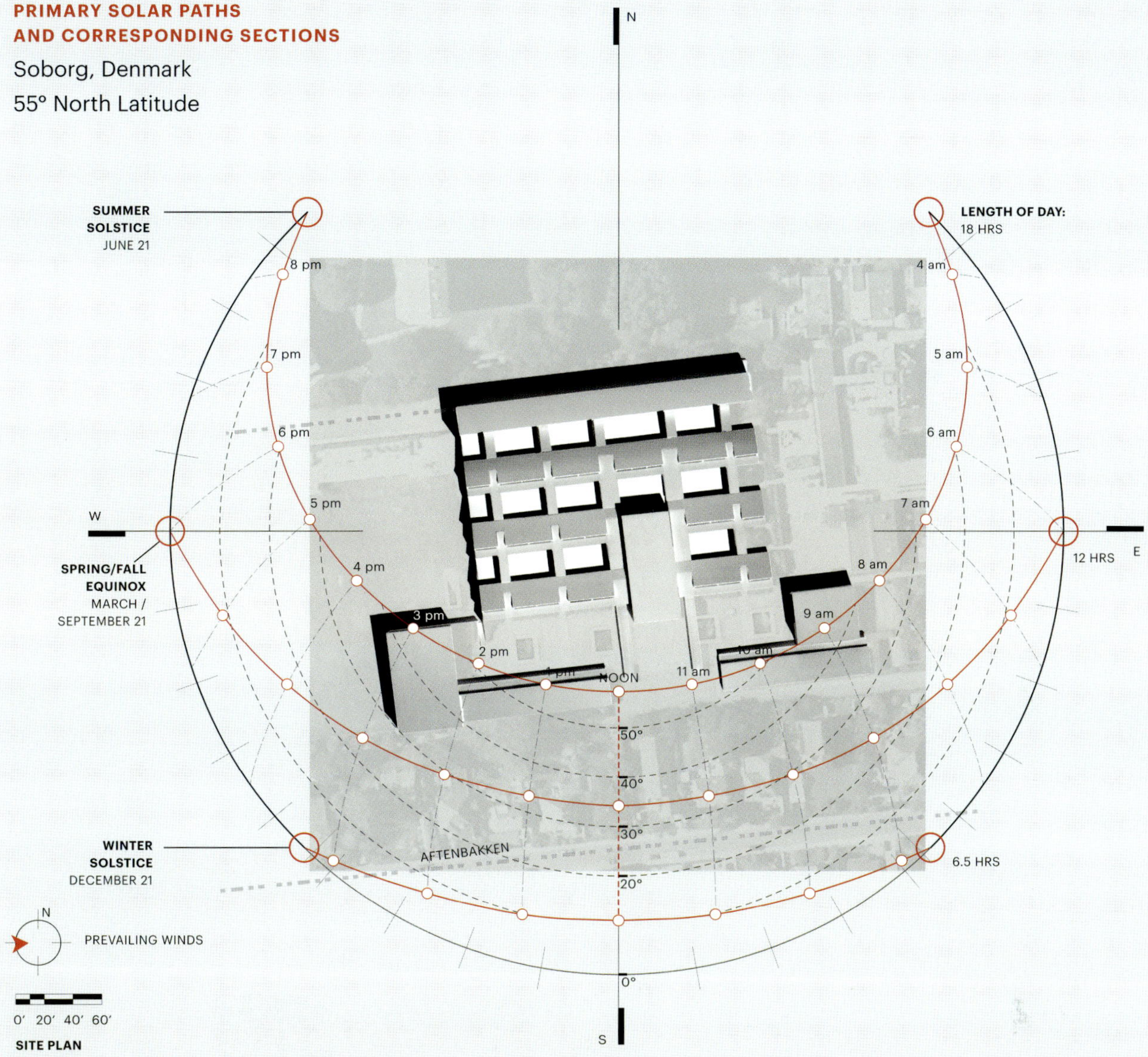

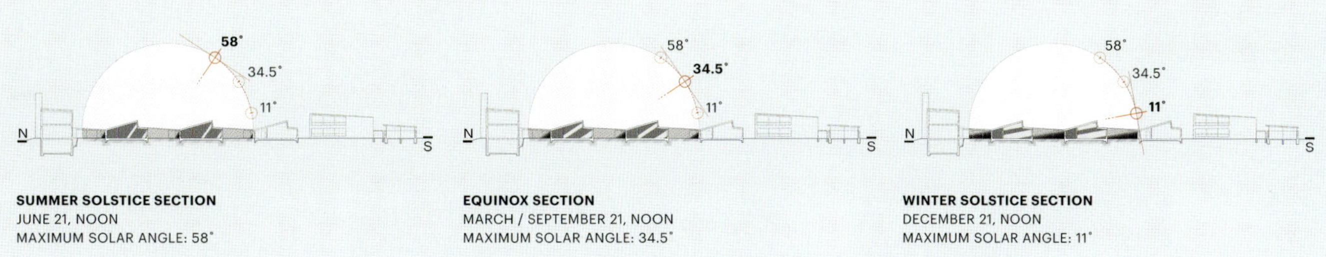

SUMMER SOLSTICE SECTION
JUNE 21, NOON
MAXIMUM SOLAR ANGLE: 58°

EQUINOX SECTION
MARCH / SEPTEMBER 21, NOON
MAXIMUM SOLAR ANGLE: 34.5°

WINTER SOLSTICE SECTION
DECEMBER 21, NOON
MAXIMUM SOLAR ANGLE: 11°

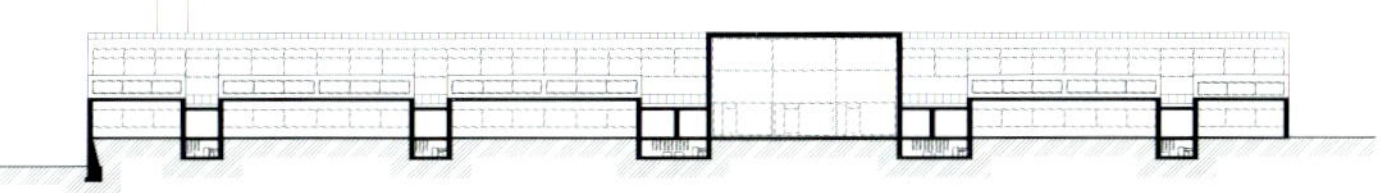

SECTION A – A

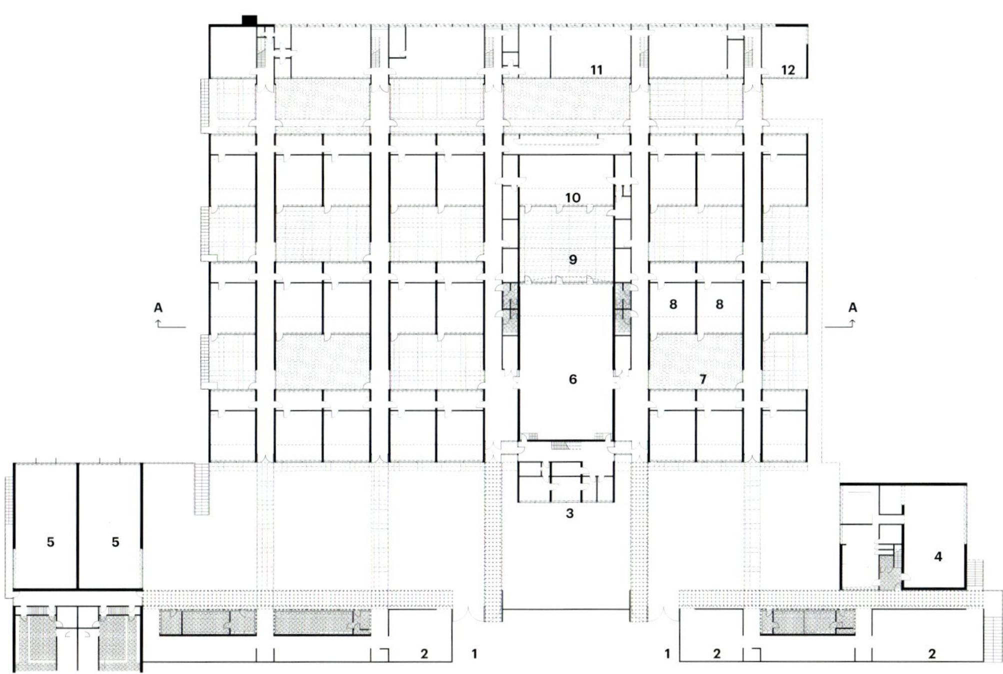

GROUND LEVEL

1 Main entrance
2 Bicycle storage
3 Offices
4 Gymnasium for younger children
5 Gymnasium for older children
6 Assembly hall
7 Outdoor classroom
8 Indoor classroom
9 Teachers' courtyard
10 Teachers' lounge
11 Special classroom
12 Classroom

0 2   5   10m

Cocoon House
Paul Rudolph + Ralph Twitchell

YEAR
1957

LOCATION
Sarasota, Florida
27°18'5"N 82°33'33"W

CLIMATE ZONE
Humid Subtropical

PROGRAM
Beach House

Located on a bayou adjacent to Sarasota Bay, the Cocoon House is a lightweight structure with a minimal footprint that demonstrates an inventive use of readily available building components and materials.

Cantilevered over the bulkhead at the edge of the water, the structure is supported by five main beams that rest on raised concrete piles. These beams extend beyond the perimeter of the interior living space, which is enclosed by post and lintel framing along the east and west facades. The framing is secured with metal struts, which are tied to the end of the main beams below.[1] The framing of the east and west facades is infilled almost entirely with wooden jalousies, allowing for maximum ventilation from the southwestern breezes when opened and affording complete privacy when closed.

During his years of service in the Navy during World War II, Rudolph learned of the practice of "moth-balling," the wrapping and sealing of gun turrets on warships when they were taken out of service. A thin metal frame sprayed with a mixture of saran and vinyl plastics, followed by a final coat of clear vinyl, or Cocoon, provided a weather-tight, flexible membrane. Rudolph drew from this process for the roof for the Cocoon House. Cold rolled steel straps measuring 1/2 by 1/8 inches were spaced 12 inches apart and draped across the 22-foot span, their weight over this distance forming a catenary curve. Thin insulation board was clipped to the straps and then covered with additional flexible insulation. The exterior and interior of the assem-bly was sprayed with a lightweight vinyl compound. The result is a thin, semi-rigid tensile roof. A lightweight steel truss at the northern and southern ends of the house provides the stiffening necessary for the extensive glaz-ing on those facades.[2] With the drape of the roof at its lowest point at the center of the house, the roof further accentuates the expansive views of the water and natu-ral surroundings to the north and south.

The main living and dining areas are defined by an open plan. A bedroom and bathroom are located at the north end of the house. A study, which also doubles as a second bedroom, is located at the center. A deck proj-ects to the west, cantilevered over the water. Steps lead down from the southern edge of the deck to a modest boat slip.[3]

Rudolph recognized the opportunity of adopting industrial technology and new materials to create modern, lightweight, and graceful structures that were well adapted to the humid subtropical climate of the Florida Keys.

1. Tony Monk, *The Art and Architecture of Paul Rudolph* (Chichester, West Sussex: Wiley-Academy, 1999), 27–28.

2. Ralph Twitchell and Paul Rudolph, "Cocoon House," *Architectural Forum* 95, no. 6 (1951): 157–58.

3. Monk, 28.

PRIMARY SOLAR PATHS
AND CORRESPONDING SECTIONS
Sarasota, Florida
27° North Latitude

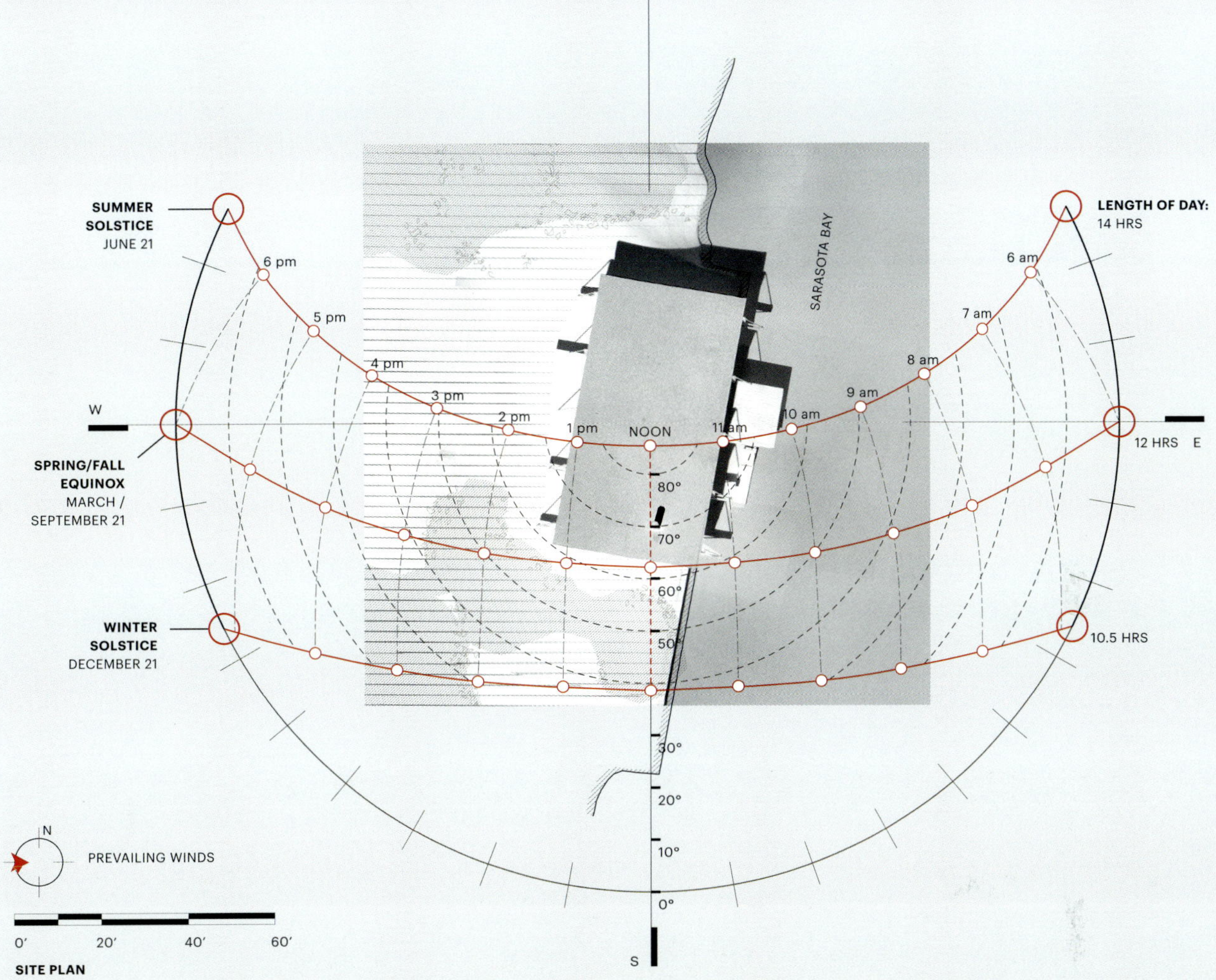

N
S
W
E

SUMMER SOLSTICE
JUNE 21

SPRING/FALL EQUINOX
MARCH / SEPTEMBER 21

WINTER SOLSTICE
DECEMBER 21

LENGTH OF DAY:
14 HRS

12 HRS
10.5 HRS

SARASOTA BAY

6 pm
5 pm
4 pm
3 pm
2 pm
1 pm
NOON
11 am
10 am
9 am
8 am
7 am
6 am

80°
70°
60°
50°
30°
20°
10°
0°

N
PREVAILING WINDS

0'   20'   40'   60'
SITE PLAN

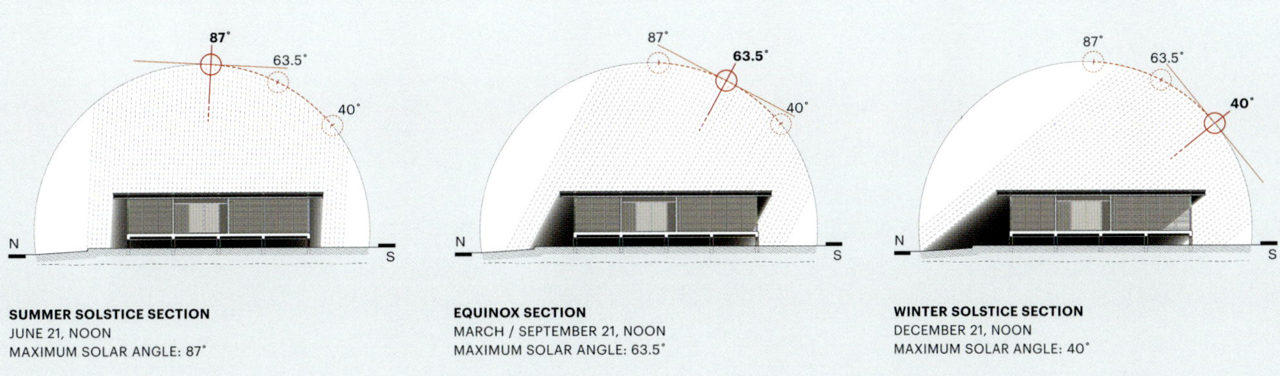

87°
63.5°
40°
N   S
SUMMER SOLSTICE SECTION
JUNE 21, NOON
MAXIMUM SOLAR ANGLE: 87°

87°
63.5°
40°
N   S
EQUINOX SECTION
MARCH / SEPTEMBER 21, NOON
MAXIMUM SOLAR ANGLE: 63.5°

87°
63.5°
40°
N   S
WINTER SOLSTICE SECTION
DECEMBER 21, NOON
MAXIMUM SOLAR ANGLE: 40°

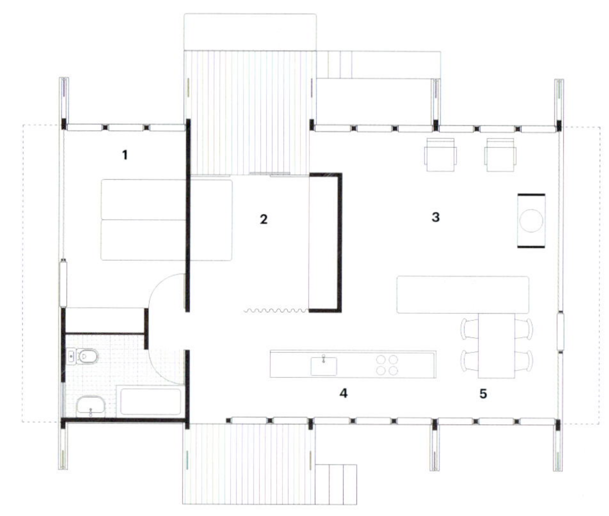

GROUND LEVEL

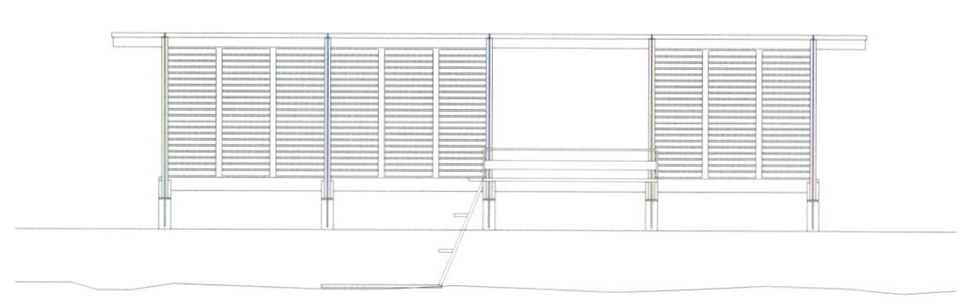

EAST ELEVATION

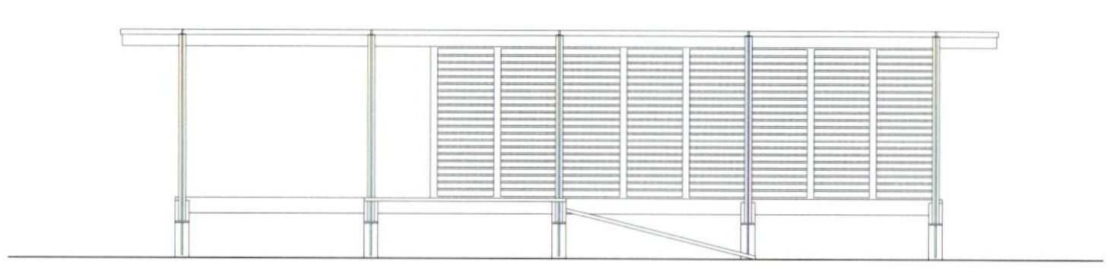

WEST ELEVATION

1 Bedroom
2 Bedroom/study
3 Living area
4 Kitchen
5 Dining area

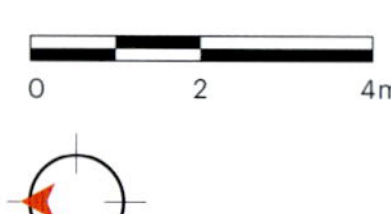

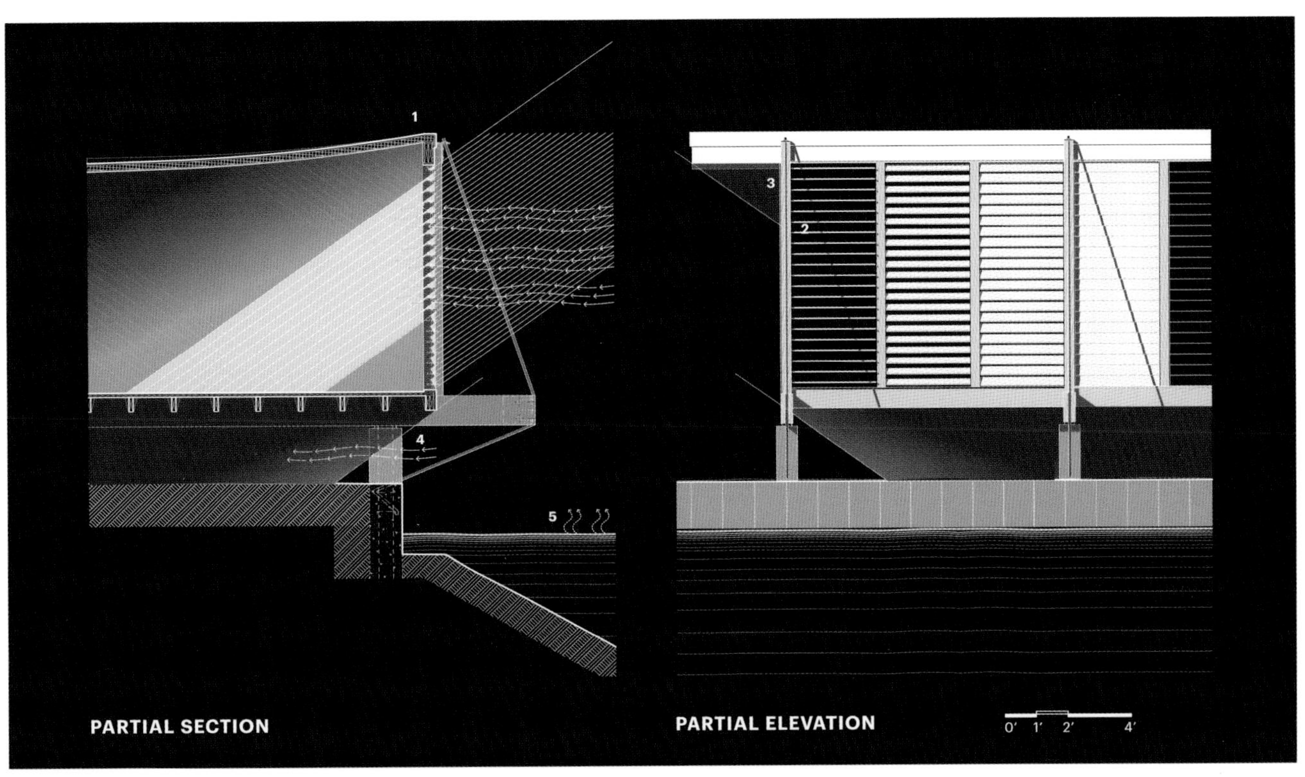

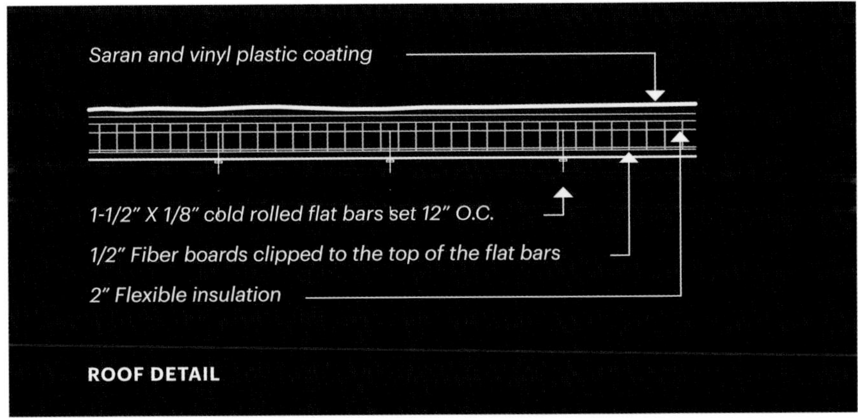

1 *Reflective roof*
2 *Operable jalousies*
3 *Shading overhang*
4 *Elevated building ventilation*
5 *Evaporative cooling*

Pavilion on the Lagoon Rodrigo de Freitas
Affonso Eduardo Reidy

YEAR
1957

LOCATION
Rio De Janeiro, Brazil
22°57'55"S 43°12'58"W

CLIMATE ZONE
Tropical Savannah

PROGRAM
Park Services

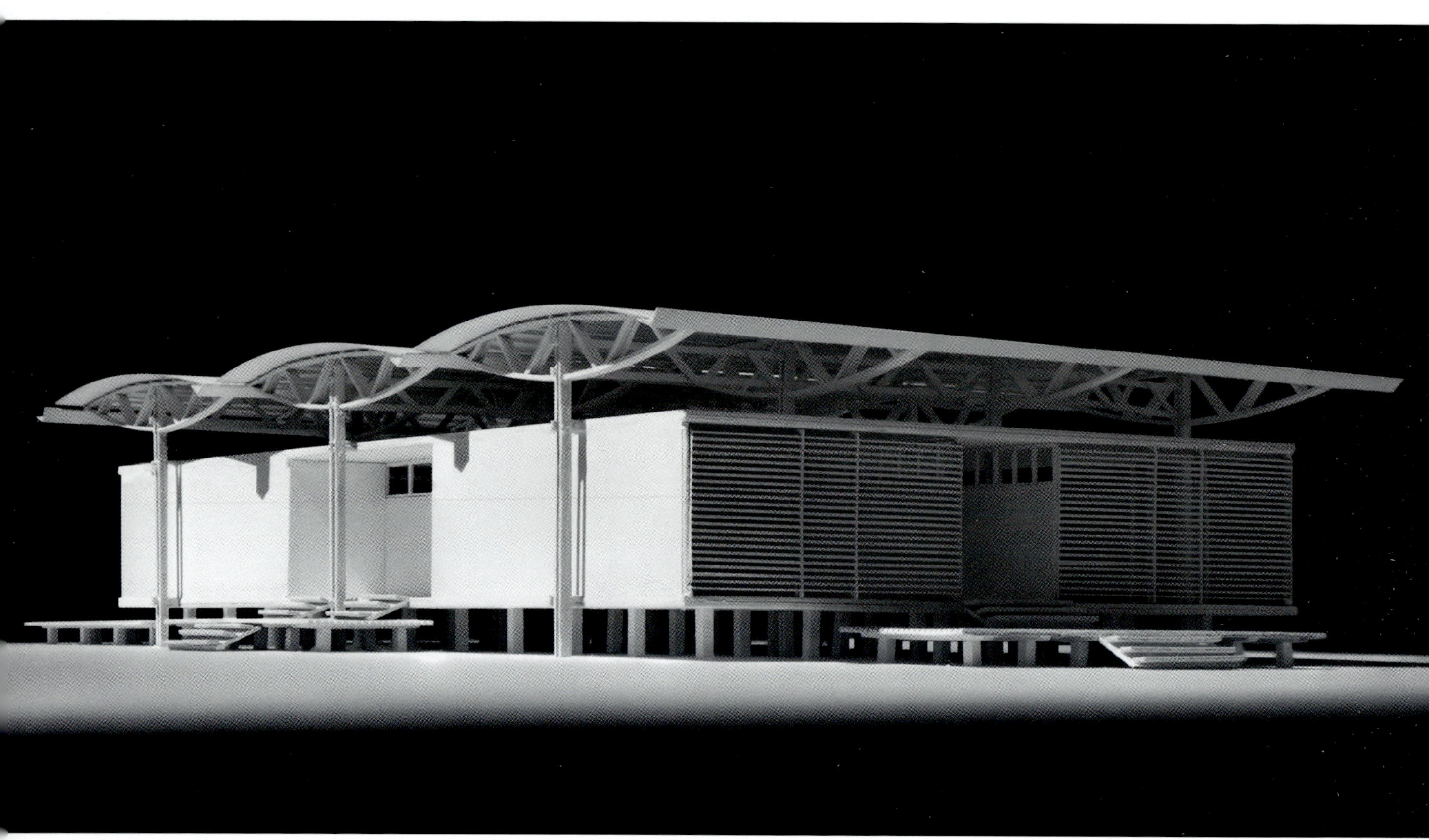

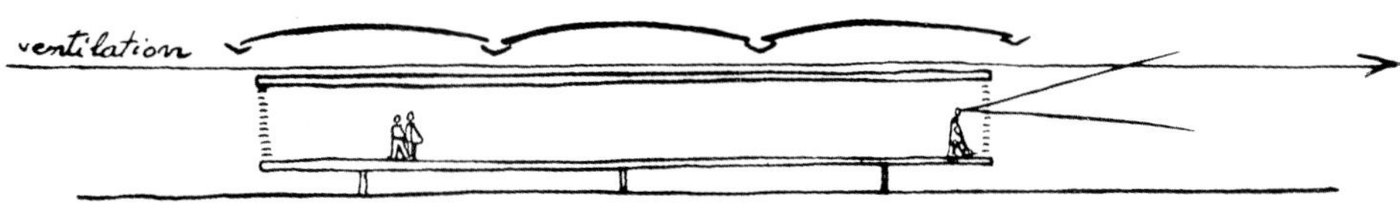

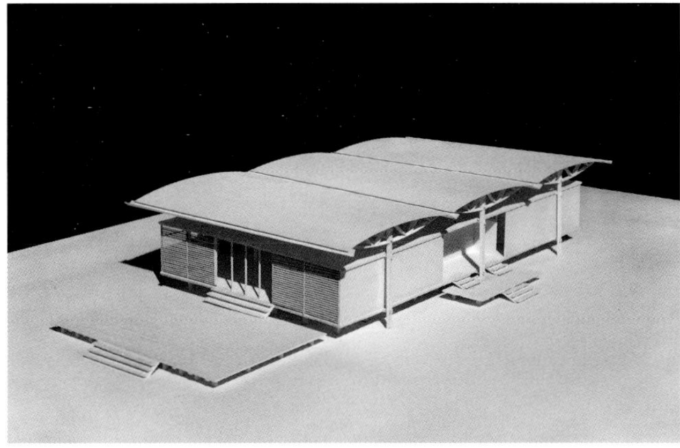

The Pavilion of the Special Technical Service for Lagoons was commissioned by the local government as the headquarters for oversight and management of the preservation of Rio de Janeiro's many lagoons. Never built, this project is a proposal for an ecological awareness center, jointly run by city and community, and intended to monitor and encourage a better understanding of the vitality of urban waterways within the context of town planning and tourism. Proposed for the northwestern edge of the Lagoon Rodrigo de Freitas, the design incorporates strategies to regulate solar gain, maximize natural ventilation, and improve comfort in and around the building.[1]

The pavilion was to be constructed primarily of wood. It includes a secondary parasol roof with three bays of lightweight, wing-like lenticular trusses. Supported by twelve columns, the primary envelope remains shaded, and as Reidy asserted, "the aluminum sunshade will ensure good conditions for thermal comfort by means of a permanent ventilation between the covering and the ceiling."[2] The floor plane is raised on piles four feet above the ground, providing ventilation that transports heat away from the structure and mitigates the impact of the tropical Brazilian climate. Similarly, the adjustable aluminum shutters, fitted to the building's exterior, provide a further barrier against the sun. The south side of the building, not vulnerable to direct sunlight, enjoys a glazed facade overlooking the lagoon.

This pavilion is one of Reidy's smaller projects, but its program and his architectural response is a comprehensive testament to the architect's environmental convictions.

1. Klaus Franck, *Affonso Eduardo Reidy—Bauten und Prokekte* (Stuttgart: Verlag Gerd Hatje, 1960), 50.

2. Affonso Eduardo Reidy, interview with Jayme Mauricio in Nabil Bonduki and Carmen Portinho, *Affonso Eduardo Reidy: Brazilian Architects* (Lisbon: Editorial Blau, 2000), 196.

PRIMARY SOLAR PATHS AND CORRESPONDING SECTIONS

Rio De Janeiro, Brazil

22° South Latitude

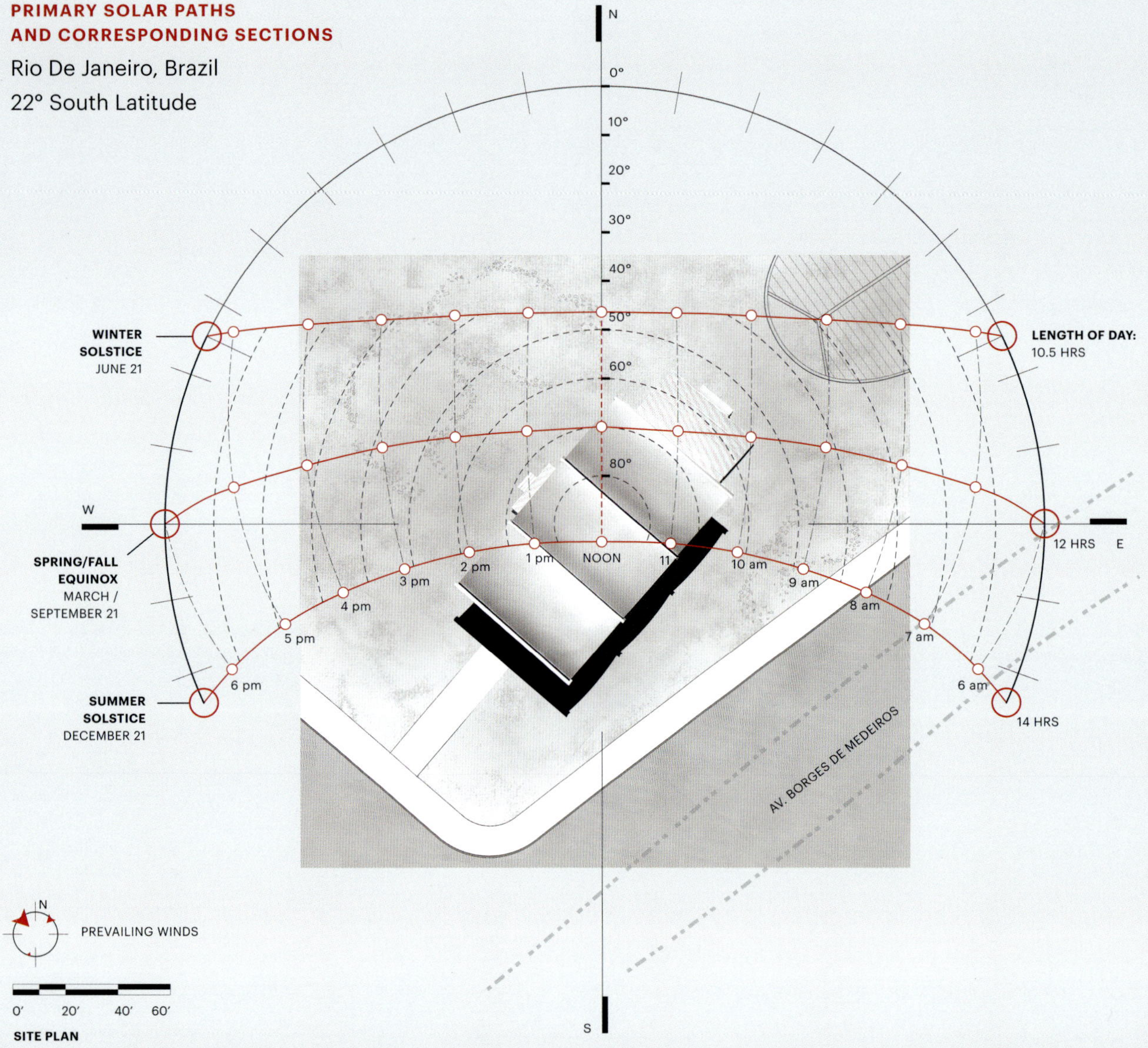

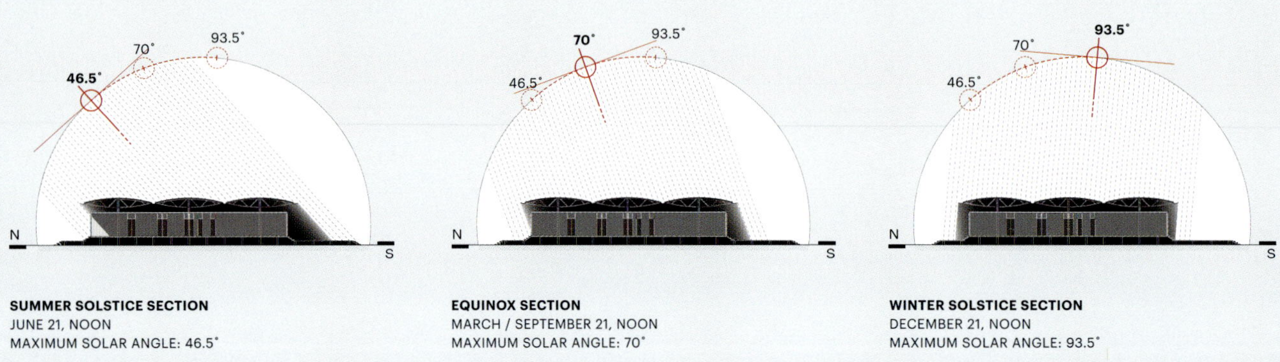

SUMMER SOLSTICE SECTION
JUNE 21, NOON
MAXIMUM SOLAR ANGLE: 46.5°

EQUINOX SECTION
MARCH / SEPTEMBER 21, NOON
MAXIMUM SOLAR ANGLE: 70°

WINTER SOLSTICE SECTION
DECEMBER 21, NOON
MAXIMUM SOLAR ANGLE: 93.5°

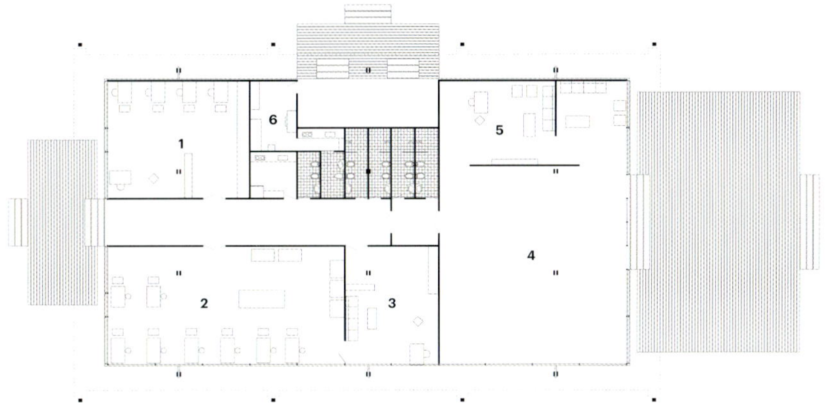

GROUND LEVEL

NORTHEAST ELEVATION   **SOUTHWEST ELEVATION**

1 Office
2 Technical department
3 Chief engineer's office
4 Assembly room
5 Administrative office
6 Caretaker's office

0 1 2   5m

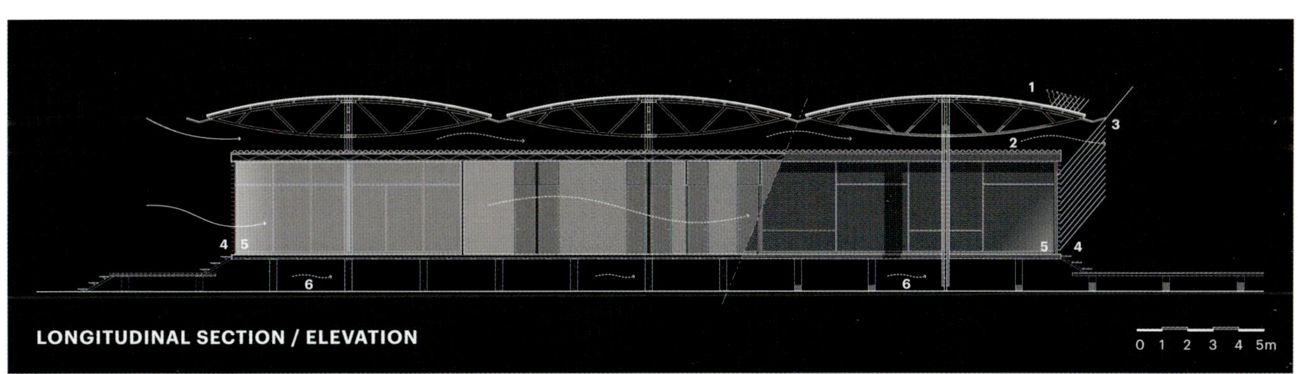

1 Solar reflective roof structure
2 Ventilation between roofs
3 Solar shading overhang
4 Exterior shading blinds
5 Cross-ventilation
6 Elevated building ventilation

Valéria P. Cirell House
Lina Bo Bardi

YEAR	LOCATION	CLIMATE ZONE	PROGRAM
1958	Morumbi, São Paolo, Brazil 23°36'43"S 46°42'48"W	Humid Subtropical	Single-family Residence

The Cirell House is the middle child of three houses built by Lina Bo Bardi. The first was the Glass House of 1950, which, despite being materially a polar opposite of the Cirell House, gave the later house its organizational strategy. The Cirell House directly adopts the formal prototype of Le Corbusier's 1924 design for mass-produced artisans' dwellings,[1] but Bo Bardi transforms the Corbusian diagram into a unique, hand-crafted object. The ideal vision of a pure and optimized dwelling on an abstracted flat ground is transformed into a site-specific architecture that seeks to embrace its climate, its physical setting, and its vernacular heritage and culture.

The land under the Valéria P. Cirell House slopes gently on a north-south axis. The alignment of the slope with a cardinal axis governs the logic of the site plan, the internal spatial organization of the house, and environmental considerations.

The vegetative roof is at the same level as the higher ground shouldering the house, providing insulation and cooling and establishing a natural continuity. This is not so much a green roof as an extension of the adjacent landscape over the house. Cisterns on the roof collect rainwater to be used in the bathrooms. An outdoor pool is situated at the lowest point of the site, providing evaporative cooling as rising warm air passes over the basin and enters the building envelope. An awning that wraps the entire perimeter links the house and the service quarters. This sunshade is framed with wood, supported by log columns, and covered with sapé grass, a traditional material used for thatching in rural Brazil. The two volumes create a heavy thermal mass that stabilizes the interior temperature. Openings are fitted with sunscreens that allow air flow, filter the sunlight, and protect the interior from overheating. Their placement is strategic for cross ventilation. The two apertures adjacent to the pool bring in the cooled air. The uninterrupted interior space (both in plan and section) promotes the free flow of air.

1. Magdalena Reches Peressotti, "Una Casa a la Vista" (Masters thesis, Universidad Politécnica de Catalunya, 2009), 33.

PRIMARY SOLAR PATHS AND CORRESPONDING SECTIONS

São Paulo, Brazil
23° South Latitude

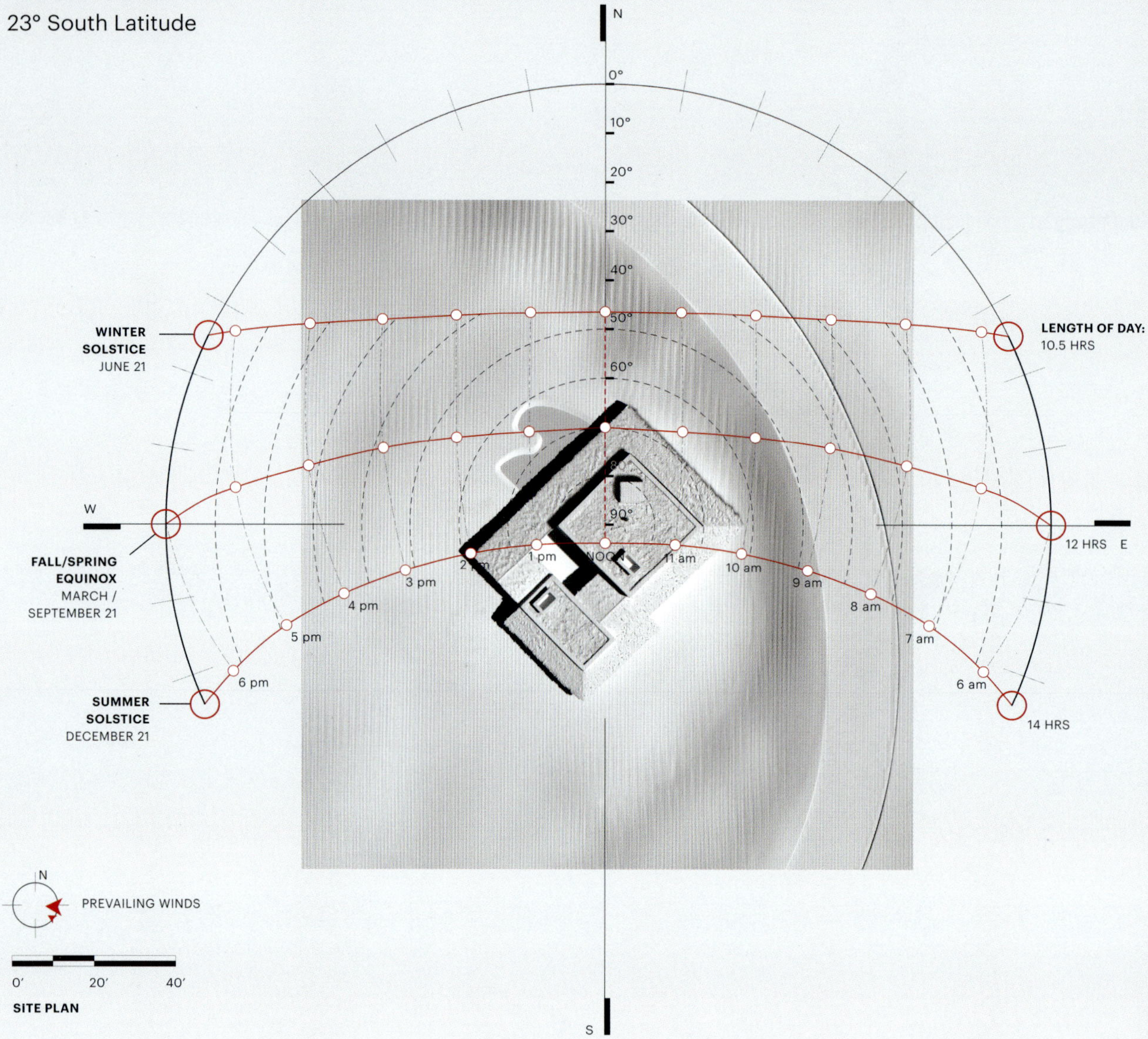

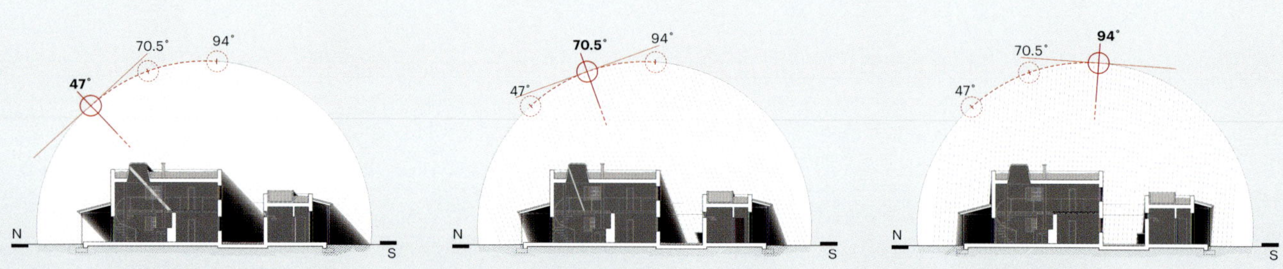

SUMMER SOLSTICE SECTION
JUNE 21, NOON
MAXIMUM SOLAR ANGLE: 47°

EQUINOX SECTION
MARCH / SEPTEMBER 21, NOON
MAXIMUM SOLAR ANGLE: 70.5°

WINTER SOLSTICE SECTION
DECEMBER 21, NOON
MAXIMUM SOLAR ANGLE: 94°

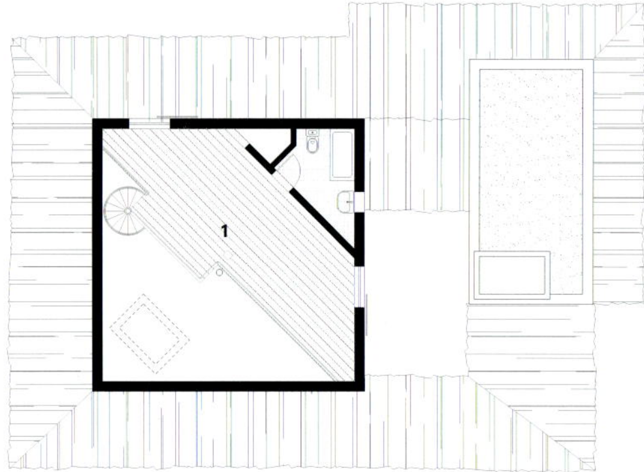

SECOND LEVEL

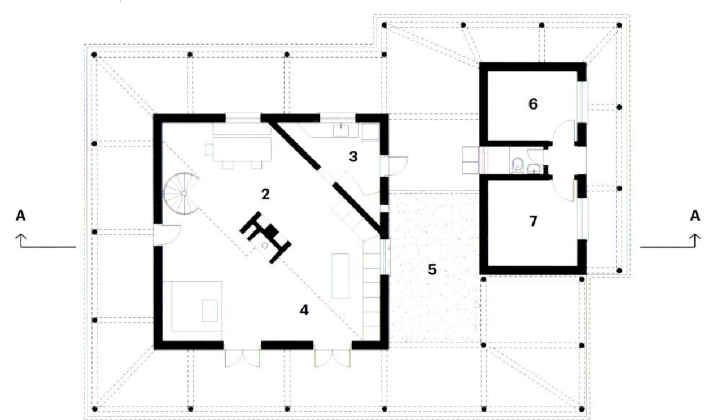

GROUND LEVEL

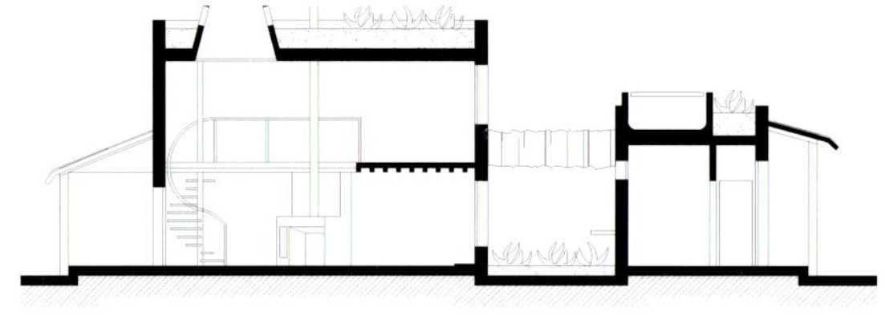

SECTION A – A

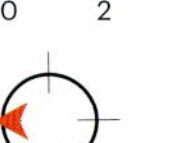

1 Bedroom
2 Dining area
3 Kitchen
4 Living area
5 Patio
6 Housekeeper's bedroom
7 Housekeeper's living room

Siedlung Halen
Atelier 5

YEAR
1961

LOCATION
Bern, Switzerland
46°58'21"N 7°24'46"E

CLIMATE ZONE
Temperate Oceanic

PROGRAM
Multifamily Housing

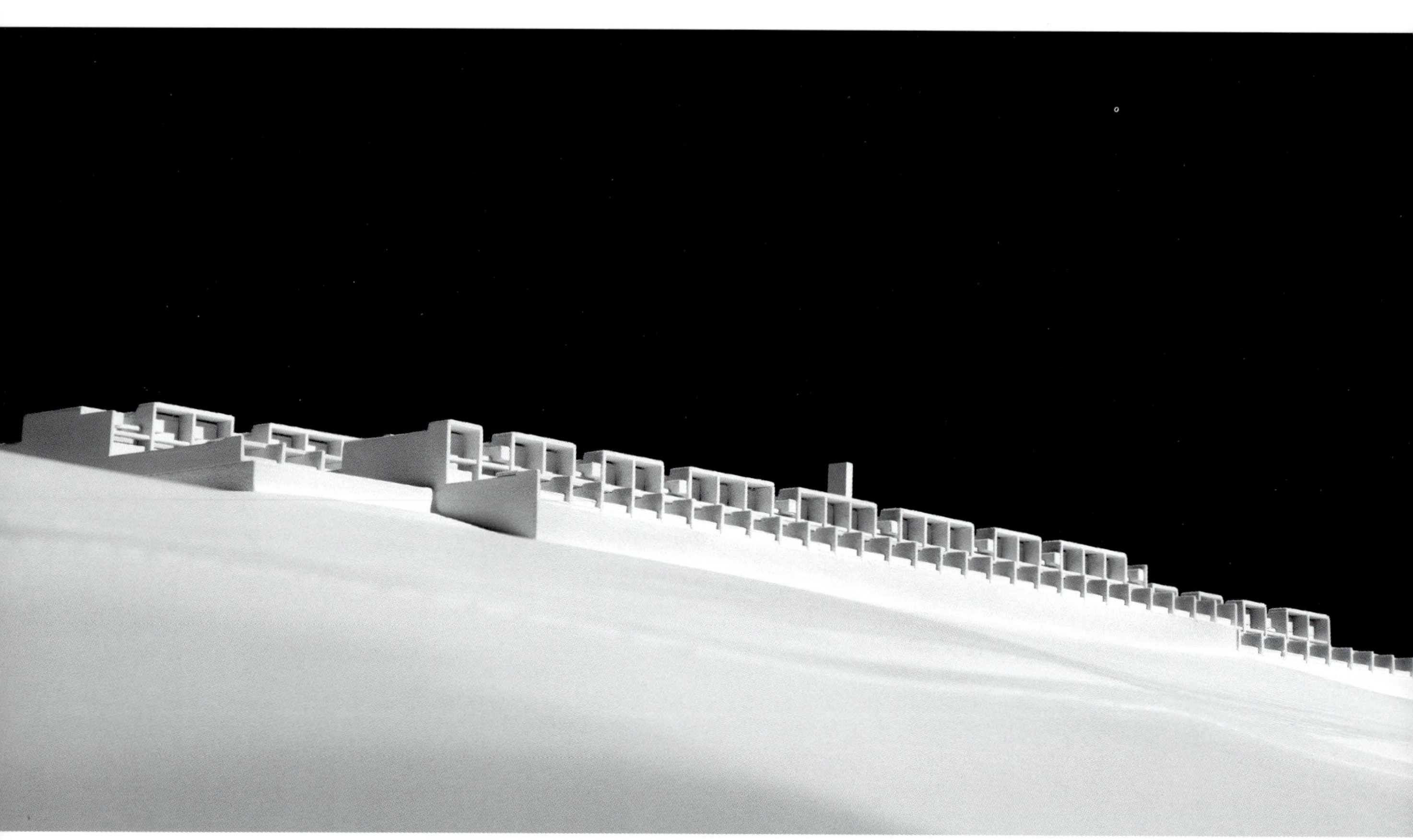

Atelier 5 was founded in 1955 by architects Erwin Fritz, Samuel Gerber, Rolf Hesterberg, Hans Hostettler, and Alfredo Pini; Niklaus Morgenthaler and Fritz Thormann joined the practice in 1956 and 1959, respectively.[1] Siedlung Halen was the first large-scale housing complex designed by the firm. The concept was to provide cooperatively owned housing for the middle class with a careful consideration of the relationship between public and private space and a strong integration with a natural site. The result is a high-density, low-rise housing complex nestled in the forest near the city of Bern, located on a sloped, south-facing site to maximize passive heating provided by the winter sun. Eighty-one units housing approximately 280 residents are organized into three stepped terraces. Tree-lined pedestrian paths between the terrace blocks act as community space for socialization and recreation, as well as entry passageways to the units themselves. A plaza occupies the center of the complex, and step and ramp passageways between blocks allow movement along the slope of the site. Other than the main entrance and parking garage, there are no streets on the site that accommodate cars. The complex occupies more than seven and a half acres.[2]

Individual owners also own a share of the communal facilities. These include an athletic field, playground, public pool, laundry facilities, automobile service station, parking, roads, paths, and the surrounding woods. An owners association is responsible for maintaining the property, with one caretaker's residence (a unit on the lowest level of the housing block) on site.[3]

There are two primary types of units, each three stories high, with subtle differences in configuration. Each features an enclosed or covered private courtyard garden on the lower level and a balcony on the first level. Entrances are from the north elevation, at the first level. The second level is either fenestrated directly to the south or onto an open-air south facing solarium. There are also a small number of studios and combined house/studio units. The Siedlung Halen design employs the landscaped terraced green roofs as outdoor space available for residents of the upper units. Seen from above, the project blends visually with the surrounding forest and meadowlands.

The project is constructed primarily of concrete slabs and concrete block walls. For construction efficiency, foundations and roof slabs are continuous across

multiple units. To maximize acoustic privacy, the individual units are separated by double party walls, each measuring five inches thick with a three-inch hollow space between them.

Siedlung Halen builds on the tradition of low-rise high density housing characteristic of the *siedlungen* built in Germany in the late 1920s. Like them, this project aspires to be a place of healthy living, where apartments are provided abundant light and air and where residents have access to green space. The Swiss project went beyond the earlier expressions of this new settlement type, as each dwelling is spatially generous, and each resident is provided with a direct connection to nature via their own outdoor living space. The project's emphasis on communal amenities, common dining areas, and other shared facilities offers an alternative to the more common bedroom community, automobile-based, suburban housing solutions.

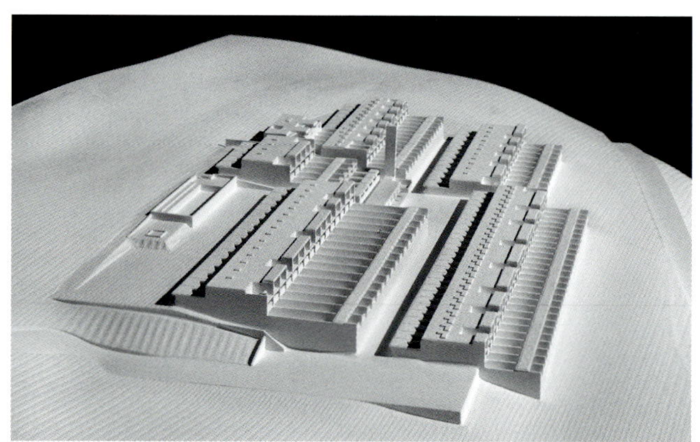

1. Atelier 5, "Atelier: Geschichte," http://www.atelier5.ch/de/Atelier/Geschichte.php (accessed on January 29, 2013).

2. "Atelier 5, "Wohnort Halen," quoted in Niklaus Morgenthaler, "Atelier 5," *GA: Global Architecture* 23, (1973).

3. Ibid.

PRIMARY SOLAR PATHS AND CORRESPONDING SECTIONS

Bern, Switzerland

46° North Latitude

SITE PLAN

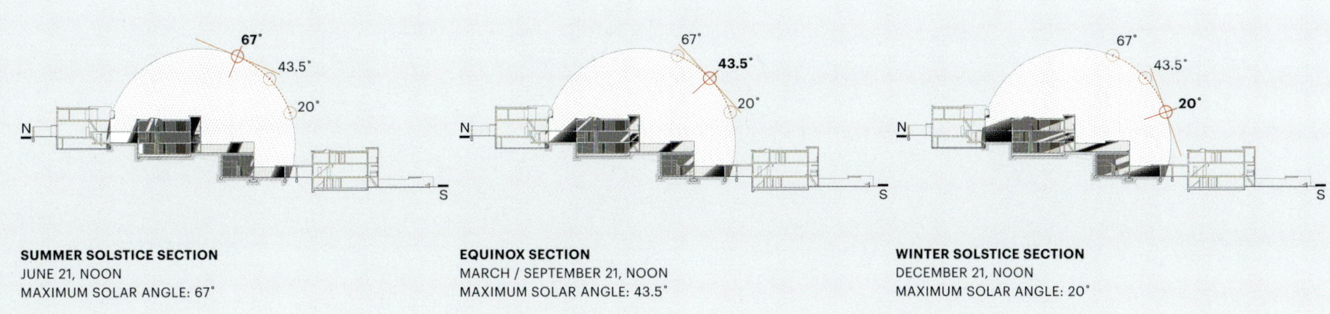

SUMMER SOLSTICE SECTION
JUNE 21, NOON
MAXIMUM SOLAR ANGLE: 67°

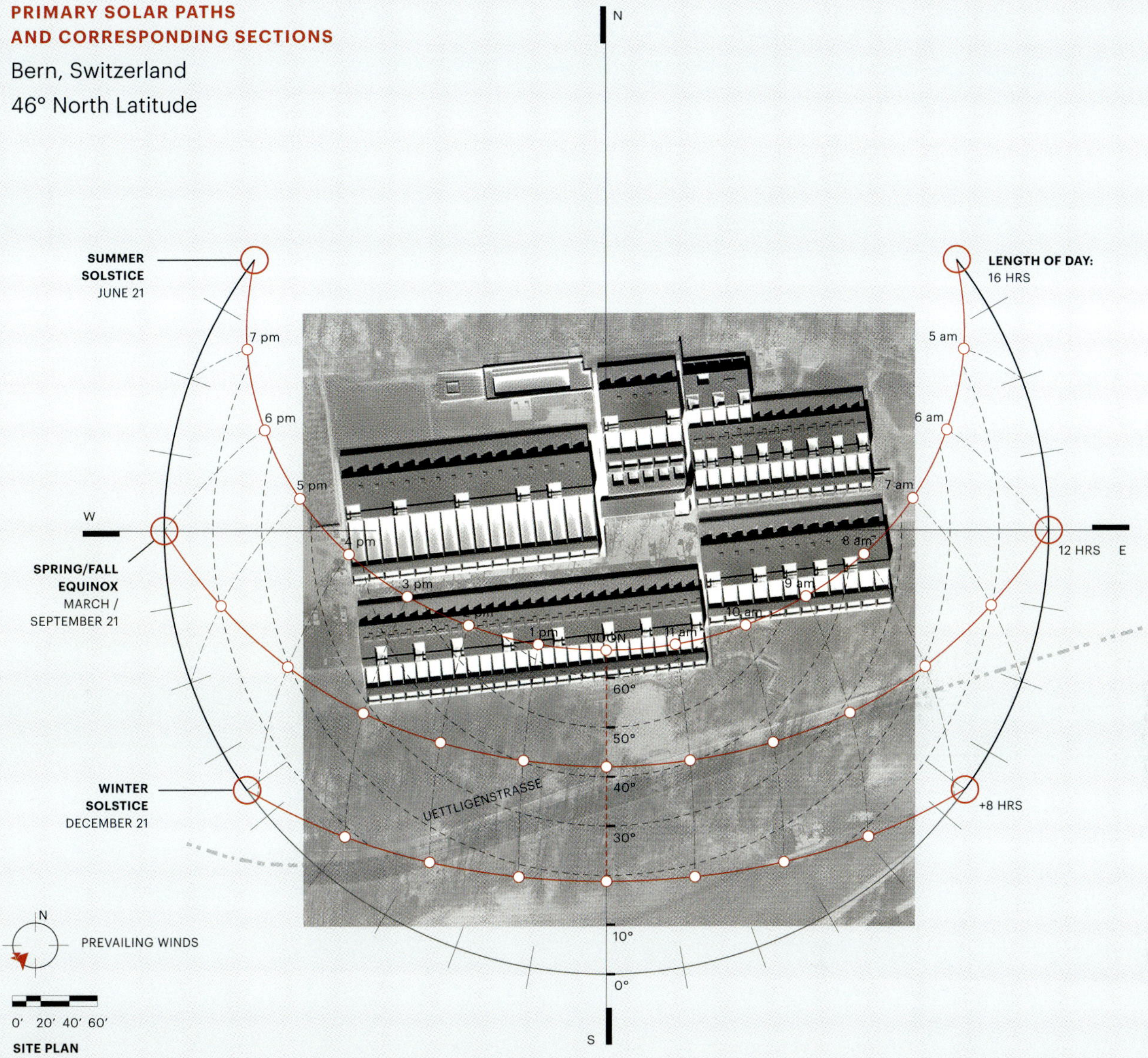

EQUINOX SECTION
MARCH / SEPTEMBER 21, NOON
MAXIMUM SOLAR ANGLE: 43.5°

WINTER SOLSTICE SECTION
DECEMBER 21, NOON
MAXIMUM SOLAR ANGLE: 20°

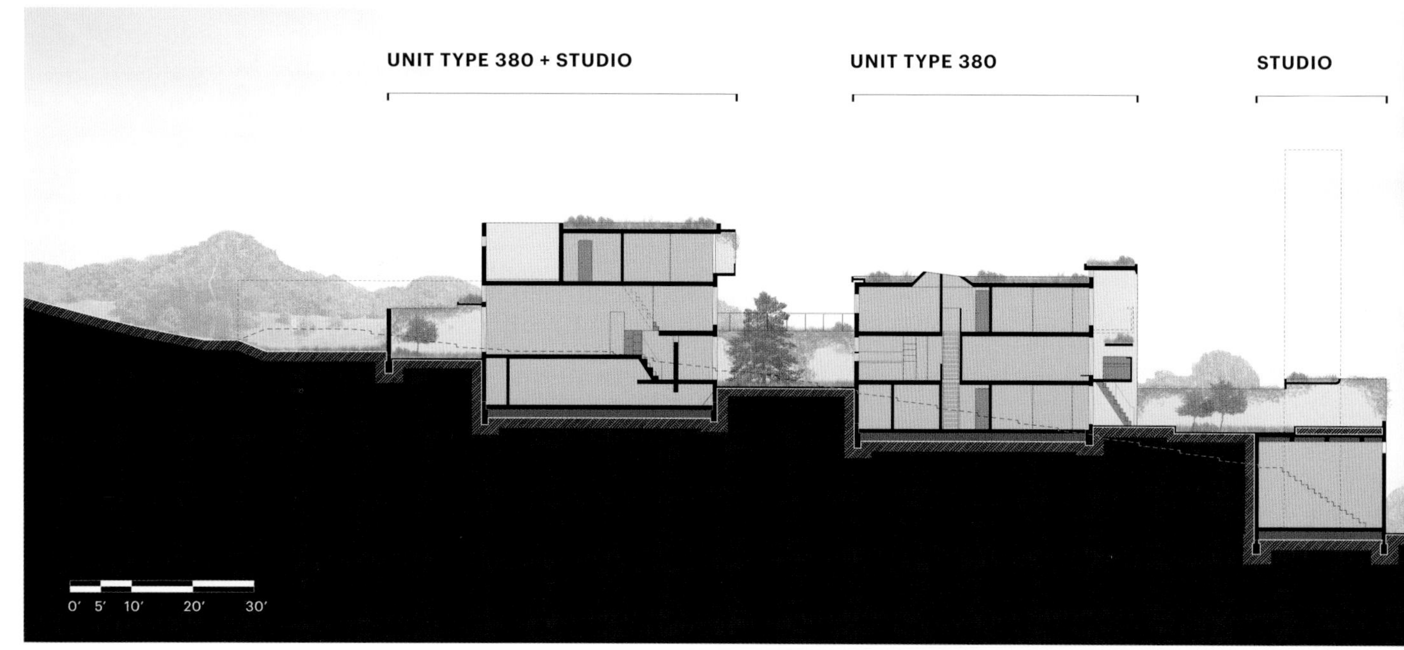

UNIT TYPE 380 + STUDIO
UNIT TYPE 380
STUDIO
0' 5' 10' 20' 30'

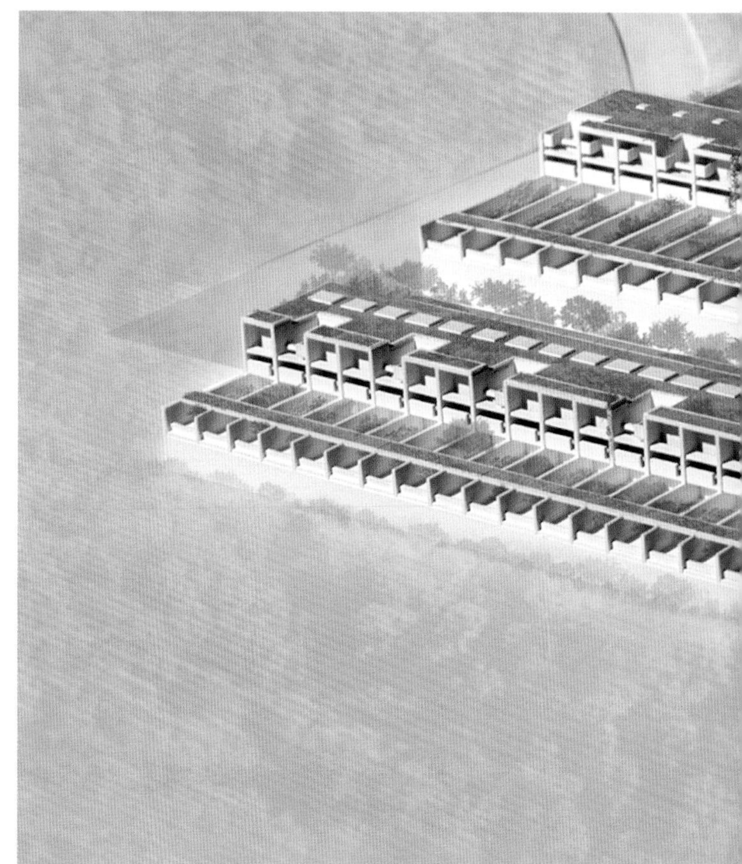

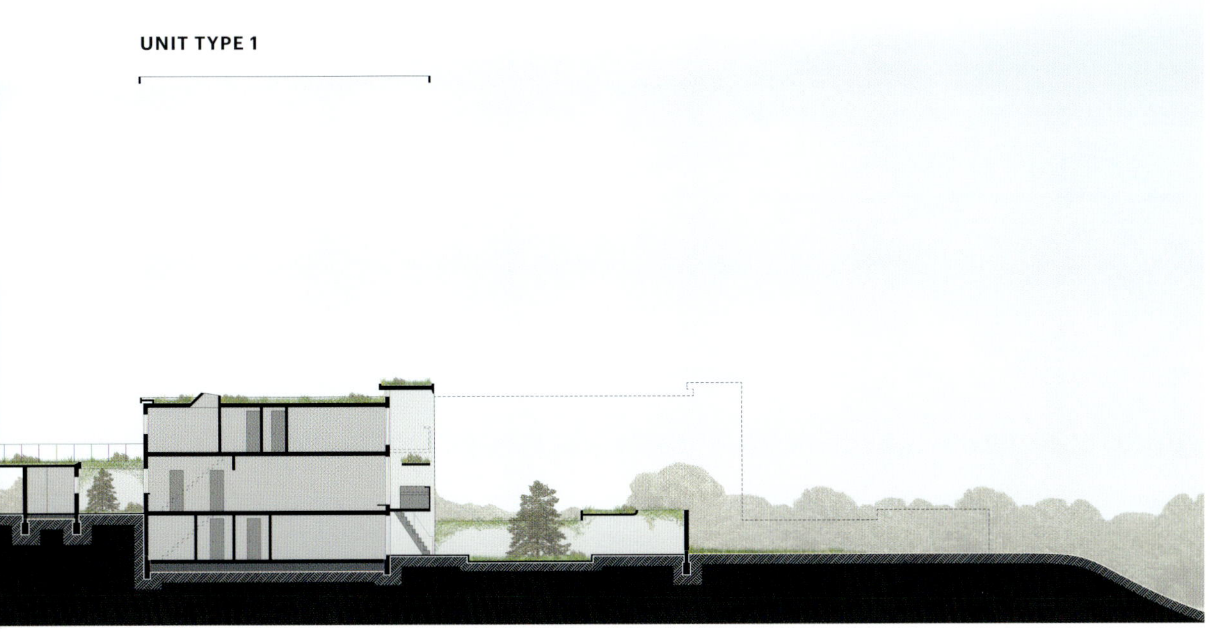

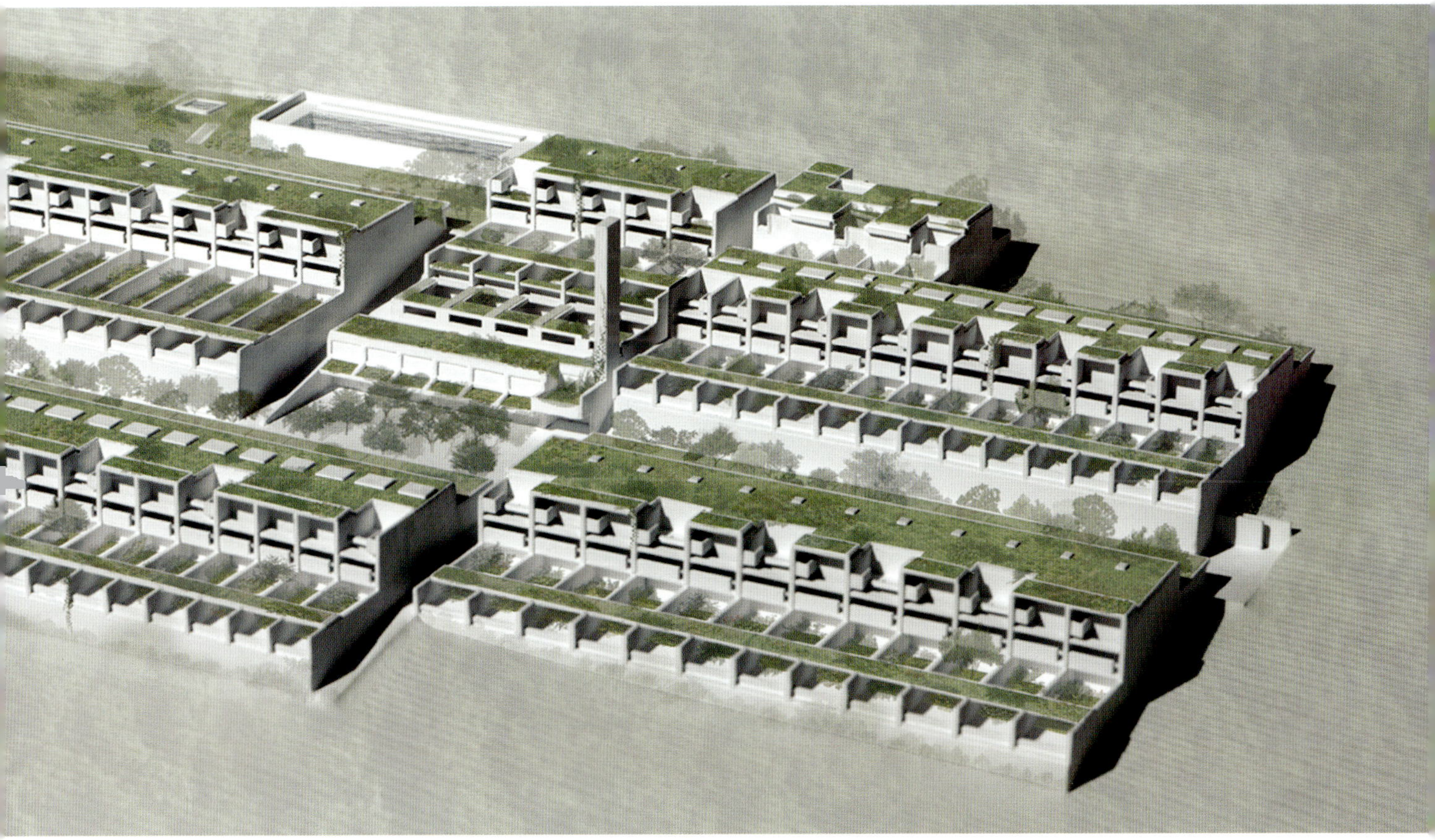

School of Plastic Arts, National Arts School
Ricardo Porro

Following the Cuban Revolution in 1959, Fidel Castro and Che Guevara, in an act of political theater, played a round of golf at the defunct Havana Country Club. Admiring the rich tropical landscape aside the Quiba River, Castro proclaimed that the grounds would be the site for the national schools of the arts. He hired the young Cuban architect Ricardo Porro to oversee the entire project, which was designed to accommodate the five separate schools. Porro would design the School of Plastic Arts and the School of Modern Dance, while Italian Architect Roberto Gottardi designed the School of Dramatic Arts, and fellow Italian Architect Vittorio Garatti designed the School of Music and the School of Ballet.

Of the five schools, Porro's School of Plastic Arts, consisting of ten studios, exhibition spaces, offices, and classrooms, is the most visible and accessible, and the project most often identified with the complex. Porro and his colleagues worked with a palette of local materials and a common vocabulary that included the Catalonian vault. Whether this choice was ideologically motivated, as an alternative to the geometric rigidity of the International Style, or the reality of working with the limited materials what were available is difficult to determine. The U.S. imposed trade embargo on Cuba had left building materials such as steel and reinforced concrete in short supply and there were few options for off-island sources. So the schools were built using locally produced materials: brick for the walls and terra-cotta tiles for the Catalonian-inspired domes and roof vaults.[1] Porro hired skilled traditional craftsmen to train the construction crew in the art of Catalonian construction. The result was a hand made, organic form that integrated with the surroundings.

The school uses outdoor vaulted corridors to connect the domed studios and classrooms. The covered arcades provide deep shade along the perimeter of the complex and prevents heat from radiating into the buildings. Most pathways also channel rainwater into the fountain in the central courtyard, a gathering place for the entire academy.

Throughout the day, the domes of the School of Plastic Arts heat up, with more heat accumulating on the side more directly oriented towards the sun, enhancing the natural upward flow of air. The domes are vented with operable skylights at the crowns. Smaller skylights provide natural daylight throughout the studios.

Construction on the National Arts Schools ceased in 1965 for political and economic reasons: the expressive and exuberant designs were reconsidered by the political class and came to be seen as embodying bourgeois and elitists values. Even though the Schools of Plastic Arts, Modern Dance, and Ballet were nearly complete, the Castro regime shut the work down and expelled the architects from the country. The campus fell into disarray and suffered decades of vandalism until the mid-1980s, when international interest in the projects began to build momentum. By 1999 various Cuban cultural ministries and councils began to throw their support behind preservation of the complex and the architects were invited back. In 2010 the campus was granted status as a national monument by the Cuban government, and architect Norman Foster was invited in by Carlos Acosta, native of Cuba and one of the première ballet dancers of our time, to develop a controversial program to redevelop Garatti's School of Ballet. The controversy over what many see as an inappropriate privatization of a cultural treasure has put the project on hold; Porro's School of Plastic Arts was in the process of restoration when work was interrupted by the global recession.

1. John Loomis, "Castro's Dream," *Icon Magazine,* Winter 2002–2003: 27.

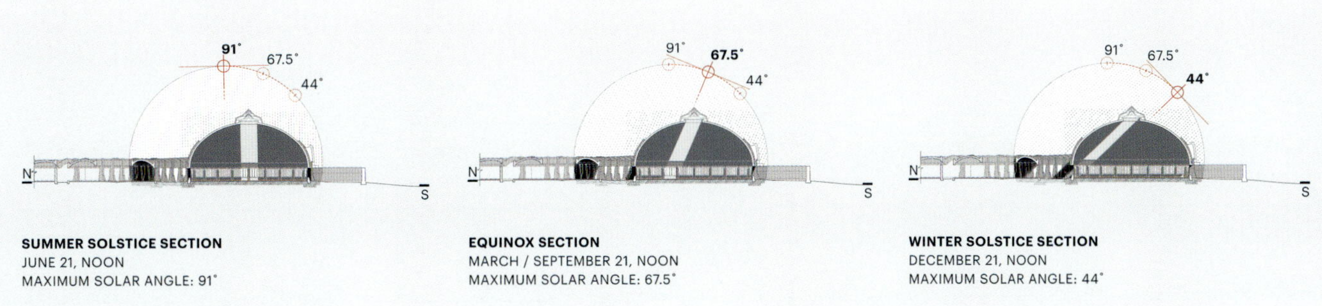

SUMMER SOLSTICE SECTION
JUNE 21, NOON
MAXIMUM SOLAR ANGLE: 91°

EQUINOX SECTION
MARCH / SEPTEMBER 21, NOON
MAXIMUM SOLAR ANGLE: 67.5°

WINTER SOLSTICE SECTION
DECEMBER 21, NOON
MAXIMUM SOLAR ANGLE: 44°

1 Guastavino tile dome
2 Skylights with operable windows
3 Shading overhang/gutter
4 Operable pivot windows
5 Convection air circulation
6 Shaded exterior passage

House on a Cycladic Island
Iannis Xenakis

YEAR
Designed 1966;
Completed 1974

LOCATION
Greece
36°N 25°E

CLIMATE ZONE
Subtropical
Mediterranean

PROGRAM
Residence

In 1966, French composer François-Bernard Mâche commissioned his friend Iannis Xenakis to design a summer house for his family on a Cycladic Island. At the time Xenakis, an engineer and musical theorist, was focused almost exclusively on music compositions. Between 1947 and 1959, he had worked in the office of Le Corbusier, contibuting to the design of the volumetric and sculptural roof garden at Unite d'Habitation Nantes and to the terrace walls at the Convent de La Tourette; the language of these designs is evident in this project. Xenakis developed the design from photographs and topographical information provided by Mâche, but he did not visit the site or the island until the house was completed.

The small plot overlooks the Aegean Sea. Due to its remote location, building materials arrived mostly by small boats, and in some cases, via donkey. Construction began in 1974 and was supervised by a local architect, following traditional building methods of the Cyclades: thick masonry walls for insulation against summer heat, small openings, a flat roof, and a lime wash exterior.[1]

Sitting on a stepped plinth, typical of the vernacular architecture of the Aegean, the house makes use of the terraced slope, on which recesses serve as seating areas and balconies that overlook the sea. The house consists of a composition of five freestanding white volumes varying in size, shape, and orientation. Each is a separate room: living room/kitchen, guestroom, two bedrooms, and a bathroom laid out at the same level and on a slight curve parallel to the hill. The exterior plinth connects the rooms; circulation and outdoor space become one. The facade openings, which continue the investigation of rhythm and light that Xenakis developed for Corbusier's La Tourette, allow slivers of light into the interior in syncopation with the everyday functions within the house. In the living area, a diagonal skylight cuts through the roof, following the sun's path through the interior. The ceilings of each volume are detached from the walls, with the recesses between ceiling and wall alternating between glazed surfaces and solid mass, admitting a glow of illumination along the upper corner of the spaces.

Synthesizing traditional Cycladic building methods with modernist spatial concepts, Xenakis transforms the house into an instrument of light using principles of blocking, channelling, radiation, diffusion, refraction, and reflection. The assemblage of the five volumes is a study of living spaces and their respective requirements for natural light specific to the very particular climatic conditions of the eastern Mediterranean region.

1. Sharon E. Kanach, "Summer House for François-Bernard Mâche," in Iannis Xenakis, *Music and Architecture: Architectural Projects, Texts, and Realizations* (Hillsdale, NY: Pendragon Press, 2008), 170–76.

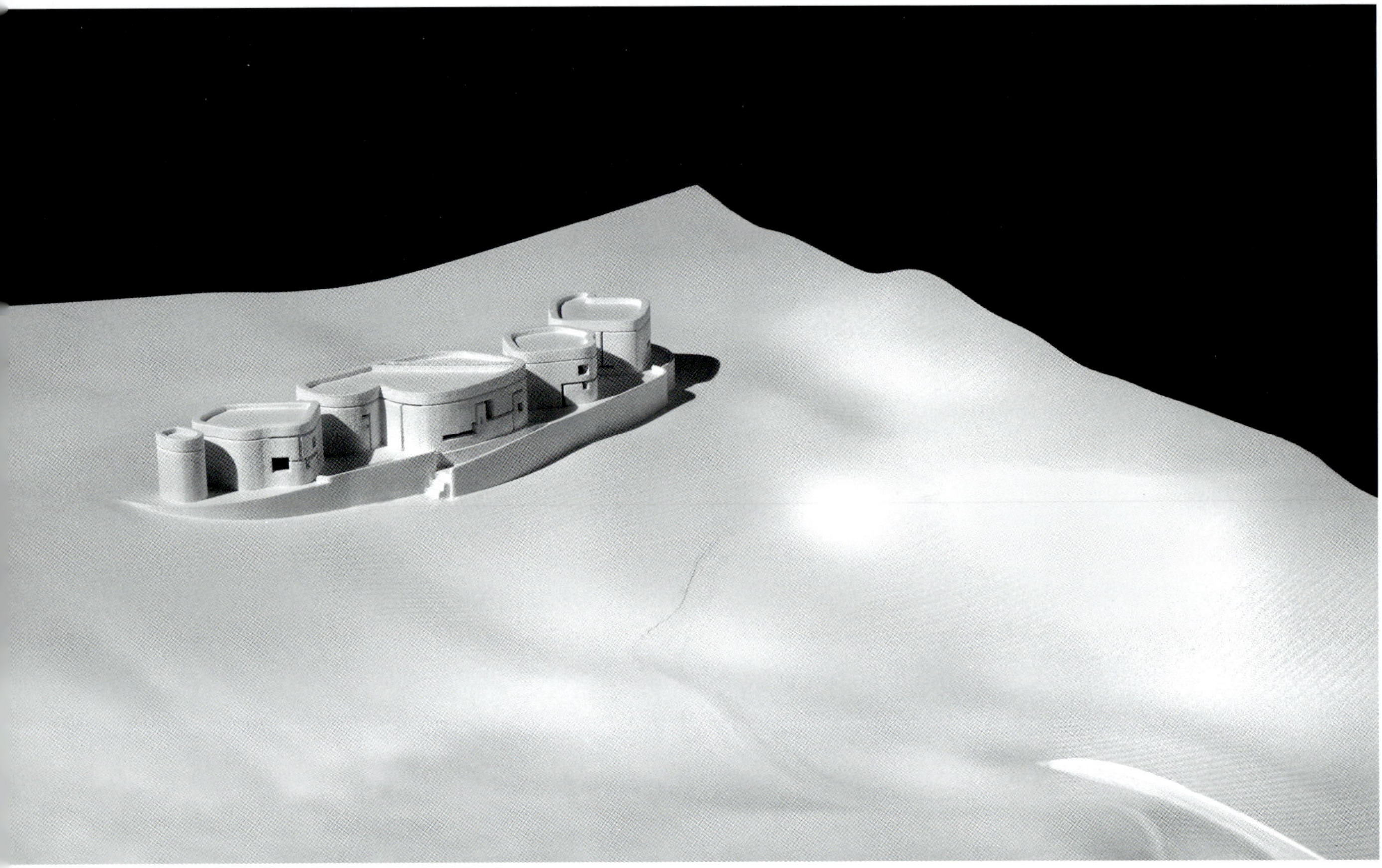

PRIMARY SOLAR PATHS AND CORRESPONDING SECTIONS

Greece
36° North Latitude

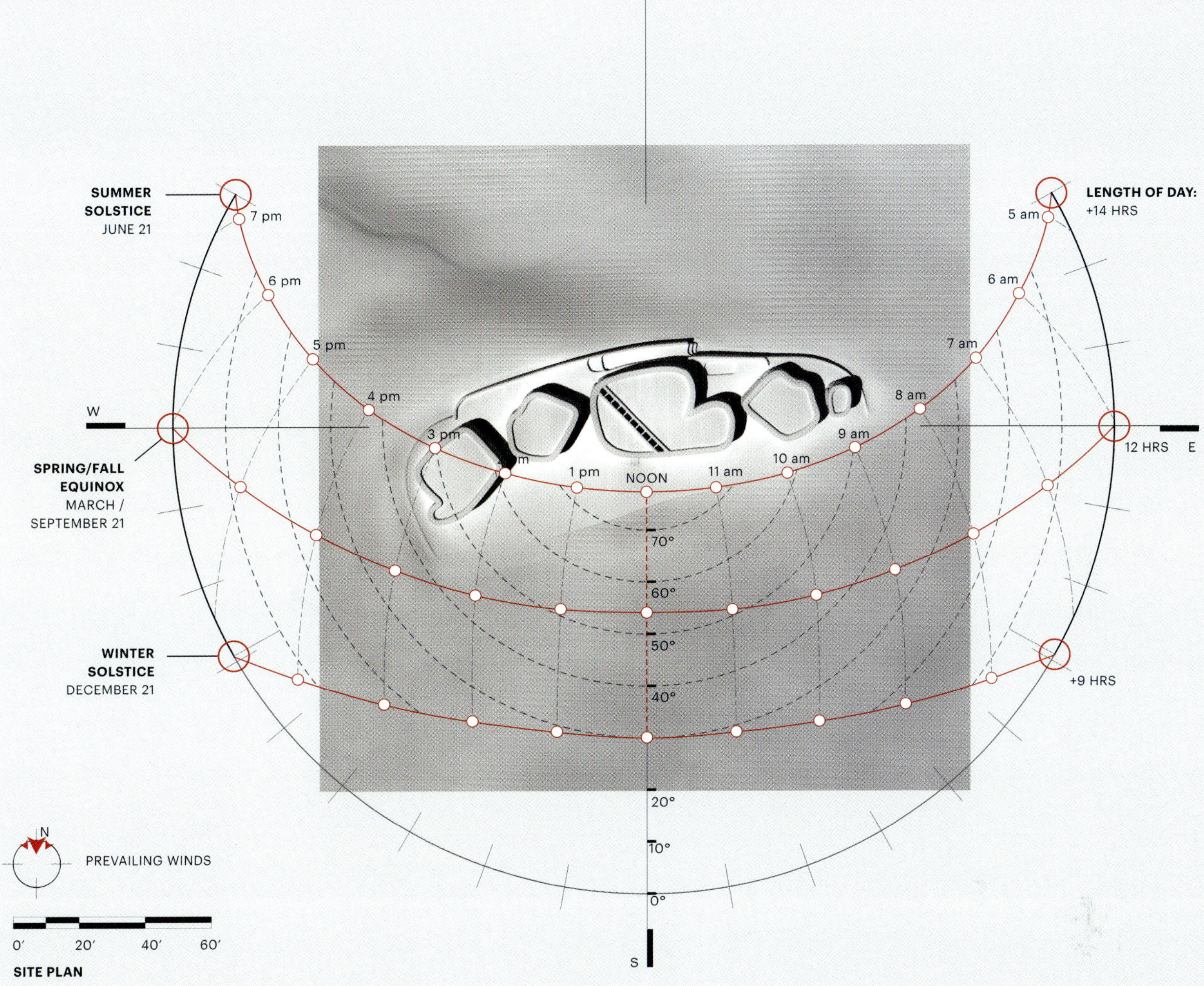

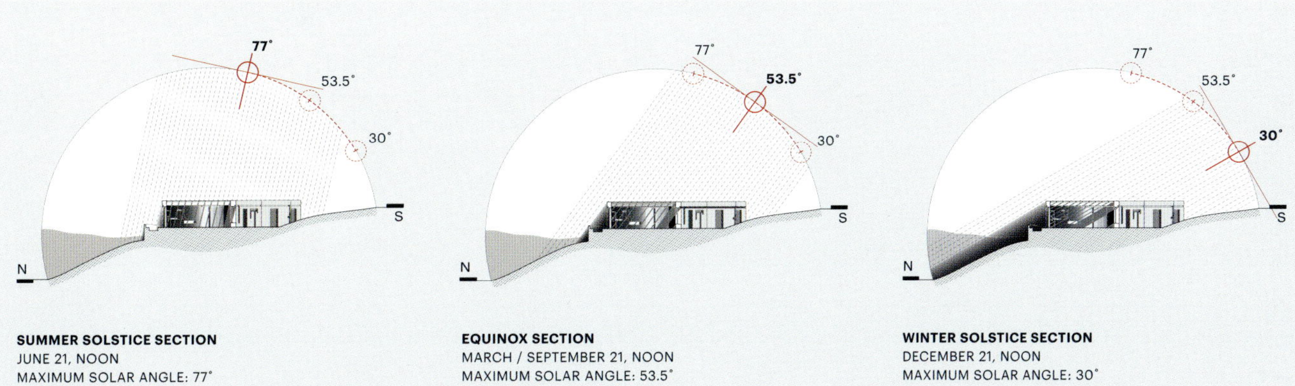

SUMMER SOLSTICE SECTION
JUNE 21, NOON
MAXIMUM SOLAR ANGLE: 77°

EQUINOX SECTION
MARCH / SEPTEMBER 21, NOON
MAXIMUM SOLAR ANGLE: 53.5°

WINTER SOLSTICE SECTION
DECEMBER 21, NOON
MAXIMUM SOLAR ANGLE: 30°

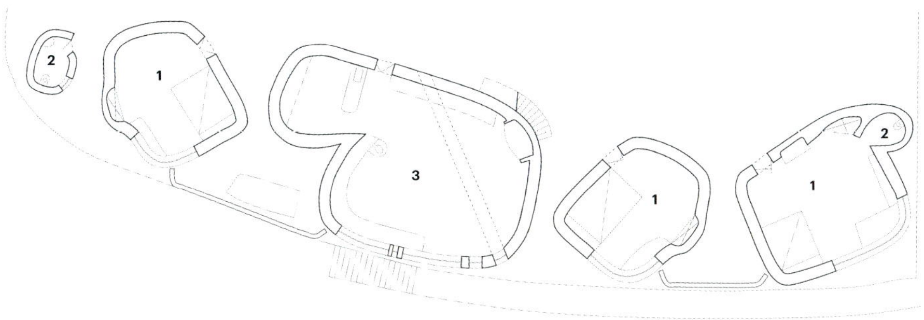

GROUND LEVEL

NORTH ELEVATION

1 Bedroom
2 Bathroom
3 Living area/kitchen

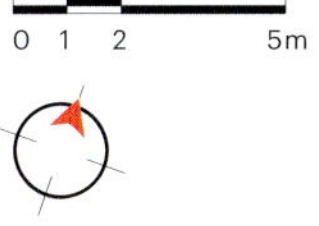

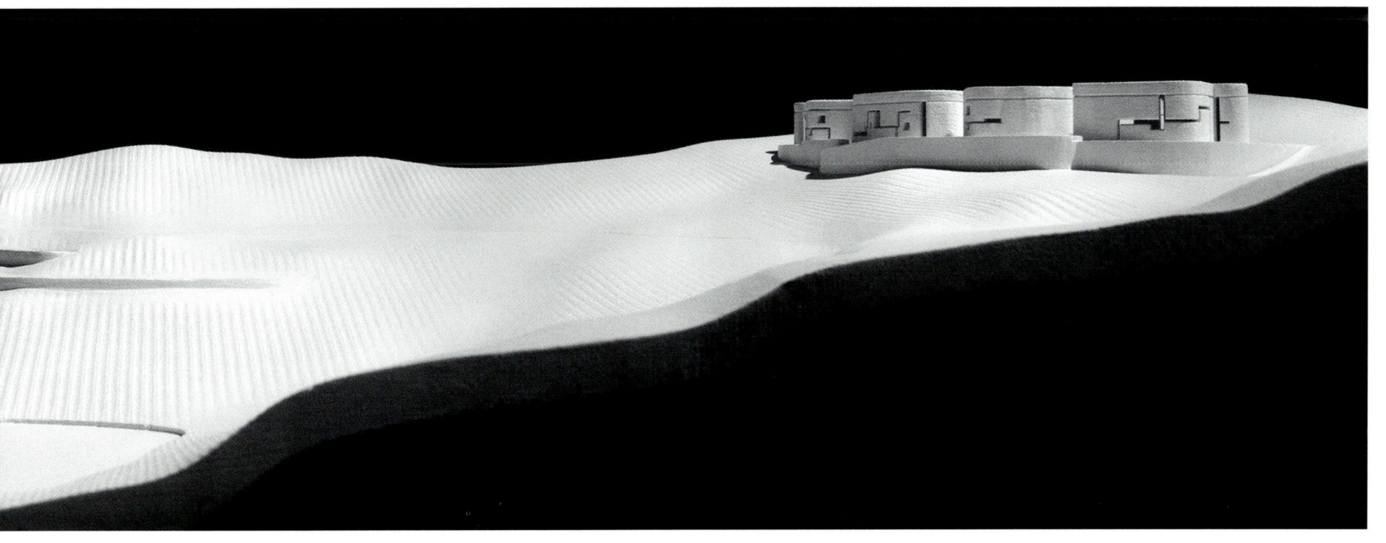

House II in Kavouri
Constantinos Decavallas

YEAR
Designed 1968;
Completed 1971

LOCATION
Athens, Attiki, Greece
37°48'56"N 23°45'42"E

CLIMATE ZONE
Subtropical
Mediterranean

PROGRAM
Single-family
Residence

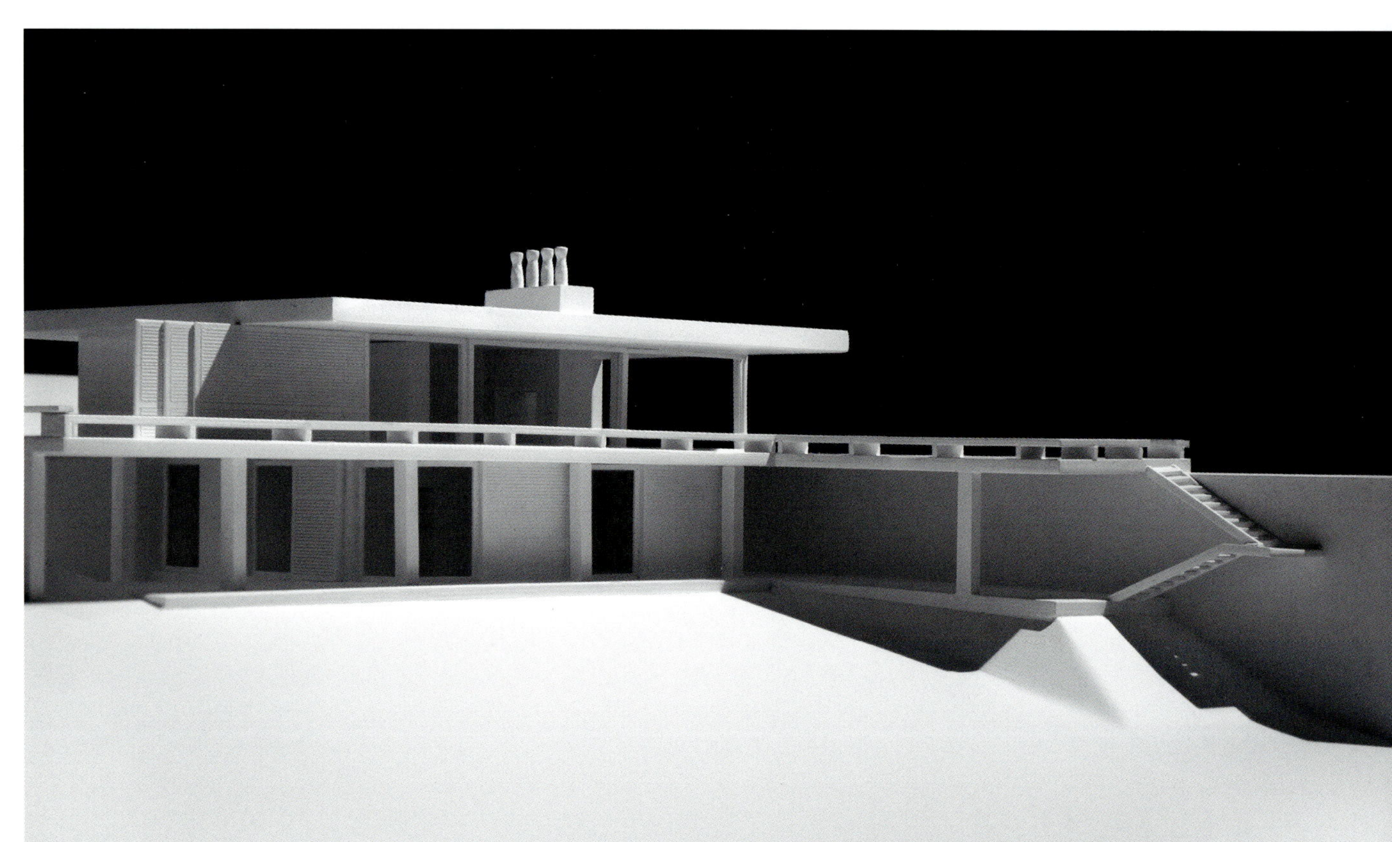

Constantinos Decavallas came to the United States from Greece in 1951 to attend school at Columbia University. At the time he arrived the emphasis on climate responsive design was gaining momentum in the United States. In 1947 James Marston Fitch published his seminal work, *American Building: The Environmental Forces That Shape It*, in which he examined how buildings responded to climate. The following year the Hungarian born Olgyay twins had immigrated to the U.S., bringing with them their research on architectural solar control. In 1951 they published their article *The Temperate House*, followed by two other important papers, *Bioclimatic Approach to Architecture* and *Solar Control and Orientation to meet Bioclimatic Requirements*. The interest in climate-based architectural studies was also taking root at Columbia University, where Decavallas had settled. An association of graduate students, working independently from the main curriculum, developed tools for measuring climate impacts on architectural forms, including airflow chambers and solar modelling devices. The group, which Dekavalles was drawn to join when he reached the school, would call itself the Form and Climate Group. The two Dekavalles projects featured here directly applied principals that he helped develop while with Form and Climate Group at Columbia University.

House II is located on the Kavouri peninsula in the southern part of Attica, overlooking the Saronikos Gulf. The orientation of the plan takes advantage of the prevailing summer winds and the gently sloping topography of the site. The design maximizes natural ventilation and passive cooling by integrating strategies of unimpeded airflow, pressure differentials in various spaces, and evaporative cooling.

A stack effect is achieved through a series of architectural operations. The roof slab diverts the sun and directs both wind and the warm air that rises up the sloped site through the interior of the house. Eight operable skylights inserted along the southern edge of the house above the living areas serve as controls for ventilation. During the winter months skylights allow daylight deep into the house, while in summer they are covered with tarpaulin to protect the interiors from solar gain. The roof slab is protected
from thermal gain with reflective white marble chips. The entire flat roof was designed so that it could be flooded with one inch of water during the summer,

PRIMARY SOLAR PATHS AND CORRESPONDING SECTIONS

Athens, Attiki, Greece

37° North Latitude

SITE PLAN

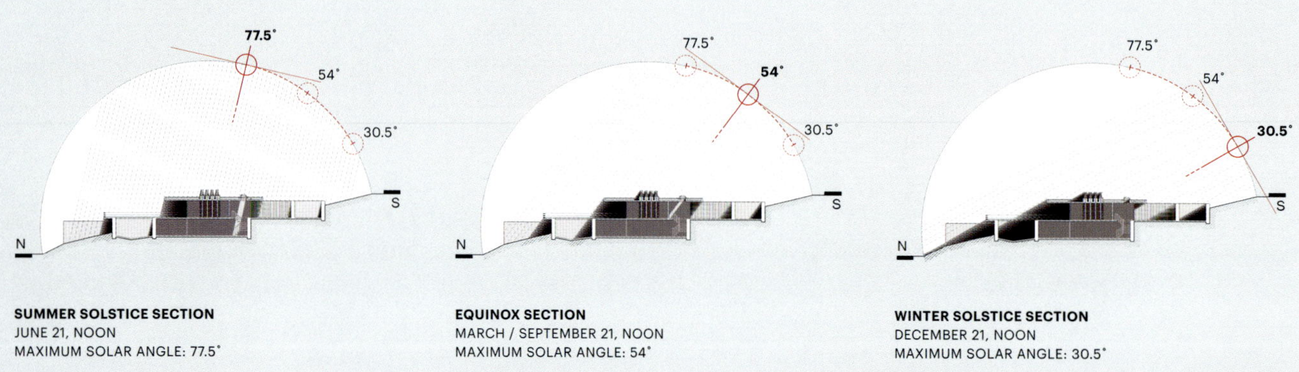

SUMMER SOLSTICE SECTION
JUNE 21, NOON
MAXIMUM SOLAR ANGLE: 77.5°

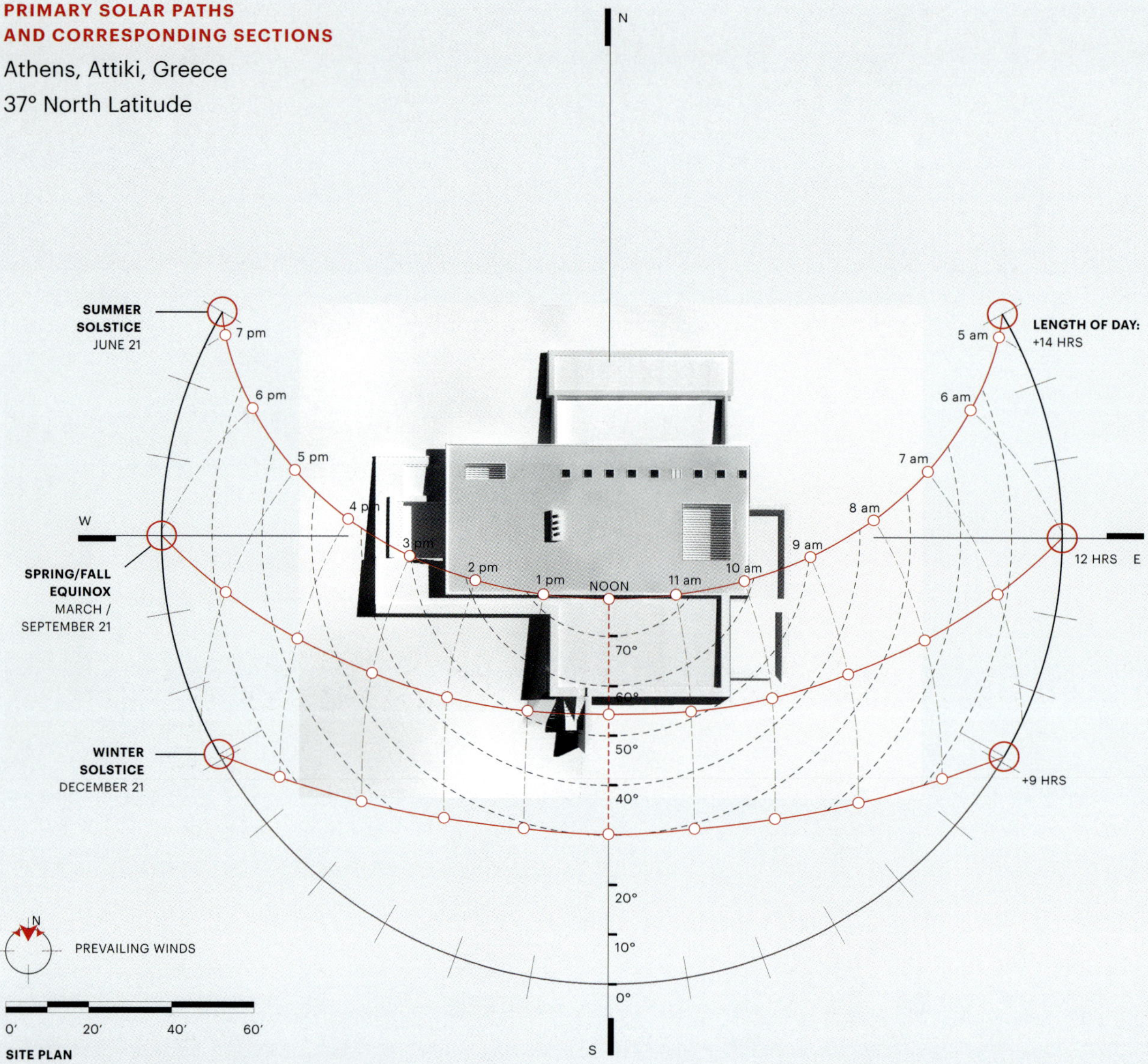

EQUINOX SECTION
MARCH / SEPTEMBER 21, NOON
MAXIMUM SOLAR ANGLE: 54°

WINTER SOLSTICE SECTION
DECEMBER 21, NOON
MAXIMUM SOLAR ANGLE: 30.5°

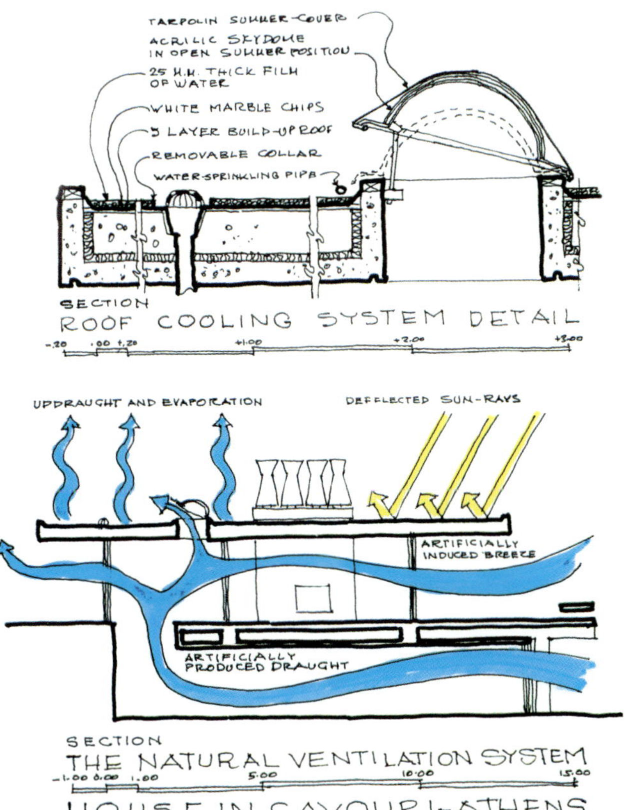

further reducing roof level air temperatures through evaporative cooling.

Sliding lightweight wooden shutters serve as partitions and provide flexibility in the delineation between inside and outside along the open side of the house. The Mediterranean climate allows evenings to be spent outdoors, while during the heat of the day the partitions screen the sun and isolate the interior from the heat. The fireplace for the house employs a unique design of four airflow chimneys. The geometry of the chimneys, which pinch to a narrow gap towards the top of the flue, increases the pressure of moving air and the rate of the smoke exiting the house.

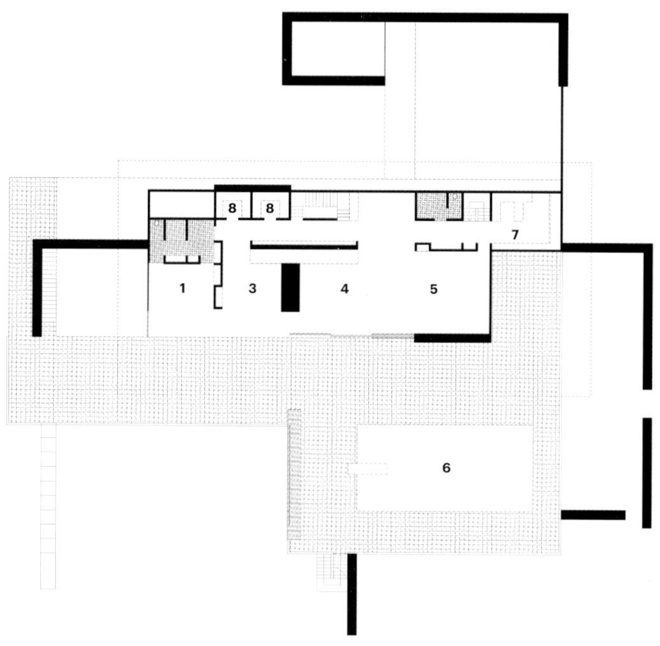

FIRST LEVEL

1 Ocean wind
2 Solar reflective roof structure
3 Operable panels allow ventilation
4 Stack effect

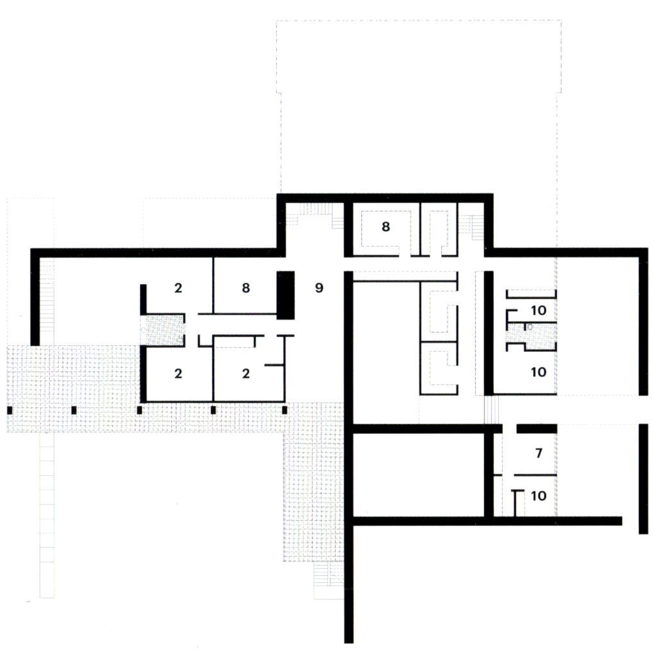

GROUND LEVEL

1 *Master bedroom*
2 *Children's bedroom*
3 *Study*
4 *Living room*
5 *Dining room*
6 *Swimming pool*
7 *Kitchen*
8 *Storage room*
9 *Secondary living quarters*
10 *Servant's quarters*

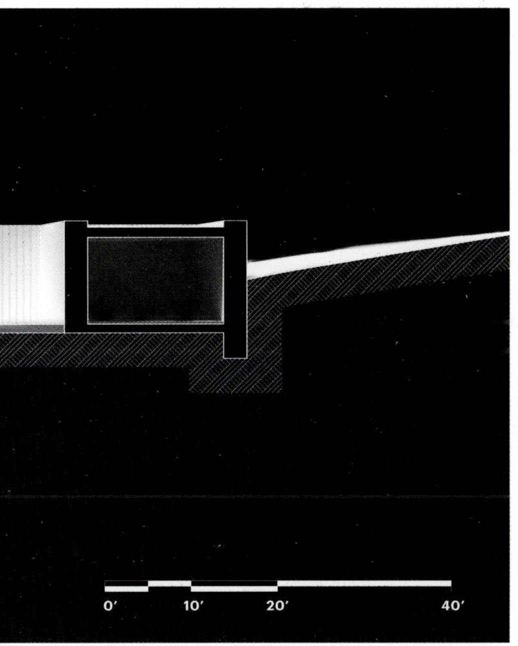

Vacation House on Aegina
Constantinos Decavallas

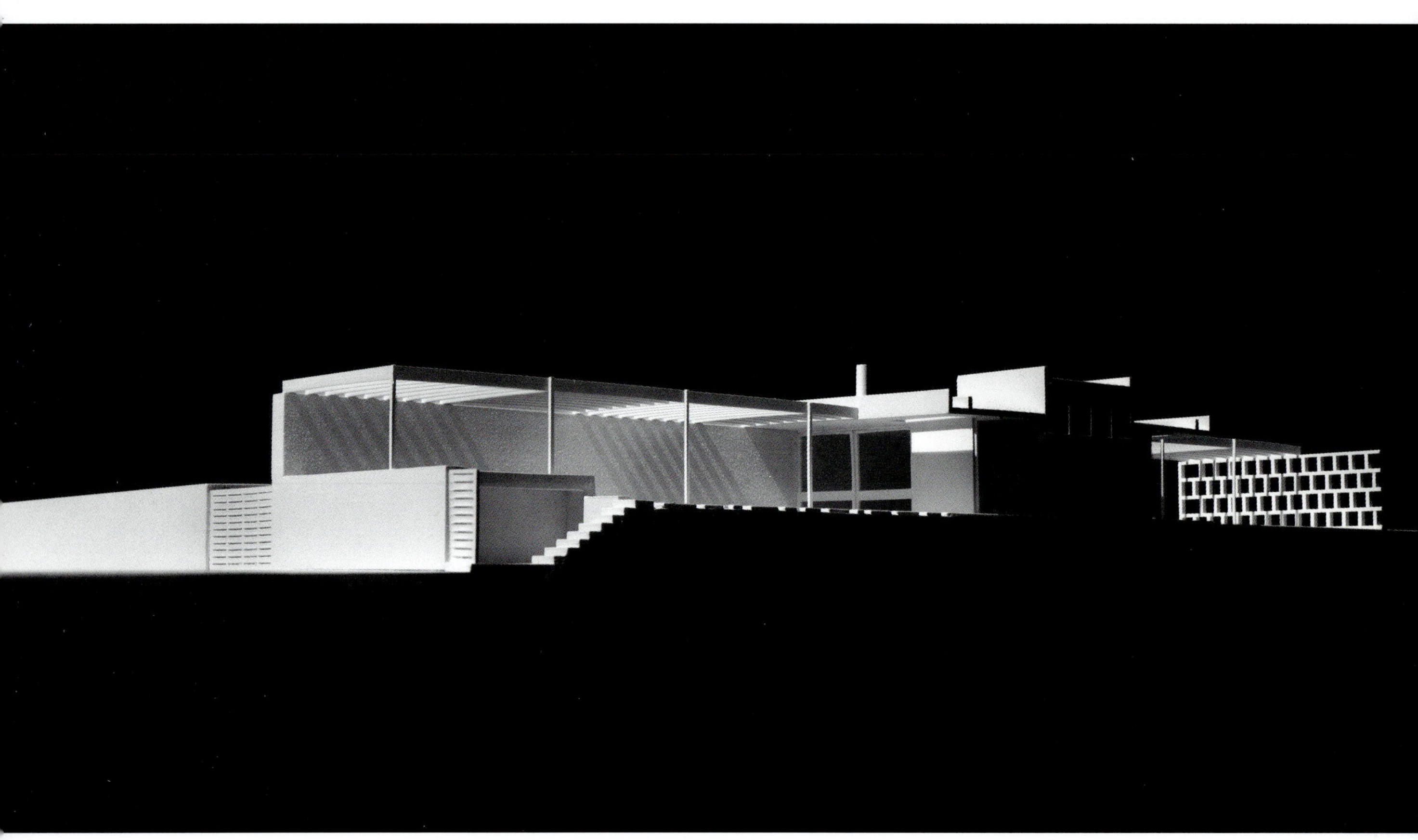

Designed as the architect's summer retreat, this house features an open-plan interior that extends both east and west from the core of the house into two partially enclosed garden areas defined by freestanding thick masonry walls and light weight wooden pergolas. The exterior areas below the pergolas continue through the north side of the interior plan, creating a linear living space that is both inside and out. The pergola-covered patios are an extension of the interior living zone, employing the same paving marble throughout. The living area can be separated from the outdoors with moveable, louvered, wooden shutters.

The main enclosure of the house is a one story, 50-foot square, topped by a raised cubic bulkhead containing four ventilation shafts. These shafts each connect to various spaces in the house, much like ductwork. Depending on the prevailing breezes (or the lack thereof), different combinations of these ducts can be opened or closed to maximize the natural movement of air through the various spaces of the house. The breeze carries air that has been cooled in the shaded outdoor spaces of the house. When there is no wind, a convective flow of air occurs from these shadowed areas around the building through the living spaces, then up to the roof and out the ventilator bulkhead. On windy days, the convection airflow is achieved by opening the small apertures on the windward side of the house and larger apertures on the protected side, setting up a pressure differential that draws air through the interior without the adverse impact of a full force wind blowing through. Water in this region is precious. Rainwater is collected from the stone pavings of the outdoor spaces and stored in a cistern under the backyard.

The design responds to two climatic conditions that typically alternate in the Greek islands over the warm seasons: extreme heat with little or no wind and strong northern winds known as the *Meltami*. The entire house was designed on the principles of natural convection and passive climate control, but it is also a precise work of modern architecture, based upon a simple modular plan, elemental geometry, and structural clarity.

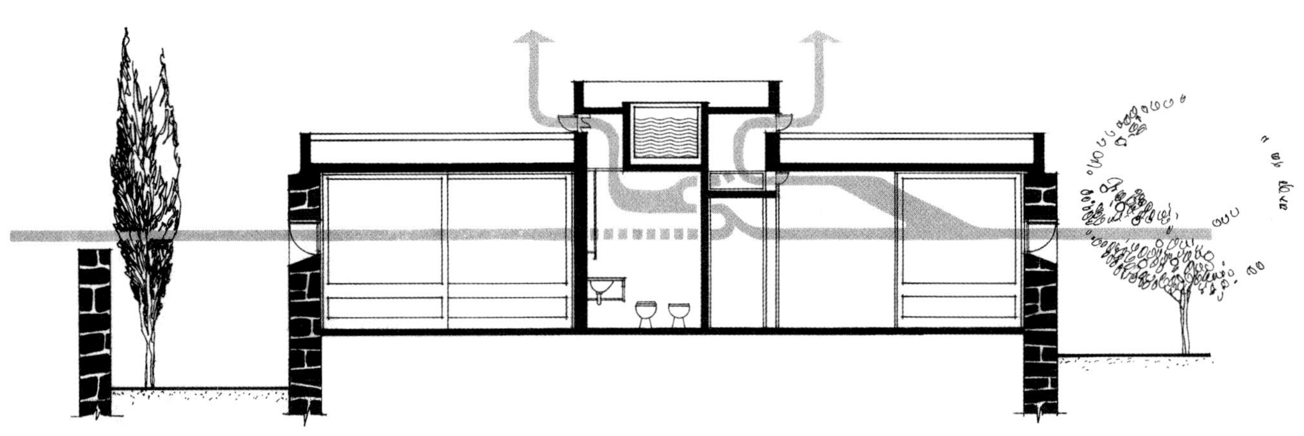

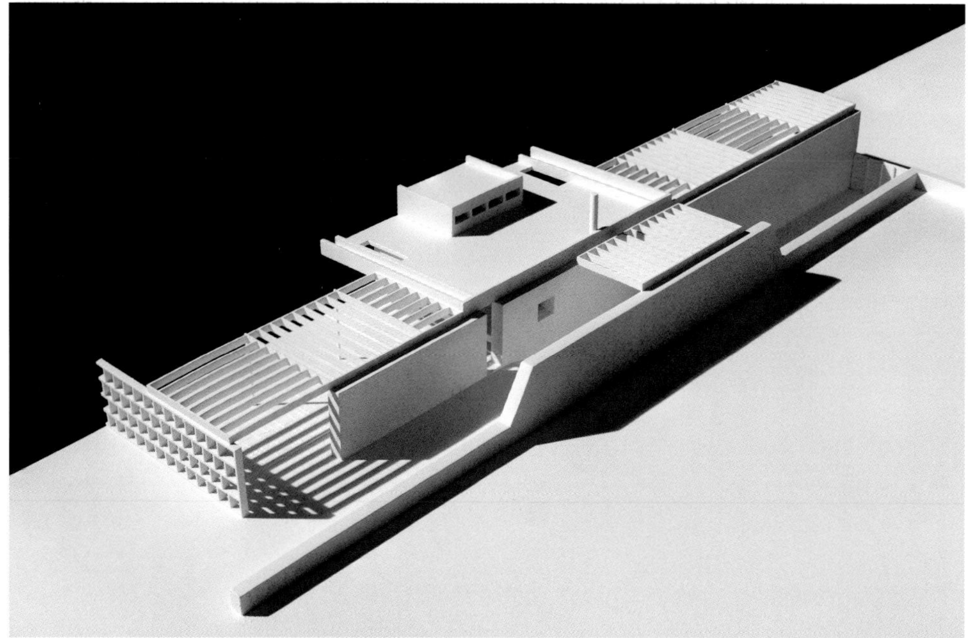

PRIMARY SOLAR PATHS
AND CORRESPONDING SECTIONS

Aegina, Greece
37° North Latitude

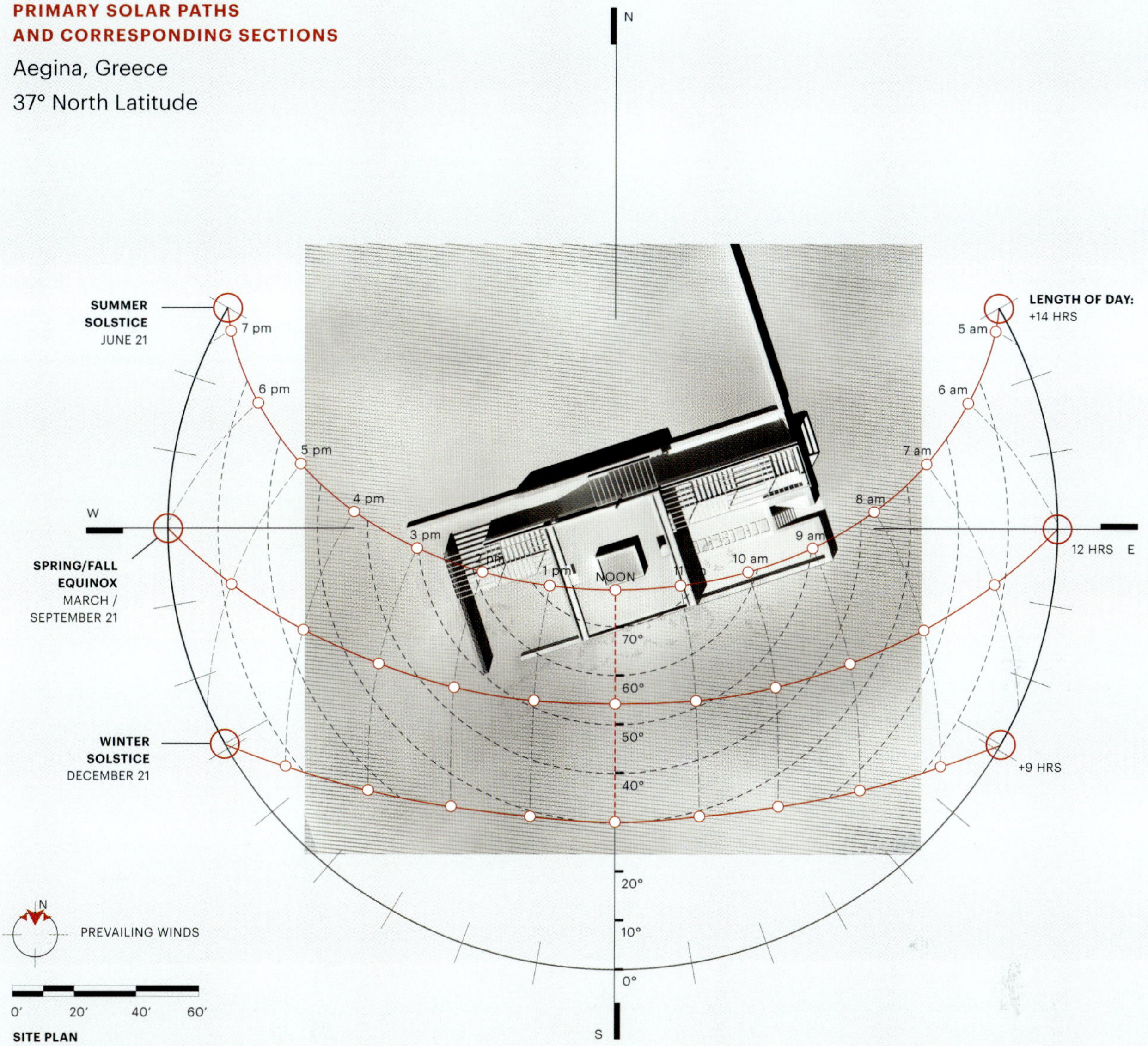

N

SUMMER
SOLSTICE
JUNE 21

7 pm
6 pm
5 pm
4 pm
3 pm
2 pm
1 pm
NOON

W

SPRING/FALL
EQUINOX
MARCH /
SEPTEMBER 21

WINTER
SOLSTICE
DECEMBER 21

LENGTH OF DAY:
+14 HRS

5 am
6 am
7 am
8 am
9 am
10 am
11 am

12 HRS   E

+9 HRS

70°
60°
50°
40°
20°
10°
0°

S

N
PREVAILING WINDS

0'   20'   40'   60'
SITE PLAN

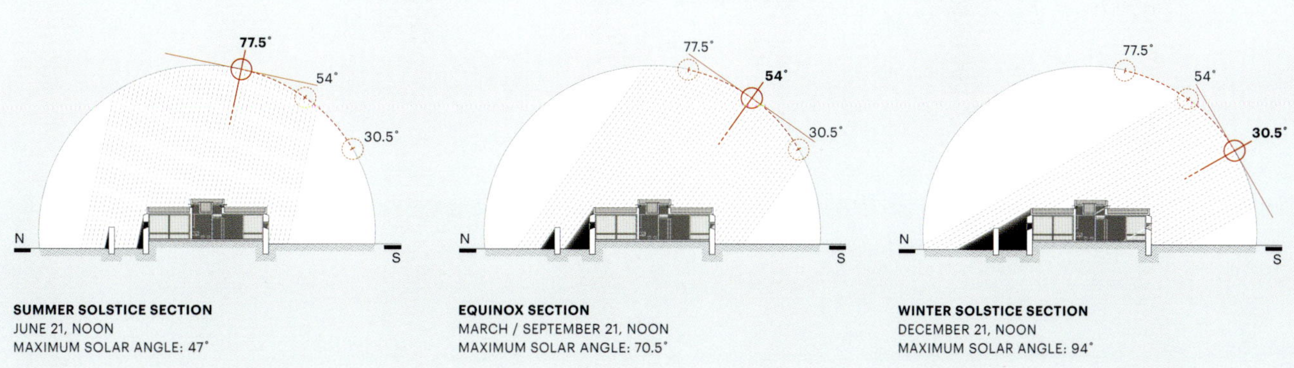

77.5°
54°
30.5°
N   S

SUMMER SOLSTICE SECTION
JUNE 21, NOON
MAXIMUM SOLAR ANGLE: 47°

77.5°
54°
30.5°
N   S

EQUINOX SECTION
MARCH / SEPTEMBER 21, NOON
MAXIMUM SOLAR ANGLE: 70.5°

77.5°
54°
30.5°
N   S

WINTER SOLSTICE SECTION
DECEMBER 21, NOON
MAXIMUM SOLAR ANGLE: 94°

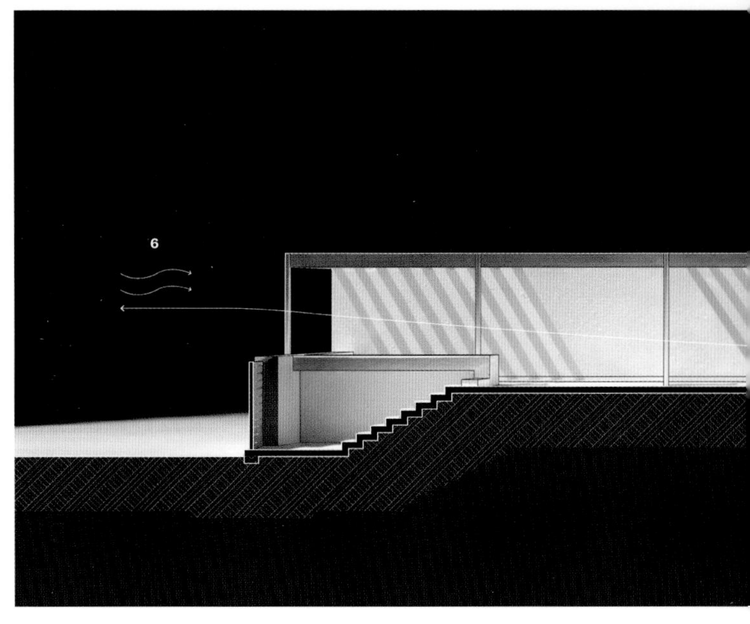

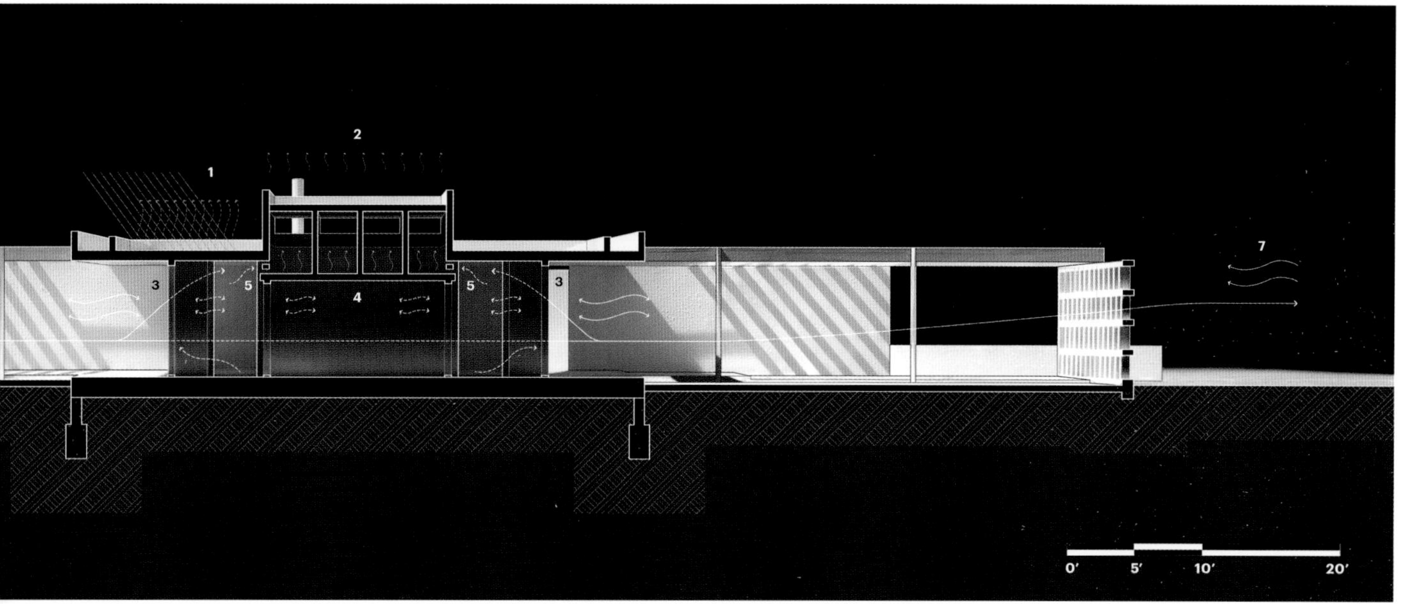

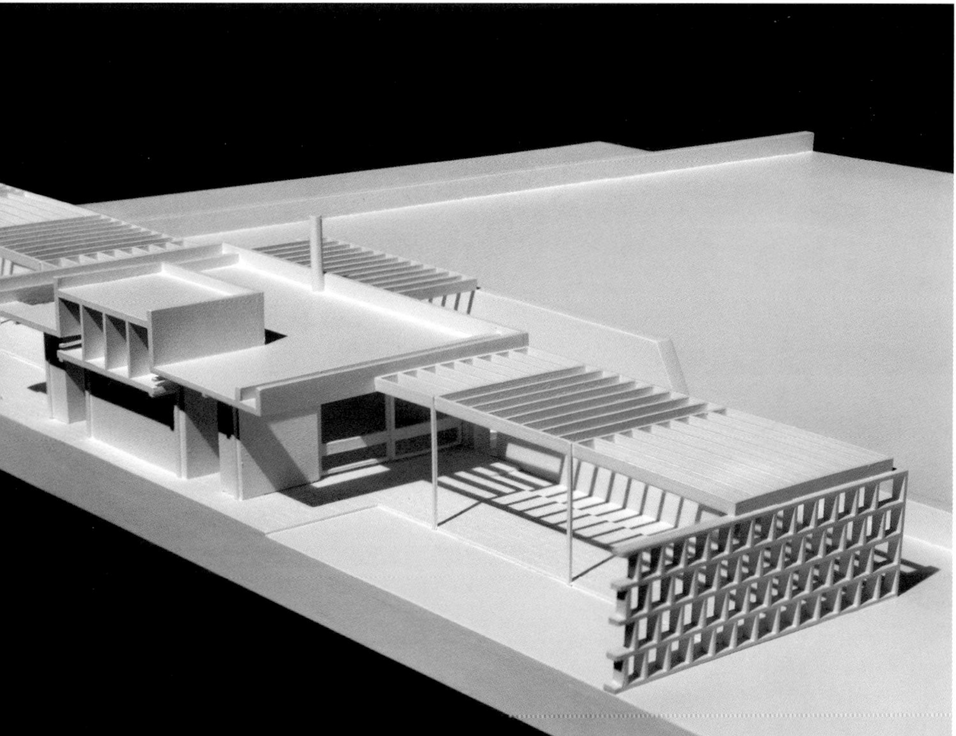

1 Solar reflective roof
2 Stack effect
3 Operable panels
allow ventilation
4 Cross-ventilation
5 Openings allow
stack effect
6 Eastern secondary wind
7 Western tertiary wind

Timeline
Selected Projects
1925–1970

1928
FIRST & SECOND GOETHEANUM
RUDOLF STEINER
Dornach, Switzerland

The Goetheanum integrates spaces for education, drama, and dance, its design embedded with symbolic references to Rudolph Steiner's view of the harmonious order of nature. Author, educator, artist, poet, and philosopher, Steiner was also the father of bio-dynamic farming, an agricultural system that embraces complete organic integration.

1925
NEW DWELLINGS
FOR BORDEAUX
LE CORBUSIER +
PIERRE JEANNERET
Bordeaux, France
(not built)

1928
SAN MARCOS IN
THE DESERT RESORT
FRANK LLOYD WRIGHT
Chandler, Arizona
(not built)

The plan of this far-flung, long-drawn-out building, owing to the placing of the levels of the sun-lit terraces, is such that each room, each bathroom, each closet, each corridor, even, has direct sunlight. Every portion of the building to be lived in is free to the sun . . . The whole building has the warm southern exposure every winter resort covets.
—FRANK LLOYD WRIGHT

1929
LOVELL HEALTH HOUSE
RICHARD NEUTRA
Los Angeles, California

Neutra also acknowledges the role of the insulating lining in controlling heat flux in both directions: "The interior shell is of caloriferic insulation material and keeps conduction of heat in both ways at a minimum." The steel deck roof was similarly insulated. Thus, in spite of dubiety about rationale of the hollow diatom floor in conjunction with hollow metal walls in winter, Neutra is undoubtedly thinking "thermal" in a very imaginative way.
—COLIN PORTEOUS

1933
SCHMINKE HOUSE
HANS SCHAROUN
Kirschallee, Lobau, Germany

Scharoun's main problem was the complete opposition of sunlight and views, which prompted him to adopt a long narrow plan for the main rooms, with windows on both facades . . . the ideal of continuity with the garden through the largest possible windows could be obtained without uncontrollable solar heat gain in summer, the south side being provided with smaller horizontal windows . . . Scharoun placed the main body of the house to face precisely south, so it lay diagonally across the site. He then turned the east and west end parallel to the site boundaries to reconcile the house with them, so incorporating a 26° angle shift.
—PETER BLUNDELL JONES

1933
KARUIZAWA SUMMER HOUSE
ANTONIN RAYMOND
Karuizawa, Nagano
Prefecture, Japan

1934
WEEKEND HOUSE
ALBERT FREY +
A. LAWRENCE KOCHER
Long Island, New York

1930

WORLD POPULATION
2.07 BILLION

1930
OPEN-AIR SCHOOL
JOHANNES DUIKER
Amsterdam, Netherlands

1931
NIGHT SHELTER FOR THE HOMELESS
AFFONSO EDUARDO REIDY +
GERSON POMPEU PINHEIRO
Rio De Janeiro, Brazil

1933
PAIMIO SANATORIUM
ALVAR AALTO
Paimio, Finland

The sanatorium is divided into four wings to maximize sunlight, with one of these being a seven-story open-air ward with a partially covered roof terrace that provides stunning views out over the forest below. The architect's humanistic concern for the patients' wellbeing goes beyond this direct physical and visual contact with nature to the materials and color used throughout and the accessibility of the communal spaces which easily orient each of the wings at the building's base.
—JAMES STEELE

1935
CORONA SCHOOL
RICHARD NEUTRA
Los Angeles, California

A prototype for open-air public schools in tropical climates. Neutra developed a series of lightweight, timber frame structures with open plans that included outdoor classroom patios shaded under the protection of vertically retractable doors. The building system provided flexibility and ease of construction, allowing local communities to erect schools with limited resources and labor.

1938
CHERMAYEFF HOUSE
SERGE CHERMAYEFF
Halland, Sussex, UK

An archetypical passive solar design . . . his house in Sussex had all the main rooms facing due south, the ground floor open to a slabbed terrace which was continued inside as thermal mass, and had a pergola to shade the bedrooms on the first floor. There is also a series of service rooms, with a lower demand in terms of temperature, along the north edge on each floor.
—COLIN PORTEOUS

1939
VILLA MAIREA
ALVAR AALTO
Noormarkku, Finland

Raised up on a plinth to lift it slightly above the surrounding forest, the garden court bracketed by the L-shaped plan blurs the demarcation between inside and outside, effectively integrating house and site. This juncture, particularly related to social space, is visually reinforced by the predominance of natural details, such as the clusters of slim columns that replicate the thin trunks of the pine trees outside, the sod on the portion of the roof, and the lake-like pool.
—JAMES STEELE

1936
HOUSING AT SUNILA PULP MILL
ALVAR AALTO
Kotka, Finland

1937
JACOBS HOUSE I
FRANK LLOYD WRIGHT
Madison, Wisconsin

1940

WORLD POPULATION
2.30 BILLION

1937
ALFRED LOOMIS HOUSE
WILLIAM LESCAZE
Tuxedo Park, New York

The most remarkable, and probably unique, feature of the structure was its double exterior walls and roof, so that in effect it consisted of one house built entirely within the shell of another house. The space between the double walls was approximately two feet, creating a corridor of air, or "shell space," that could be heated independently of the inner house.
—JENNET CONANT

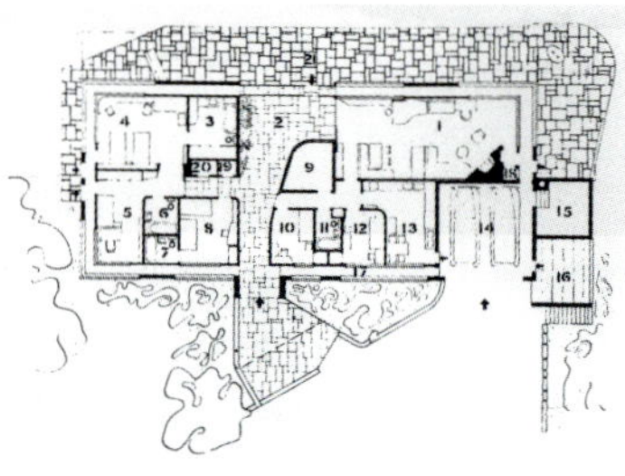

1938
PONDICHERRY DORMITORY
ANTONIN RAYMOND
Pondicherry, India

This dormitory in India is not a building in the ordinary sense, it was designed to provide a space, which is roofed, shaded and ventilated. The elevations therefore consist of a giant Persian blind, which is clearly and sincerely expressed. Here, really the shading device is the architecture.
—ALADAR AND VICTOR OLGYAY

1943
MINISTRY OF EDUCATION
OSCAR NIEMEYER,
AFFONSO EDUARDO REIDY,
LUCIO COSTA, AND OTHERS
Rio De Janeiro, Brazil

On its east and west elevations the building is closed with a veneer of pink marble. The south facade, which is not exposed to the sun, is entirely of glass. The north facade, which receives a strong insolation in Rio de Janeiro, is covered entirely with a giant sun-shade, which consists of fixed vertical concrete fins, in which three movable panels of thin concrete are connected to a level arm. This arm allows a position dependent upon the incidence of the rays of the sun. The entire system is very close to the form of Persian blinds.
—ALADAR AND VICTOR OLGYAY

1943
HOUSES IN SPACE
AMANCIO WILLIAMS
Buenos Aires, Argentina
(not built)

1940
CHAMBERLAIN HOUSE
MARCEL BREUER +
WALTER GROPIUS
Wayland, Massachusetts

Walter Gropius had arrived at Harvard in 1937, beginning a four-year collaboration with Marcel Breuer to create works that responded to regional conditions and addressed material use, while experimenting with structural and insulated wall systems. The Chamberlain house is built of a timber frame, rough-hewn stone foundation, northern glass porch, and wood cladding.

1945
HOUSE OVER THE BROOK
AMANCIO WILLIAMS
Mar Del Plata,
Buenos Aires, Argentina

1945
WICHITA / DYMAXION HOUSE
BUCKMINSTER FULLER
Wichita, Kansas

These new houses will be structured after the natural systems of humans and trees, with a central stem or backbone, from which are provided all pumping, supply, filtering units, aerial systems, nerves or reception units, with appropriate covering and temperature retention.
—BUCKMINSTER FULLER

1946
KAUFMANN DESERT HOUSE
RICHARD NEUTRA
Palm Springs, California

In this arid desert surrounding, a shaded shelter was created by horizontal overhangs and moveable vertical fins, which determine the character of this residence. The pivoted louver blades are placed 12'0" o.c. and are made up of 14-gauge aluminum. A manually operated adjustment bar allows varied amounts of breeze and light to enter.
—ALADAR AND VICTOR OLGYAY

1948
UNIVERSITY OF PUERTO RICO
GENERAL LIBRARY
HENRY KLUMB
San Juan, Puerto Rico

The Río Piedras and Mayagüez campuses of the University of Puerto Rico were the stage for architectural exercises that allowed Klumb to explore the possibilities of a social architecture adapted to the conditions of Puerto Rico. He set the standards and guidelines for a democratic architecture of open and constantly flowing spaces. He also developed several architectural strategies to tone down natural light with the use of various designs for brise-soleils, which provided light and shadow, thus modulating the homogeneous space and creating spaces suited for habitation.
—ENRIQUE VIVONI-FARAGE

1947
MENE GRANDE OIL COMPANY
OFFICE BUILDING
RALPH WALKER
Caracas, Venezuela

As the site is near the Equator, the sun, at one time or another, shines on all four walls; hence, the brise-soleil here surrounds the building entirely. Note that the exterior line of columns is actually on the outside of the structure. The windows are installed on the inner side of these, and the louvers are fixed to the outer side, a few feet away. Thus, there is created an air space with a chimney effect, which assists in ventilating the area. As can be seen from the absence of vegetation, the country is very arid; but all aluminum brise-soleil and fixtures were necessary because of the corroding influence of the salt water in the area.
—J.E. ARONIN

1948
JACOBS HOUSE II
FRANK LLOYD WRIGHT
Middleton, Wisconsin

1949
BUILDING FOR THE EMPREZAS
GRÁFICAS O CRUZEIRO
OSCAR NIEMEYER
Rio de Janeiro, Brazil

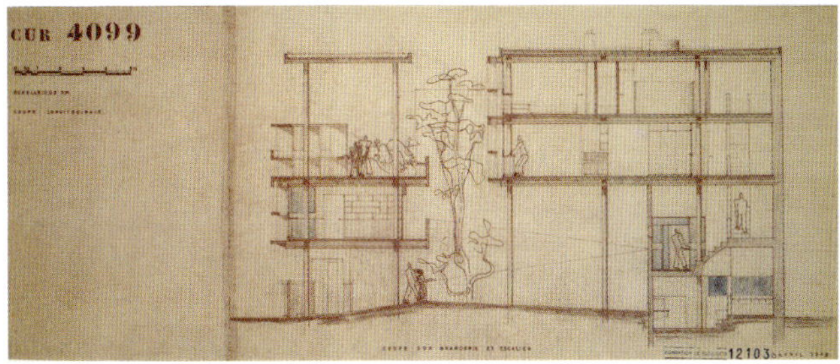

1949
MAISON CURUTCHET
LE CORBUSIER
La Plata, Argentina

Le Corbusier here incorporated reinforced-concrete sunscreens (brise-soleils) and an elevated parasol roof to modulate the South American sun and breeze. These screens not only reduce the amount of direct sunlight hitting the fully glazed "pan de verre" facades, but also manipulate the perception of frontal depth through multiple layers of built form.
—A+U

1950

WORLD POPULATION
2.50 BILLION

1949
VICTORIA COLLEGE
JOHN W. POLTOCK
Cairo, Egypt

Egypt's broiling sun made the design of the new campus . . . an expression of shading and ventilated spaces. A wide range of louvers and canopies reduce sky glare, screen direct sunlight, and also channel the air movements.
—ALADAR AND VICTOR OLGYAY

1950
SOHOLM 1
ARNE JACOBSEN
Klampenborg, Denmark

c. 1950
BACHELOR FLATS
BRONEK KATZ + REGINALD VAUGHAN
Rufisque, Dakar, Senegal

1955
PREMPEH COLLEGE
FRY, DREW, DRAKE
AND LASDUN
Kumasi, Ghana

This dormitory has an axis to the east and west, with an elaborate eggcrate brise-soleil shading the south façade against major sun penetration. The northern façade, which during certain seasons is affected by sun, is protected by continuous covered walks.
—ALADAR AND VICTOR OLGYAY

1956
PRICE TOWER
FRANK LLOYD WRIGHT
Bartlesville, Oklahoma

The structural system of the Price Tower, the taproot foundation and cantilevered reinforced concrete floor slabs, exhibits a minimization of materials in high-rise design compared to the conventional steel frame box designs of the time. The facade design allows maximum day lighting with two glass facades per unit; tinted glass with vertical and horizontal louvers filters sunlight, assisting cooling loads and reducing air-conditioning costs.

1951
DEXTER M. FERRY JR. COOPERATIVE HOUSE
MARCEL BREUER
Poughkeepsie, New York

1953
WALKER BEACH HOUSE
PAUL RUDOLPH
Sanibel Island, Florida

1953
UNESCO HEADQUARTERS
MARCEL BREUER, BERNARD ZEHRFUSS and PIER LUIGI NERVI
Place De Fontenoy, Paris

Two technical principles are introduced to solve the sun-control problem: first, the "Eyebrow" sunshade is made of slats rather than solid panels, so that the heat that accumulates outside the window can escape upward before it affects the interior of the building; and second, sheets of "solar glass" that absorb heat and reduce glare were introduced as part of the shading device.
—ALADAR AND VICTOR OLGYAY

1956
MUNKEGAARD ELEMENTARY SCHOOL
ARNE JACOBSEN
Soborg, Denmark

1957
COCOON HOUSE
PAUL RUDOLPH +
RALPH TWITCHELL
Sarasota, Florida

1957

UNIVERSIDAD CENTRAL DE VENEZUELA SCHOOL OF ARCHITECTURE

CARLOS RAÚL VILLANUEVA
Caracas, Venezuela

The building consists of a slender nine-story tower around which the lower wings are grouped and arranged in an irregular topography of folded roofs . . . The tower is a rectangular sculpture of unfolded planes and changing face. A grid of concrete brise-soleils covers the north side, housing the lecture rooms; a fine weave of perforated concrete screens veils the south side, accommodating the extensive circulation area on each floor; a slim staircase of fine vertical concrete strips stands out on the east side; and on the southwest, a crenellated elevator and stair tower rises alongside blind walls clad with a black, white, and blue tile polychromatic design.
—PAULINA VILLANUEVA
AND MACIÁ PINTÓ

1958

ART MUSEUM IN BAGHDAD

ALVAR AALTO
Baghdad, Iraq

Most of the roof garden is covered over with special sunlight reflectors. In this way the intense glare of the sun is reflected, the open-air sculpture area receives shade, and the skylights of the museum obtain uniform light. At night, the sculptures, which are set up between the skylights, can be flood lit through the latter.

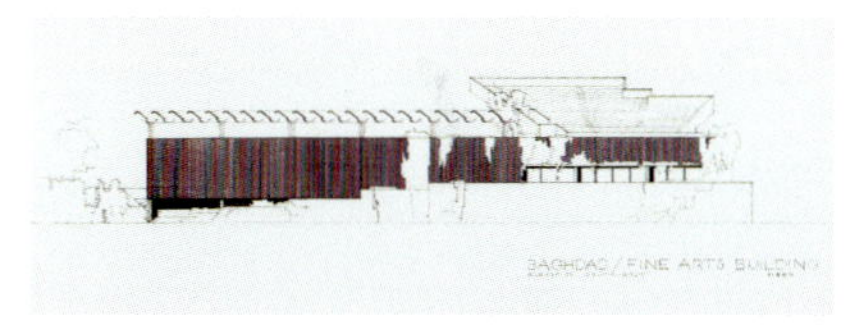

1957

PAVILION ON THE LAGOON RODRIGO DE FREITAS

AFFONSO EDUARDO REIDY
Rio De Janeiro, Brazil

1957

SENANAYAKE FLATS

MINETTE DE SILVA
Colombo, Sri Lanka

There were two identical blocks of flats, each built around an interior courtyard to ensure cross ventilation, both vertically (through the carports and courtyards) and horizontally. Any windows overlooking the courtyard were obscured to give complete privacy. Service balconies were open to a separate service courtyard. I opened out the stairs to avoid the dark, dismal, dank, depressing access stairs, normal to apartment buildings in the tropics. Each flat was designed to have a living room-like veranda with French windows, which threw open the living areas to the balconies.
—MINETTE DE SILVA

1958

VALÉRIA P. CIRELL HOUSE

LINA BO BARDI
Morumbi, São Paolo, Brazil

1959

ARCOSANTI

PAOLO SOLERI
PROTOTYPICAL CITY
Located in any Flat, Arid or Semiarid Region

Soleri consolidated several hypotheses about the increasingly urgent need to concentrate rapid population growth into ecologically harmonious earth-cast megastructures to conserve precious arable land in an urban regional plan he called Mesa City.
—JAMES STEELE

1962

US CONSULATE
AND RESIDENCE

LOUIS KAHN
Luanda, Angola (not built)

Kahn employed a second, detached, outer skin to protect the windows from glare and a raised metal roof daringly used to protect a second one below it and soak up solar heat so that it could be wicked away by the wind, as it is in the radiator of an automobile. An open central court oriented to capture the prevailing breeze was also intended to distribute it into the interior.
—JAMES STEELE

1965

CONDOMINIUM I,
SEA RANCH

CHARLES MOORE, DONLYN LYNDON, WILLIAM TURNBULL and RICHARD WHITAKER
Sonoma County, California

Moore, Lyndon, Turnbull, and Whitaker designed the iconic shed-roofed dwellings that are the image of what was originally conceived as an ecological ideal of multifamily housing. The solid volumes built with California timbers are grouped around a courtyard such that they afford the openness of the site and sun, yet provide protection from the strong Pacific winds.

1960

WORLD POPULATION
3.04 BILLION

1961

SIEDLUNG HALEN
ATELIER 5
Bern, Switzerland

1963

FREY HOUSE II
ALBERT FREY
Palm Springs, CA

I studied the position of the sun for a whole year . . . My partner and I put up a ten foot pole and we measured the shadow from it and made a diagram so we knew where the sun was at this location at any time of the year. The plan was designed so that, for instance, the glass walls are not exposed to the sun in the heat of the summer. That's what determined these overhangs. In winter, when the sun is much lower, it comes in and heats the house.
—ALBERT FREY

1965

SCHOOL OF PLASTIC ARTS,
NATIONAL ARTS SCHOOL
RICARDO PORRO
Havanna, Cuba

1966

HOUSE ON A CYCLADIC
ISLAND
IANNIS XENAKIS
Greece

1967
USA PAVILION AT
EXPO '67
BUCKMINSTER FULLER
Montreal, Canada

When I invented and developed my first clear-span, all-weather geodesic dome, the two largest domes in the world were both in Rome and were each about 50 meters in diameter. They are at St Peter's, built around A.D. 1500, and the Pantheon, built around A.D. 1. Each weighs approximately 15,000 tonnes. In contrast, my first 50-meter diameter geodesic all-weather dome installed in Hawaii weighs only 15 tonnes—one-thousandth the weight of its masonry counterpart. An earthquake would tumble both the Roman domes, but it would leave the geodesic unharmed.
—BUCKMINSTER FULLER

1968
HOUSE II IN KAVOURI
CONSTANTINOS DECAVALLAS
Athens, Attiki, Greece

1969
CHANDIGARH
LE CORBUSIER
Chandigarh, India

Besides the administrative and financial regulations there was the Law of the Sun in India: a calendar of sensational temperature, extraordinary heat, dry or humid according to the season or the location. The architectural problem consists first of all to make shade, second to make a current of air (to ventilate), third to control hydraulics (to evacuate rain water). This necessitated a real apprenticeship and an unprecedented adaptation of modern methods.
—LE CORBUSIER

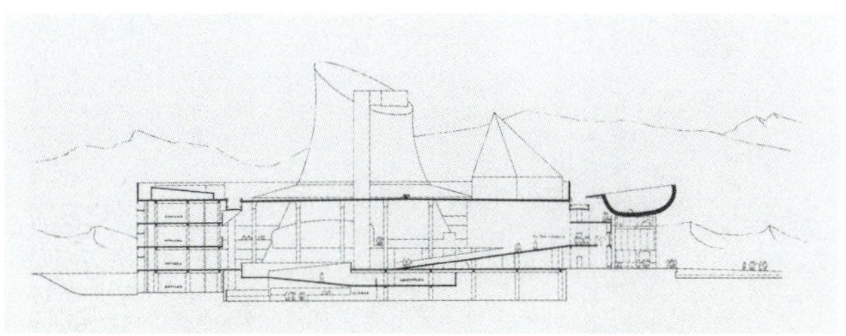

1970
VACATION HOUSE
ON AEGINA
CONSTANTINOS DECAVALLAS
Aegina, Greece

1970

WORLD POPULATION
3.71 BILLION

Lessons from *Lessons from Modernism*

Daniel A. Barber

We have learned many lessons from modernism, a number of which have been unexpected. The material collected in this book falls in that category. It makes clear that a surprisingly large number of those architects in the midcentury period engaged in formal and material experimentation were also concerned with issues we now call environmental—be they relative to material efficiencies, relationship to site and climate, or other forms of energy efficient potential. How can we understand this particular lesson from modernism, place it in the context of other lessons, and get some sense of how these lessons have, or have not, been learned?

This last concern is, perhaps, the most important to address. It can be rephrased as follows: Why do we need to learn this particular lesson from modernism—let's call it the lesson about climate—at this particular time? It is self evident that architects of the mid-twentieth century had no cause to be concerned about climate change; the geopolitical dynamics of fossil fuel combustion were not on the table. What we now consider to be climatic or energy efficient strategies were, in the 1930s, 1940s, up to the 1970s, pursued in order to allow the building envelope to best mitigate the effects of the exterior on the interior. The strategies highlighted here were developed in order to encourage comfortable living in challenging climates, from the arctic to the desert, and in the context of a much wider, if often less aggressive, interest in shading devices, thermally active materials, and other means of allowing the building to collaborate more effectively with its natural surround.

This is no doubt an important lesson. Architects cared about climate and designed according to climatic regional parameters long before the mechanical systems that inhabit most buildings were understood to be impacting global climatic conditions. Architects cared about climate because, as the historian Paul Overy made clear in his 2008 book *Light, Air and Openness: Modern Architecture Between the Wars*, modern architecture was seen by many clients and bureaucratic agencies as a means to improve the health of the building's occupants. Health was, here and elsewhere, an important argument for the cultural acceptance of the new style. Johannes Duiker's Cliostraat Open-Air School of 1930 is seen by Overy as a crucial insertion into a lively modernist discourse on the relationship of light and air to the promise of more healthful forms of life. "A strong hygienic power," Overy quotes Duiker, "is influencing our life, one which develops into a style, a hygienic style!"[1] His generous use of glass and integration of interior and exterior spaces can also be seen as something of an architectural analogue to the Waldorf, Montessori, and other alternative education models then being experimented with across Europe, as means to rethink the structures and parameters of cultivating modern life, and to see its socially inflected technologies as productive of completely new and heretofore unexpected modes of being in the world. This hygienic style came to condition much of the architecture of the early twentieth century, as buildings by Neutra, Mies, Le Corbusier, and many others responded to this imperative for an architecture focused on healthy living.[2]

Still, beyond the specific concern regarding the details of this climatic lesson is the more compelling question of why we are learning this lesson again now—a question not only of architectural method, but also of historical inquiry. What I want to demonstrate is that the lesson from modernism that underlies *Lessons from Modernism* is this: disciplinary obstacles have prevented architects from effectively learning this lesson in the past. The lesson we need to learn is about historical method rather than technological method. How do we understand the relationship between architectural innovation and historical change? I will return to this question below, but first I need to clarify the extent to which the climatic lesson has already been offered to modern architects as a potent site for their self-education.

Lessons from Modernism can be seen as a re-presentation of the second half of Victor and Aladar Olgyay's *Solar Control and Shading Devices* published in 1957.[3] That the current version is significantly more aesthetically engaging I will also return to below. The Olgyays' book, part of a larger research agenda aimed at understanding the potential of modern design strategies to mitigate climatic effects, established the methods of analysis and representation developed in this book—the mapping of the solar path, the careful placement of the building in its climatic zone—and also sought to integrate these strategies into contemporary design practice.

The story of the Olgyays is an interesting one, and deserves some attention as an object lesson on how lessons from modernism have or have not been learned. Twin brothers, the Olgyays were born in Budapest in 1910 and trained as architects at the Royal Hungarian Polytechnic. They won a

1. Paul Overy, *Light, Air and Openness: Modern Architecture Between the Wars* (New York: Thames and Hudson, 2007), 129.

2. See for example Richard Neutra, *Architecture of Social Concern in Regions of Mild Climate* (Sao Paulo: Gerth Todtmann, 1948); some of these issues have been engaged in more recent analyses including Thomas Hines, *Architecture of the Sun: Los Angeles Modernism 1900–1970* (New York: Rizzoli, 2010) and Colin Porteous, *The New Eco-Architecture: Alternatives from the Modern Movement* (London: Taylor and Francis, 2002).

3. Aladar Olgyay and Victor Olgyay, *Solar Control and Shading Devices* (Princeton: Princeton University Press, 1957).

number of commercial, government, and institutional commissions right away, and became known for a 1939 apartment building in Budapest, called the Reverse House, in which they faced the more prominent facade away from the street, orienting the building to the garden rather than to the city.[4] The project also exhibits a dynamic use of shading devices to seasonally manage solar incidence. By this time they had already entered the international scene of modern architecture, having been collectively awarded the Rome prize in 1934 and then, starting in the fall of that year, spending a year on a fellowship at Columbia University. It is possible that at Columbia they first began to engage the question of climate, as the planner Henry Wright, at Columbia in those years, spent some time in the 1930s researching the relationship of climatic patterns to the plot organization and design orientation of his many garden city-type experiments.[5] Of course by the late 1930s, as this book demonstrates, concern over climate—over the relationship of building design to site, and to light and air—was ubiquitous, a claim further substantiated by the discussion on "Rational Site Planning" at the third CIAM meeting in Brussels in 1930.[6]

The Olgyays returned to the United States in 1947, through an invitation from Marcel Breuer, who had managed to secure them a position at Notre Dame. In 1949 they moved to MIT, at that time a vibrant center for integrating technological and design analysis. Among the many proponents of new determinants for architecture at MIT was the semi-independent Bemis Foundation, which had, since before the war, focused on facilitating the design and manufacturing of prefabricated houses.[7] Burnham Kelly, who took over the foundation in 1945, came in with strong ties to the federal government and submitted grant applications to the Housing and Home Finance Agency (HHFA) and the Building Research Advisory Board for research into building design and materials relative to the different climates of the country. Both grants identified the Olgyay brothers as primary researchers. The result of the research carried out under these grants was multivalent. It informed the regional climatic charts developed by Paul Siple, of the Army Corps of Engineers, who was assisting the American Institute of Architects (AIA) and the editors of *House Beautiful* in developing recommendations to consumers, organized under the rubric of a "Climate Control" project that ran in the magazine from 1949 to 1951.[8] Siple's charts were organized relative to regionally specific, seasonally adjusted climate data, and later widely distributed by the AIA to provide a starting point for the kinds of climatic analyses architects could perform. The AIA/*House Beautiful* project is further indication of the widespread interest in climatic methods, now extended into the immediate postwar years, which resulted in a number of journal issues and technical manuals focused on the subject.

The Olgyays' research for the HHFA also resulted in an article by Victor Olgyay in *Architectural Forum* in March 1951 entitled "The Temperate House." It laid out their basic methodological premise: that a careful regional analysis was necessary to develop a climatically appropriate architectural response, and that the building shape and orientation

4. *The Work of Architects Olgyay and Olgyay: with a preface by Marcel Breuer and an Introduction by Peter Blake* (New York: Reinhold, 1952). The cover of the book was designed by Gyorgy Kepes.

5. See Howard T. Fisher, "A Rapid Method for Determining Sunlight on Buildings," *Architectural Record* 12 (December 1931): 445–54. See also Waclaw Turner-Szymanowski, "A Rapid Method for Predicting the Distribution of Daylight in Buildings," *University of Michigan Engineering Research Bulletin* 17 (January 1931).

6. See Eric Mumford, *The CIAM Discourse on Urbanism, 1928–1960* (Cambridge, MIT Press, 2000): 49–58.

7. Burnham Kelly, *The Prefabrication of Houses: A Study by the Albert Farwell Bemis Foundation of the Prefabrication Industry in the United States* (Cambridge, MA: MIT Press, 1955).

8. See for example Elizabeth Gordon, "What climate does to YOU and what you can do to CLIMATE," *House Beautiful* (October 1949).

should conform to the specifics of this analysis.[9] They also participated in a "Research Correlation Conference" on "Weather and the Building Industry" at the National Academy of Sciences in January 1950—at which Carl Koch and James Marston Fitch were also participants—and at a conference on "Housing and Building in Hot-Humid and Hot-Dry Climates" at the University of Texas in 1952, which was hosted by Harwell Hamilton Harris and included a presentation on the "Practical Aspects of Tropical Living" by Ralph Walker.[10] They further propounded on their basic theories by developing a series of more focused methodological proposals, including "The Theory of Sol-Air Orientation" published in March 1954 and considerations of climate and "building shape" in August of the same year.[11]

The main project of their best-known books—*Solar Control and Shading Devices* (1957) and *Design with Climate: A Bio-Climatic Approach to Architectural Regionalism* (1963)—was the development of a method for adapting a building to its climatic conditions. I am not going to describe that method in great detail, but I do want to suggest its complexity. The method involved a contextual analysis of built and natural shading conditions and careful investigation into regional and seasonal variation in solar path and solar incidence to determine not only the building shape and orientation, but also the possible selections from a typological array of shading devices.

They also proposed a number of basic principles. First, as a refutation of the use of shading devices and screens as purely ornamental, they insisted that a bioclimatic building necessarily had a different shading treatment on different facades, and second, they asserted that the best way to manage solar radiation was to block it *before* it came into the building—demonstrated here diagrammatically and, in the introduction to the 1957 book, by reference to the climatically challenged conditions of a number of recent buildings.

The Olgyays' research was central to the material collected in Jeffrey Aronin's *Climate and Architecture* for Progressive Architecture books in 1953, and their influence is also evident in Breuer's *Sun and Shadow: the Philosophy of an Architect* (1955).[12] Furthermore, their interests are reflected in the international discussion on climate, as perhaps best represented in the work of so-called Tropical Architecture, which developed out of a group of architects, scientists, and sociologists from the UK working in the former British colonies of West Africa from the late 1940s, and which directly applied the principles of architectural modernism to the climatic challenges they faced. There was a Tropical Architecture conference in London in 1953, and by 1955 the Architectural Association was offering a one-year diploma in Tropical Studies. Maxwell Fry and Jane Drew, prominent practitioners, summarized the discourse in their *Tropical Architecture in the Humid Zones* (1956).[13]

During this period, the Olgyays designed a number of houses across the Northeast and consulted on projects assisting other architects on issues of climatic mitigation. Their project for the American Association for the Advancement of Science in Washington, D.C., with Faulkner, Kingsbury, and Stenhouse was especially well received in the press and by the clients;

9. Victor Olgyay, "The Temperate House," *Architectural Forum*, (March 1951).

10. Building Research Advisory Board, *Proceedings: Housing and Building in Hot-Humid and Hot-Dry Climates, November 18 and 19, 1952* (Washington, D.C.: National Academy of Sciences National Research Council, 1952).

11. Victor and Aladar Olgyay, "The Theory of Sol-Air Orientation," *Architectural Forum*, (March 1954), 132–34.

12. Jeffrey Aronin, *Climate and Architecture* (New York: Reinhold/Progressive Architecture, 1953) and Marcel Breuer, *Sun and Shadow: The Philosophy of an Architect* (New York: Dodd, Mead, 1955).

13. See *Conference on Tropical Architecture: A Report on the Proceedings of the Conference held at University College, London, March 1953* (London: Allen and Unwin, 1954) and Maxwell Fry and Jane Drew, *Tropical Architecture in the Dry and Humid Zones* (Huntington, New York: Kreiger, 1956).

it still stands as the Tunisian Embassy. They also collaborated with O'Connor and Kilham to design the shading screen for Lehman Hall at Barnard College, currently threatened with demolition. Aladar designed a house for the solar engineer Maria Telkes in 1960, which was not built. A few years earlier Aladar and Telkes built an experimental campus to test solar heating devices in Princeton and also proposed a solar energy suburb in Westchester County, New York. Both were based on the introduction of the "solar wall" as a device to be sold to developers and builders for insertion into a number of possible house designs. Aladar presented the solar wall at the Conference on New Sources of Energy sponsored by the UN and held in Rome in 1961, a conference which also saw the presentation of solar houses in Japan and Sweden, ways of increasing the use of geothermal energy in buildings, and the development of thermally active materials, among a number of lessons from the wide range of modernisms then on display.[14]

In 1953 the Olgyays moved from MIT to Princeton to take up positions as research professors in the Princeton School of Architecture. Most of the climatic analyses they came to be known for were performed in the Princeton Architectural Laboratory, recently established by Robert McLaughlin, dean of the School of Architecture. With McLaughlin, they worked on how to adjust their analytic mechanism, tooled for free standing houses in the suburbs, for curtain walls, and for other building techniques more readily used in dense urban environments.[15] Beyond these specific methodological innovations, they also developed a new model for architectural engagement with academic institutions. They were hired as research professors, and the bulk of their salary came through grants from the Ford Foundation, the Rockefeller Foundation, the National Science Foundation, and a number of building industry consortia. The notion of design research, while being developed in a number of institutions and arenas in this period, was here a means to integrate architectural and scientific knowledge about climate.

The Princeton Architectural Laboratory became the site for their major project of the late 1950s, the design and construction of the Thermoheliodon device. The Thermoheliodon offered a marked improvement on the heliodons that had been utilized in architectural schools since the late nineteenth century. Here, able to control not only the arc of the sun's path, but also wind, humidity, and soil conditions, a significantly more detailed model of the climatic world became available to the designer. A problem quickly arose, however, having to do with the thermal capacity of materials. The buildings they inserted into the device were tested for shape and orientation, but the internal climatic conditions could not be adequately monitored because of challenges to scaling up the thermal capacity of different materials from the model to the building. Indeed, a significant portion of the report they submitted to the National Science Foundation, which had funded the project, involved indications of the calculations necessary to clarify the performance of a given building as a result of this materials problem.[16] When seeking additional funding, they proposed to build identical test houses in Princeton, Montreal, and Los Angeles and maintain constant data analysis in order to adjust their calculative matrix

14. Aladar Olgyay, "Design Criteria for Solar Heated Houses," in *Proceedings of the United Nations Conference on New Sources of Energy: Solar Energy, Wind Power, and Geothermal Energy, Rome 21-31 August 1961* (New York: United Nations Publications, 1964), 154–55.

15. Aladar Olgyay, *Thermal Behavior of Curtain Walls in Relation to Cooling Costs and Shading Devices* (Princeton, NJ: Princeton University School of Architecture, 1957).

16. Victor and Aladar Olgyay, *Report on the Thermoheliodon: Laboratory Machine for Testing Thermal Behavior of Buildings through Model Structures* (Princeton, NJ: School of Architecture and School of Engineering, June 1956), 32.

according to the recent historical record of climatic conditions. Their funding was not renewed.

This brief chronicle makes clear the Olgyays were not outliers in a modernist milieu that emphasized form, or materials, or social concerns. Rather, their research was at the heart of the modern project and engaged in understanding how new forms of architectural research could make the field more relevant to the social and political challenges of the rapidly globalizing postwar period. There are two reasons why this climatic lesson, their decade-long investigation of the climate performance of modern design techniques, was not, at this moment, learned. The first appears to be straightforward. Though more or less unwittingly, the climatic lesson was mostly applicable to a conception of architectural design that did not rely on the fossil-fuel-based HVAC systems that were then ascendant. Once these mechanical systems were adequately developed and affordable, and once the global flow of oil had been instantiated through a wide range of economic, political, military, and diplomatic machinations, the perceived need to mitigate the climatic impacts on building largely evaporated. So the first reason that the climatic lesson was not learned in the 1950s and 1960s is based on developments external to the discipline, having to do with the ready availability of oil for use in heating systems. This also explains why interest in climatic strategies briefly returned in response to the oil turmoils of the 1970s, and have emerged again today relative to global concerns over carbon emissions.

The second reason the climatic lesson was not learned in the 1950s and 1960s, and the reason that it might not be learned again today, is a result of the internal dynamics of the discipline of architecture. How do we learn lessons, as a professional field and as a cultural discourse, and how do we apply them? The case of the Olgyays is telling. They were not ignored in the period of their most aggressive research and publication; rather, as with other environmentally sustainable approaches to architectural form-making, they were aggressively rejected by protagonists of the emergent postmodern movement.[17] For the Olgyays this is especially germane, given their position at Princeton in the late 1950s and early 1960s when they likely met, or at least came across, many of these protagonists. From this perspective, fraternal debates between the Grays and the Whites for example, are belittled by the broader debate over the relevance of architecture to wider social issues.[18] The rise and fall of the post-critical claim to the continued relevance of architecture's internal logic, and Bjarke Ingles's recent invocation of a "Hedonistic Sustainability" are two disparate examples of how this dichotomy between environmental relevance and novel form is still being negotiated today.[19]

It is important in this context to recognize that *Solar Control and Shading Devices* was also concerned with history, albeit a bit haphazardly. While the first half established the analytic parameters for a climatically engaged design practice, the second half of the book—a 106-page spread on "Architectural Examples"—traced the emergence of shading devices for the formal, material, and climatic innovations they were seen to allow.

17. For other attempts in this regard, see Daniel A. Barber, "Making Design Environmental: The Correctional Facilities Studios at the UC Berkeley College of Environmental Design, 1965-67," *Pidgin (Journal of the Princeton University School of Architecture)* Vol. 10 (May 2011): 54–67.

18. The debate between the Grays and the Whites was an early moment in the stylistic debates of postmodernism. For details see Robert A. M. Stern, "Gray Architecture as Post-Modernism, or, Up and Down from Orthodoxy," *Architecture Theory Since 1968*, ed. Michael Hays (New York: Columbia Books on Architecture, 1998), 242–46; originally published 1976. See also Felicity D. Scott, "Architecture or Techno-Utopia" in *Grey Room*, no. 3 (Spring 2001): 112–26.

19. The post-critical discourse developed as an apparent rejection of the formal and theoretical tropes of the "critical architecture" practiced by Peter Eisenman and others. It led to a lively debate on the role of theory in architecture and a renewed discussion on the relationship between architecture and social change. See Robert Somol and Sarah Whiting, "Notes around the Doppler Effect and Other Moods of Modernism," *Perspecta* 33 (2002): 72–77; Reinhold Martin, "Critical of What?: Toward a Utopian Realism," *Harvard Design Magazine*, no. 22 (Spring, Summer 2005): 1–5 and Daniel A. Barber, "Militant Architecture: Destabilizing Architecture's Disciplinarity," *The Journal of Architecture*, 10, no. 3 (June 2005): 245–53.

Following the chains of influence, Le Corbusier was explicitly modeled as the *genus loci* of this global interest in the brise-soleil, and the Olgyays' trace of the use of shading devices through Brazil, West Africa, and eventually to other parts of the global south as well as the United States and Europe can itself be mapped across Le Corbusier's travels and the trajectory of those under his influence. The Olgyays were seen to be playing out the spatial, technological, and social influence of Le Corbusier. We could go so far as to frame their second book *Design with Climate: A Bioclimatic Approach to Architectural Regionalism* as an insistence on the Climatic Basis of Modern Architecture, a sort of virtual rejoinder to Peter Eisenman's "Formal Basis of Modern Architecture," written, as is well known, as a dissertation at Cambridge in 1962.[20] Which is to say, the climatic lesson was intended not only as a lesson about architectural method and technology, but it was also a claim about the relevance of a given perspective on the historical narrative of modern architecture.

Given the extent to which *Lessons from Modernism* reasserts the mechanisms offered by the Olgyays in the 1950s and 1960s, I submit that the power of historical narrative is the imperative lesson at hand. At stake in the discourse generated by the exhibition and book, rather than the precise lessons of the technological and formal issues themselves, is a new framework for disciplinary change. How do we learn lessons? And more importantly, how do we allow for our disciplinary concerns to transform according to those lessons that we need to remember?

This is a question that has been important to theorists for some time, particularly theorists of history and pedagogy. In a landmark essay from 1987, entitled *The Ignorant Schoolmaster: Five Lessons in Intellectual Emancipation*, Jacques Rancière argues against the notion that in order for "comprehension to take place, one has to be given an explication." Rather, he proposes, "explication is not necessary to remedy an incapacity to understand;" more data points, more knowledge, and more interpretation, will not necessarily render more clear the lessons being discussed.[21] This is especially the case in our current disciplinary condition, when those architects valued by the discourse and by the common culture have very little to teach about the relevance of the climatic lesson. Indeed, in many cases, their careers were constructed in order to render this lesson irrelevant. We are stuck in the conundrum that Ranciere describes, in which our disciplinary condition (and not any given pedagogue) is that of the ignorant schoolmaster, attempting to teach things and to value perspectives about which, collectively, we know surprisingly little and value even less.

But there is hope. As Rancière insists, this position of ignorance encourages the schoolmaster and the student to *look around*: "Whoever looks away finds," Rancière writes. "He doesn't necessarily find what he was looking for, and even less what he was supposed to find, but he finds something new to relate to the thing he already knows."[22] What this exhibition and book provide—which the Olgyays were unable to—is something attractive to look at, to draw the gaze of the student or young architect. Insofar as *Lessons from Modernism* is a repetition, a lesson we should have already

20. Eisenman's thesis was published as *The Formal Basis of Modern Architecture* (Baden, Switzerland: Lars Muller, 2006); the dissertation was initially written as a repost to that of Christopher Alexander, published soon thereafter as *Notes on the Synthesis of Form* (Cambridge, MA: Harvard University Press, 1964).

21. Jacques Rancière, *The Ignorant Schoolmaster: Five Lessons in Intellectual Emancipation* (Stanford, CA: Stanford University Press, 1991), 6.

22. Rancière, 32.

learned, it is one with an important difference: it looks good. Really good. And really good in a specifically high modernist, bleached white, spatially inquisitive way that has the potential to appeal to architects of many different orientations. The tools used to convince the viewer of the relevance of the climatic lesson, this time, are not the quasi-scientific charts of the solar path and the sun-mask, nor the awkward placement of a chipboard model in a domed technological device, but a beautiful and dynamic image of climatic engagement. This image rewards careful analysis and sustained engagement, and makes the argument, implicitly, that an architecture that is consumed by the concerns of the broader social and environmental world *can also be beautiful*, and relevant to the internal debates of the discipline. And by extension, a discipline seemingly insistent, even today, on maintaining ignorance as to its potential role in addressing these wider social problems is forced to look at itself, and to extract new lessons from the old.

Modern Legacy /
Sustainable Culture

Carl Stein

Modernism, in its true sense, offers a comprehensive framework to accept, evaluate, and integrate issues of sustainability into contemporary architecture, not to say all aspects of contemporary action. There are, of course, within the modern panoply, many examples of specific responses to environmental forces and concerns for sustainability. Component design includes forms of solar control such as brise-soleil, deep-set windows, and operable louvers and awnings. Non-mechanical ventilation can be induced by taking advantage of differential pressure on opposite sides of buildings and by the convective effects of differential air temperature. Vegetation, both interior and exterior, filters the air, augments inadequate humidity, and mitigates the effects of excessive storm water. These processes directly reduce negative impact of building operation on the natural environment, reduce energy and other resource usage, reduce discharge of objectionable materials, and reduce demand for finite essential resources.

At a larger scale, design strategies integral to modernism incorporate elements of the natural environment into the experience of the architecture and provide quality of life enhancements at little or no environmental cost. Prominent examples include the operable glass walls of Le Corbusier's Villa Savoye and Mies Van der Rohe's Villa Tugendhat and the siting of Frank Lloyd Wright's Fallingwater. These qualitative measures also provide quantitative contributions to sustainability. For example, architecture that exploits natural water-flow patterns to enhance user experience can also reduce damage that results from flooding. Reduced building size is inherent in design resulting from the careful matching of building to program. This and the use of devices such as pilotis minimizes the incompatibility between the building and the natural ground plane. A thoughtful dialogue between architecture and nature generates buildings whose physical forms are visually appealing and readily communicate sustainable principles.

The environmental benefits that accrue with reduced use of material resources are a direct outgrowth of modernism's insistence on efficient planning and design. This, as well as the rejection of applied ornament, produces architecture that requires less material and therefore uses less energy, less natural resources, and releases less carbon—all significant environmental metrics. Reduced resource use optimizes relative programmatic return; however, for the calculation to be meaningful, all resources committed to the process must be considered. Identifying the gamut of these resources, particularly those that are less commonly recognized, such as the ambient historical culture, is key to understanding the relationships between modernism, building preservation, and sustainability.

Further, any evaluation of efficiency, in this case a modern-based evaluation of the sustainable efficiency of resource utilization in delivering programmatic solutions, must take into account both expenditures and resulting product. Expenditures include the physical resources that go into construction, many of which originate at a considerable distance from the project and also include the intellectual and creative efforts inherent in the design process. Product includes not only the physical aspects of construction but also non-physical assets, including reinforcement of the built and urban fabrics and connection to the cultural and historic continuum. Additionally, there is the full scope of program criteria articulated by the modern movement, criteria that are frequently overlooked. There is a widely held opinion that modernism advocates a mechanistic view of the purpose of architecture due, perhaps in large part, to a misreading of Le Corbusier's famous statement, "une maison est une machine à habiter" ("a house is a machine for living in"), from *Vers une architecture*, first published in 1923.[1] The characterization of this statement as a call for narrow pragmatism may be an honest misunderstanding or an intentional distortion, but in either case, it is wrong. In the same book, in fact in the same chapter, Le Corbusier writes:

> *The business of Architecture is to establish emotional relationships by means of raw materials.*
> *Architecture goes beyond utilitarian needs.*
> *Architecture is a plastic thing.[2]*
> *My house is practical. I thank you, as I might thank Railway engineers, or the Telephone service. You have not touched my heart.*
> *But suppose that walls rise toward heaven in such a way I am moved. I perceive your intentions . . . This is architecture.[3]*

In other words, the "machine for living in" is intended to provide not only shelter and safety but also, and equally important, joy and fulfillment. With this in mind, any evaluation of the efficiency with which resource

1. Le Corbusier, *Towards a New Architecture*, trans. Frederick Etchells (London: Architectural Press, 1927; New York: Praeger, 1960), 10. Citations refer to Praeger edition.

2. *Towards a New Architecture*, 140.

3. *Towards a New Architecture*, 165.

application solves program requirements must consider not only all of the resource expenditures but also the full breadth of program issues—cultural, emotional, spiritual, and intellectual, as well as pragmatic.

In the current context with the now-widespread understanding that complex environmental effects may produce dire results, modern practice demands that sustainability be a fundamental, integrated component of the design process—not an afterthought. In this light, modernism's connection to and use of the natural environment and its expanded understanding of program would, by themselves, serve as significant examples of sustainable planning and design and offer significant lessons for contemporary practice. However, there is another and perhaps more fundamental connection between modernism and sustainability. This is the modern process or methodology itself, which is holistic, comprehensive, and seeks to involve and address all aspects of life. While this goal is highly ambitious, if not impossible, the inclusiveness provides the basis for connecting sustainable thought and action with the totality of architectural design. The full range of these concerns has been given physical form in the grid prepared by the International Congress of Modern Architecture (Congrès Internationaux d'Architecture Moderne or CIAM), originally published in *L'Architecture d'Aujourd'hui* in 1948. The grid was created to identify the interrelationships between three sets of criteria. One set, identified as the four primary concerns of modern architecture, are "Living, Working, Care of the Body and Spirit, and Circulation." Intersecting and interacting with the four primary concerns are, first, "themes or general avenues" and, second, specific architecture and planning opportunities and techniques for dealing with those concerns.

Unlike traditional programming matrices, which typically use words and numbers to describe the conditions that occur within the cells created at the intersections, the CIAM grid also uses photography, drawing, montage, and other graphic tools, which support qualitative as well as quantitative input, evaluation, and proposal development. In the context of program as presented in *Vers une architecture* and as seen throughout the work of the modern masters, this approach allows for the recording and presenting of issues and solutions that touch the heart, as well as those that address the practical.

Much of environmental design deals with absolute limits on resource availability, either in terms of total quantities (as in the case of non-renewables) or the rate of supply (as in the case of renewable resources). Because of the catastrophic consequences of ignoring these limits, there are potential risks in introducing qualitative considerations into the discussion, particularly the possibility of sustainable architecture and planning becoming subject to capricious decision-making. On the other hand, the modern process that requires the satisfaction of qualitative demands figures heavily in measuring the success of architectural and planning projects, especially in projects that entail the commitment of vast resources.

The quantitative evaluation of environmental issues may be seen as a matter of the first law of thermodynamics: consideration of absolute quantities without regard to the quality of the units involved. For resource input, or, in this case, energy input, the First Law says that a Btu is a Btu (or kilowatt-hour or joule) whether in the form of heat or light, kinetic energy, or electricity. Similarly, if the product of this resource commitment were a building, its quantity would be defined in terms of square feet of floor area, or perhaps cubic feet of built volume. The second law makes the distinction between high and low quality resources and high and low quality products. For the products of construction, there is particular relevance in the modern assertion that an essential measure of architecture is that it elevate the spirit.

Every day the glazed openings in the south wall of the chapel at Ronchamp receive a finite amount of solar energy. This solar energy, as manipulated by Le Corbusier, provides a profound architectural experience. If the same finite quantity of energy were captured by solar hot-water collectors, it would generate enough hot water for slightly less than two baths. While both experiences (the architecture of the chapel and the effects of a bath) have value, there are significant qualitative differences. Similarly, the dynamic use of shadows to create changing surface patterns, of sunlight to model surfaces, and of transparency and reflection to speak to conditions of containment and edge, are, or should be, fundamental elements of architectural vocabulary. They are examples of solar energy used for building operations delivering high level second law product.

Ongoing interactions between built form and natural phenomena create architectural experience. The making of built form requires resource expenditure. This expenditure becomes the embodied resource in buildings: the sum total of all resources that are required to obtain and process raw materials, to transport them, and, finally, to assemble them on the building site. It is the capital cost in resources of making buildings. Embodied resources create embodied value. Just as the sunlight striking a building can heat bath water or create the experience of the chapel at Ronchamp, the product resulting from resources embodied in building construction can be seen in quantitative terms such as square feet of built space, a first law measure, or as qualitative effects, in the creation of joy or transcendence, a second law measure.

The modern analytic process requires that the culture, or perhaps the intellect or creativity that shapes architecture, be recognized as embodied resource, and the results, particularly those that touch the heart, as embodied value. Here, the modern imperative—that architecture serve higher ends—becomes a strong basis for preservation, particularly of significant buildings. This argument should not be taken to mean that new or modern works cannot serve the spirit and heart. There is no question that they can and do. Rather, any evaluation of historically or architecturally important building—ancient, medieval, renaissance, modern, or other—must consider the embodied culture as well as the more conventional embodiments, such as material resources, carbon sequestration, and energy.

The modern paradigm provides guidance for placing cultural resources into context, including discussions on the meaning of architectural history and contemporary planning and building design. In 1939 Walter Gropius called for "studies in the history of art and architecture, intellectual and analytical in character [to] make the student familiar with the conditions and reasons which have brought about the visual expression of the different periods: i.e., the changes in philosophy, in politics, and in the means of production caused by new inventions."[4]

Gropius was talking about visual expression, perhaps the most ephemeral of architectural descriptors. But the broader point is that the most potent aspects of historical structures were driven by factors—technical, cultural, pragmatic, and political—in ways that can be identified and articulated rather than by capricious applications of *a priori* style; and, through the understanding of these factors, significant works of architecture offer meaningful lessons for contemporary building. Gropius was arguing for an approach to the consideration of modernism's predecessors. The same approach is valid for the evaluation of modern buildings as well as of modernism itself, particularly as it applies to sustainable architecture. This study is well-served by a methodology that considers proposed use, building performance, renovation and reconstruction techniques, historic and urban context, natural context, and embodied resources in both quantitative and qualitative terms. Although current analysis relies heavily on digital tools, the manually generated multi-format notational system developed for the CIAM grid offers a suggestion for combining quantitative and qualitative commentary within an evaluation process.

In order to properly apply the underlying principles of modernism to sustainable practice, it is essential, first and foremost, to reassert that modern is not a style. It is a broadly inclusive method, a process, a state of mind, and a fundamental conceptual foundation that deals with the full range of human endeavors. Gropius, describing the essence of modernism, wrote that his life was marked by "the strong desire to include every vital component of life instead of excluding them for the sake of too narrow and too dogmatic an approach."[5] This is to say that modernism has the capacity to accommodate the entire scope of architectural endeavor and that an extension of this comprehensiveness is the possibility of a unified structure that rationally organizes all activity affecting the physical environment, built and natural.

4. Walter Gropius, *Scope of Total Architecture* (Abingdon: Taylor and Francis, 1954), 62.

5. From a May 1953 talk delivered at the Illinois Institute of Technology published in Gropius, *Scope of Total Architecture*, 14.

The Search for a Healthy Living Environment and the Roots of Modernism

Alan Berman

The design revolution of the early twentieth century was largely driven by deeply held social and moral convictions. The early modernist architects were one group in a widespread movement that included medical, social, political, and artistic reformers determined to create better living conditions for urban workers suffering the consequences of the industrial revolution. This was a moral crusade, and it underpinned radical innovations in architecture and town planning.

Much of the developed world is no longer concerned with the basic conditions necessary for a healthy life. The nineteenth century battles for fresh air, natural daylight, sunshine, and sanitation have largely been won. Today's environmental concerns include global issues such as climate change, ecosystem protection, and resource management. Nevertheless, much can be learned from the relationship between early environmental health problems and the modernist design revolution that contributed to their resolution. If we are to have an architecture that supports human endeavours, lifts the human spirit, and promotes the fulfilment of human potential without further undermining natural systems, then we need an architecture that is equally underpinned by environmental principles. We need to abjure environmental design that is merely stylistic and become rooted instead in an idealism and vision that leads to real solutions.

The idealism of the twentieth century modernists was born of the political, social, and economic upheaval of the industrial revolution. The dreadful living conditions of the urban poor led to the emergence of an era of reforming philanthropists who sought better building solutions. Concurrently, the expansion of medical knowledge, particularly the role of hygiene in health and an intellectual and artistic awakening to the restorative powers of nature all nourished the new architecture.

The industrial revolution in Europe and the Americas (and beyond) led to many innovations, fast-changing economies, and population growth, but the towns and cities into which working people crowded were densely packed and unsanitary. Their meagre water supplies were contaminated, their limited foods lacked nourishment, the air was often toxic with factory effluents, and there was no open space or greenery. Before 1870 most inhabitants of towns were within walking distance of a field, but the newly triumphant barons of industry, in their unbridled pursuit of wealth, swept away everything, not only restrictive (and also protective) trade practices such as the old guilds, but also market places, allotments, and orchards, virtually any place where greenery and open space existed. "Thousands of families have only a single room to dwell in where they sleep and eat, multiply and die . . . [I]t is difficult to exaggerate the misery which such condition[s] of life must cause . . . [T]he depression of the body and mind which they create is an almost insuperable obstacle to the action of any elevating or refining agencies."[1] By the 1880s Manhattan's Lower East Side had an estimated 520 people per acre, possibly the most crowded area in the world at that time: "These industrial cities were man-heaps, machine-warrens, not [as some would have them] agents of human association for the promotion of a better life but rather . . . dark hives, busily puffing, clanking screeching, smoking, sometimes around the clock. The slavish routine of the mines . . . became the normal environment of the new industrial worker."[2]

In the mid-nineteenth century the extremes of private wealth and public squalor had reached such proportions that intellectuals and a small element of the educated population began to question how life could have become so bestial for so many yet so luxurious for others. This scrutiny fuelled a mix of practical ideas for reform as well as utopian visions for a better world. Thinkers such as Denis Diderot, François-Noël Babeuf, Henri de Saint-Simon, Edmund Burke, and John Locke were in general agreement that the lot of man needed improvement. This urge did not come from only intellectual and moral indignation; everyone, not just the worker, suffered the unsanitary and pestilent conditions of towns and cities. Raw sewage was everywhere, tipped into streets and basements, and spreading diseases like cholera and tuberculosis.

During the Age of Reform (1815–70), philosophers, artists, and political and social thinkers determined that human suffering was so great it must be against the natural order. This determination, and advances in the understanding of disease, inspired many of the philanthropist reformers of the era. Obvious as it may seem to us today, it took time for the connection to be made between a healthy workforce and productivity. But once that connection was made, a few enlightened industrial barons came to see value in improving the living conditions of their workers and set about constructing model houses and villages for healthier living environments.

1. Robert Arthur Talbot Gascoyne-Cecil, 3rd Marquess of Salisbury, "Labourers' and Artisans' Dwellings," *National Review*, November 1883, quoted in Andrew Roberts, *Salisbury: Victorian Titan* (London: Weidenfeld & Nicholson, 1999), 283.

2. Lewis Mumford, *The City in History: Its Origins, Its Transformations, and Its Prospects* (New York: Harcourt, Brace & World, 1961), 446.

One of the first and most extraordinary examples of an ideal village, directly inspired by the Encyclopaedists and other influential thinkers such as François-Noël Babeuf and Denis Diderot, was Claude Nicholas Ledoux's 1793 complex for workers at the salt mines at Chaux in northeastern France. Ledoux built an entire community planned along the egalitarian principles that he set out in his *Prospectus* of 1802: accommodation for the work force was separated from the industrial buildings by open space, all had gardens for the production of food; the houses were of different sizes according to workers' status, and all incorporated sanitary conditions with drainage and access to running water. Other idealist communities were proposed in France around this time as well, such as François-Marie-Charles Fourier's experiments in communal living with sleeping, living, eating, and child care arrangements separated from the debilitating pollution of factories. Most subsequent ideal settlements were driven less by formal and symbolic architectural preoccupations than by the will to create better living conditions.

Another influential model community was Robert Owen's mill town at New Lanark, England, where Owen settled in 1802. A mill owner, he, like Ledoux, was influenced by Enlightenment ideas. By 1825 Owen had established a model community where power for the factory was generated by the waterfalls nearby. He gained an international reputation because of his avowed mission to create the best possible conditions for his workers: "everyone should be placed in the midst of those external circumstances, that will produce the greatest number of pleasurable sensations, through the longest life, that man may be truly intelligent, moral and happy,"[3] and, specifically, in 1842, to "preserve health . . . pure air is necessary . . . [A]ll who understand the cause of disease know that an impure atmosphere is most unfavourable to the enjoyment of health . . . [D]ecisive measures should be adopted to ensure to all a pure atmosphere, in which to live."[4] He also intended that inhabitants "will be surrounded by gardens, have abundance of space in all directions to keep the air healthy and pleasant. They will have walks and plantations before them."[5]

Like Robert Owen, other industrialist reformers backed their ideas with their own money. The model village Saltaire was built by Sir Titus Salt in 1851 with basic, sound housing that had outdoor toilets and drainage, and in 1894 Lever Brothers, a British manufacturer, built the garden village Port Sunlight. Basic as all this accommodation was, it was significantly better than the slum dwellings of the vast majority of city workers. There were communal facilities, including open space and land allotments on which fresh vegetables could be grown. While these men, and other reformers such as the businessmen Joseph Rowntree, Arthur Guinness, and John Cadbury, fully understood the benefit to their enterprises, they were also deeply imbued with the religious and moral imperative to improve the lot of the working poor. It was through these reformers that the link between idealistic vision, social reform, and architecture was forged.

A similar track followed reformist efforts to improve hospitals and the quality of life for the sick. Traditional hospital buildings were based on monastic cloister forms organized around a central church, as the power

3. Robert Owen, *A Development of the Principles and Plans on which to Establish Self-supporting Home Colonies* (London: Home Colonization Society, 1841), 35.

4. Robert Owen, *The Book of the New Moral World Containing the Rational System of Society* (London: Home Colonization Society, 1842–44), 15.

5. Robert Owen, *The Life of Robert Owen*, vol. 1A (London: Effingham Wilson, 1858), 90.

of healing was left largely to God and virtue. But the small cells were unsatisfactory for nursing care, and there was little ventilation to remove germ-laden air. In response, experimental buildings with larger wards were developed in quiet locations with abundant fresh air. One model facility that recognized the need for fresh air was the Hôtel Dieu in Paris. Proposed in 1787 by the architect Charles-François Viel, the design incorporated individual ventilation shafts for each sick bay. It was influenced by the ideas of the foremost hospital designer of the time, Jacques-René Tenon (1724–1816) a physician, and architect Antoine Petit (1722–94). They had proposed an architectural cross-section that gave each sick bay a domed ceiling and a roof-top ventilation shaft similar to passive strategies in use today.[6]

The critical importance of improved environmental conditions for the health of patients inspired doctors, like industrialists, to put reforms in place. It is clear from their writings that they had a practical understanding of the environmental performance of buildings, and they complained that many architects were only interested in academic matters of style and form. In 1872 John Drysdale and John Hayward not only wrote a book entitled *Health and Comfort in House Building*, but they also had the vision to construct ventilated and sanitary model homes.[7] Of particular interest in terms of natural ventilation systems was the adaptation of the kitchen chimney flue to draw air away from other rooms through ingenious devices such as holes in the crown mouldings disguised as classical dentils. In one example the house was planned with central lobbies on each floor, one above another, with floor and ceiling grills between each lobby, the lowest room in the stack acting as a warming chamber. This allowed warm air to rise, creating a stack effect and drawing air from adjacent rooms, an effective strategy for natural ventilation.

The thinker, artist, and writer John Ruskin was also concerned with the wellbeing of the poor and was deeply disturbed by the effect of industry on the countryside in places such as his native Sheffield and other manufacturing centers. In the 1860s he was persuaded by the English reformer Octavia Hill to fund projects for social housing. What allied these two was a combination of sensibilities that were not uncommon in the latter part of the century: a concern for the social conditions of the working classes together with a passionate interest in the countryside and all things natural. Hill's work eventually led to the formation of the National Trust for the Protection of Rural England and the preservation of open green spaces in London.

The interest in the beneficial effects of nature, the idealism behind the model settlements, and support for egalitarian ideals for the rights of workers led to the garden city movements in the late nineteenth century. In England, Barry Parker and Sir Raymond Unwin's designs at Letchworth Garden City in Hertfordshire, England, and Hampstead Garden Suburb were rooted in the ideals of the early reformers: "All dwellings should be available to all classes of people and income groups . . . have wide tree lined roads . . . [and] houses should be separated by hedges not walls, and woods and public gardens should be available to all, and it should be quiet."[8] According to Parker and Unwin, "The essential thing is that every house

6. Helen Rosenau, *Social Purpose in Architecture: Paris and London Compared 1760–1800* (London: Studio Vista, 1970), 52–58.

7. John James Drysdale and John Williams Hayward, *Health and Comfort in House Building* (London: E & E.F. Spon, 1872).

8. Henrietta Barnett, "A Garden Suburb at Hampstead," *Contemporary Review* 87, no. 2 (1905), 235.

should turn its face to the sun, whence comes light, sweetness and health."[9] This type of planning ensured that residential areas were established well away from polluting industries. Similarly, the influential town planner Patrick Geddes, a biologist by training, sought to start with "primary human needs," stating that "man's interaction with a natural environment . . . produced stable healthy homes [which are] essential conditions to allow children to fully 'participate in life.'"[10] He put his theories into action in buying slum houses and transforming them by "weeding out the worst of the houses . . . [and] widening narrow closes into courtyards" so as to improve sunlight and airflow.[11]

The garden city architects envisioned a design ethos without artifice, one guided by the nature of their materials, and offering, as a result, a moral and healthy existence. These ideas were part of the intellectual convictions of the latter half of the nineteenth century that would give birth to the arts and crafts movement and, as Nikolaus Pevsner established in his *Pioneers of the Modern Movement*, would have great influence on the development of the Bauhaus and modernism. Like their antecedents at Chaux, New Lanark, Saltaire, and Port Sunlight, the garden cities manifested their idealistic roots and benign purpose, similar to the idealism behind Le Corbusier's projects in the 1920s for La Ville Radieuse and the agricultural community of New Dwellings for Bordeaux. In these projects, residences are set in open green spaces in order to provide a healthy life for modern workers and city dwellers. At the same time, in Le Corbusier and Amédée Ozenfant's influential publication *L'Esprit Nouveau*, various authors expounded on the health benefits of sport, proclaiming "La Physiologie est tout!" and affirming that sport can make "Le Corps Nouveau: The body will re-appear, naked in the sunlight, cleansed, muscled, supple."[12] This is the same emphasis on hygiene that Le Corbusier advocated: "Put the kitchen at the top of the house to avoid smells, demand ventilators in the windows for every room. Demand a bathroom looking south."[13] In these calls for improved conditions we see the same passion and drive among modern architects as those of the eighteenth and nineteenth century reformers.

Public awareness that tuberculosis was a major killer developed at the same time as late nineteenth century notions of the benign social role of design and craftsmanship, along with visions of healthy living conditions that could be created in garden cities. Discoveries regarding the nature of infections, and surveys like those by the Sanitary Institute of Great Britain, which reported that disease was 50 percent more prevalent in back-to-back housing that lacked through-ventilation, asserted the need for better environmental living conditions. Indeed, in the United States and Britain, government agencies set up programmes to fight disease.

Starting in the mid-nineteenth century, practitioners and healers in England, France, and central Europe promoted fresh air and nature baths for health. Doctors, such as Vincenz Priessnitz in Silesia (1799–1851), Richard Barter in Ireland (1802–70), David Urquhart in England (1805–77), and Arnold Rikli in Switzerland (1823–1906), built reputations on their successes in treating tuberculosis with bathing cures. Their knowledge of

9. Raymond Unwin and Barry Parker, "Cottage Plans and Common Sense," *Fabian Tract*, no. 109 (1902), 3.

10. Patrick Geddes, "Town Planning in Kapurthala. A Report to H.H. the Maharaja of Kapurthala, 1917," in *Patrick Geddes in India*, ed. Jacqueline Tyrwhitt (London: Lund Humphries, 1947), 26.

11. Geddes, 57.

12. Dr. Pierre Winter, "Le Corps Nouveau," *L'Esprit Nouveau*, no. 15 (1755), quoted in Reyner Banham, *The Architecture of the Well-Tempered Environment* (London: Architectural Press, 1969), 146.

13. Le Corbusier, *Towards a New Architecture*, trans. Frederick Etchells (London: Architectural Press, 1927), 114–115, quoted in Banham, *The Architecture of the Well-Tempered Environment*, 147.

the healing properties of fresh water and sunlight was later at the core of the back-to-nature and nudist movements that became popular in Europe, particularly in Germany, after 1900.[14]

A spate of sanatorium building followed in the early decades of the twentieth century, driven by the need to improve popular health. These buildings had a significant influence on the architecture of the time, and their design was influenced by 150 years of ideas about what was necessary for healthy living. Sanatoriums were sited away from towns amid greenery, often at high altitudes, and oriented south to take in the winter sun. To take maximum advantage of the sunlight and air, plans included large projecting balconies with glass walls that opened, allowing patients to recover in the open air. There were communal sun terraces on stepped sections at each level or on the main roof. The most notable and influential of these buildings were Johannes Duiker and Bernard Bijvoet's Sonnenstraal Sanatorium in Hilvershulm, Holland (1925) and Alvar Aalto's sanatorium at Paimo, Finland (1930). Many other examples were built in Europe, primarily in Germany, Switzerland, and Holland. These buildings deployed the latest developments in concrete and glass technologies to create large cantilevered terraces and expanses of glass.

This set of architectural forms was driven by the principles of clean, healthy living and answered modernism's demand for plain, unadorned forms and surfaces. All these ideas were evident in the designs for model workers' housing built by the Stuttgart municipality in 1927 at the Weissenhof Siedlung, where Mies van der Rohe, acting as the lead architect, invited young idealistic architects of the period to set out their visions for social housing. Undecorated smooth surfaces were made of easily cleaned timber or steel with a minimum of dust-collecting padded upholstery. Everything was light, white, and smooth, and brightly lit by the large expanses of glass or exposed electric light bulbs.

Publications like *L'Esprit Nouveau* and Siegfried Giedeon's *Befreites Wohnen* from 1929 reveal that architects were allying themselves with health professionals and reformers. This was a new design impulse for healthy, disease-free living conditions. It was not a matter of design style but a sensibility driven by a social mission to create health in body and mind. This ethos is the foundation of the aesthetic, and it remains today a paradigm of design as a consequence of human need. If we are to learn from the lessons of modernism, the same paradigm should be applied to an environmentally sustainable building culture today.

14. Sigfried Giedion, *Mechanization Takes Command: A Contribution to Anonymous History* (New York: Oxford University Press, 1948), 628–712.

Towards a New Architecture?

Michael Ben-Eli

"A great epoch has begun. There exists a new spirit."

Thus proclaimed Le Corbusier in his 1923 book, *Towards a New Architecture*.[1] The book, a milestone exposition of the modern movement in architecture, was an impassioned personal manifesto that called for a new interpretation of the possibilities and needs of the time. It argued for an architecture free from clutter and stylish clichés that would reflect the integrity of the machine age.

Le Corbusier derived much of his inspiration from the great historical monuments of the past. The ancient pyramids and temples of Egypt, the towers of Babylon, the Parthenon, the Coliseum, Santa Sofia, the designs of Brunelleschi and Michelangelo—these and other classical buildings provided valuable lessons about plan, function, and form. But the early-twentieth-century feats of engineering and technology—the new factories, granaries, hangars, cranes, the giant ocean-going ships, the airplanes, automobiles, and other mechanical devices—provided the impetus and driving elements for the new vocabulary he was advocating. Technology offered a fresh promise and the machine emerged as the new icon. Le Corbusier's declaration that "a house is a machine for living in," was the inevitable result.[2]

Materials —reinforced concrete, steel, and glass—as well as mechanical innovations like the elevator were changing the landscape of possibilities, and other leading architects of the time were similarly engaged in

1. Le Corbusier, *Towards a New Architecture* (London: Percy Land, Humphries, 1927).

2. Ibid.

developing a new language befitting the emerging new world. Mies van der Rohe was reaching for a new synthesis of architecture and technology, giving expression to his rational, purist concept of the modern style. And while Frank Lloyd Wright was seeking his own authentically American expression of an "organic architecture,"[3] it was Buckminster Fuller who took the machine metaphor to a groundbreaking conclusion with his Dymaxion Dwelling Machines: the 1927 Dymaxion House, and the 1944 design of the aircraft manufacturing-based technology of the Wichita House.[4]

In discussing the period's quest for a new direction, Mies van der Rohe observed that architecture is about giving authentic expression to the particular civilization of its time.[5] What, then, will be the next expression? What should be the most appropriate design paradigm for our own time?

"Environment" and "green building" have emerged as current buzz-words, but in themselves they do not always signal something truly new. In one way or another, all buildings must respond to their environment, and in obvious ways, they always have. Indigenous structures through the ages are perfect examples. Igloos in Alaska, Bedouin tents in desert regions, mud buildings in the Sub-Sahara, stilt villages on riverbanks, the amazing living bridges of Cherrapunji in Northern India, and even cave dwellings all display remarkable adaptation to particular environments. The projects presented in this book are excellent examples of environmentally related design considerations. But do these, and similar current architectural manifestations, take us far enough?

Architecture, like civilization itself, is continuously evolving, and each people, each generation, has to integrate the relevant context of its time and synthesize the available materials, tools, issues, aspirations, possibili-ties, and culture in a unique expression of its built environment. Authentic architecture redefines itself in a process of interpreting and giving expres-sion to the particular characteristics of its era. In this regard, it appears that humanity is now faced with entirely new demands—social, economic, and environmental challenges—as well as revolutionary design possibilities that are awaiting an innovative, radical integration. To explore the contem-porary context, let us first extend the meaning of the term "design."

Extending the Meaning of "Design"

In considering our current context, we might do well to start with the biggest possible picture and turn to the Hubble Space Telescope, which has been mapping our cosmic environment. The images produced by Hubble are awe-inspiring, and their significance to the speculative understanding of our place in the universe is huge. Take, for example, the image known as the Hubble Ultra Deep Field, with its subsequent series of exposures. It is the deepest portrait of the visible universe available thus far. It penetrates to about 400 million years after the Big Bang, showing the first galaxies to emerge after the birth of the cosmos. That is to say, it presents an image of events taking place nearly 13.2 billion years ago. The image itself captures a relatively tiny region of space, about three arch-minutes across, or

3. Frank Lloyd Wright, *The Natural House* (New York: Mentor Books, 1954).

4. Robert W. Marks, *The Dymaxion World of Buckminster Fuller* (Carbondale: Southern Illinois University Press, 1960).

5. Gustavo Gili, ed., *Conversations with Mies van der Rohe* (New York: Princeton Architectural Press, 2006).

approximately one thirteen-millionth of the sky. It contains some 10,000 galaxies, giving a good sense of the immensity of the cosmic reality.

This is particularly significant if one contemplates the fact that at the time when Le Corbusier was writing his book, astronomers were still arguing whether there were galaxies beyond the Milky Way. There are now estimated to be some 200 billion galaxies in the visible universe. So the physical environment that is accessible to human awareness has expanded tremendously, both spatially and in time. Other Hubble pictures deliver images of a spectacular show, with objects at unimaginable distances and of inconceivable size. The whole is pulsating with dynamism. Now-familiar images of the Swan Nebula or the gas pillars of the Eagle Nebula—immense structures in their own right—capture regions that are hotbeds for the continuous formation of new stars. There have even been recent sightings of planets in the process of formation. Galaxies of various ages, sizes, shapes, and colors are the staging grounds of processes of birth and decay, defying any concept of a static reality.

In this total environment, one can legitimately distinguish regions and processes of two fundamentally different kinds: regions of diffusion and dissipation of energy, and regions where energy is being compounded and consolidated. Planet Earth is one such energy-compounding region, where solar radiation is instrumental in forming multiple configurations of exquisite beauty and diversity. Order and complexity are being created on our planet, manifesting in the formation of organic molecules, the evolution of living creatures and whole ecosystems, and in the flowering and promise of human consciousness. This process proceeds against all odds, defying, if only momentarily, requirements of the second law of thermodynamics. Order creation and entropy emerge as two sides of one coin, and in this context, the human mind is potentially a most powerful anti-entropic force.

This perspective leads to an intriguing sequence of thoughts. The universe, our grand context, appears as a kaleidoscopic flux of constantly inter-transforming dynamic events. This means that reality continuously reorders itself. An illuminating point, in this respect, is that human activities and potentialities are an inseparable component of this all-embracing, self-organizing process. What's more, the immanent order inherent in cosmic processes is accessible to human intelligence. It is expressible in general principles or laws which, in themselves, offer powerful tools for order creation.

The idea of order creation is central to the concept of design. In the broadest sense, design can be regarded as a process of deliberately channeling energies that otherwise would be diffused. It entails consciously applying intelligence to arranging, rearranging, and optimizing preferred configurations. Design, in this sense, is at the heart and very meaning of being human. It is our means for shaping reality, and ultimately participating, proactively and creatively, in the process of evolution itself.

A concept depicting a permanent struggle between chaos and order, between the forces of darkness and the forces of light, is at the center of many wisdom traditions. It is suggestive to interpret the prevailing global state of affairs in this context, since, even to a casual observer, it would appear that our current growth-at-all-costs civilization is flawed and entropic in nature. The consequence is a menacing disorder whereby, driven largely by un-thoughtful human activities, serious threats have emerged to the integrity of other forms of life, whole ecosystems, and to the well being of humanity itself. Ensuring a worldwide transition to an enduring sustainability regime is, therefore, the ultimate design challenge of our time.

The Sustainability Challenge

The term "sustainability," which was introduced into the language relatively recently, has quickly gained broad-based use. In the process, the underlying meaning has been watered down significantly. In this essay, the term is used in the context of the whole planet, the integrity and health of its biosphere, and the long-term well-being of humanity.

Elsewhere, I have defined sustainability as "a dynamic equilibrium in the processes of interaction between a population and the carrying capacity of its environment such that the population develops to express its full potential without producing irreversible adverse effects on the carrying capacity of the environment upon which it depends."[6]

It is this equilibrium that has been compromised in our time with the unprecedented explosion of human population and the related rapid intensification in development activity around the world. At the heart of such equilibrium are flows of energy and matter: resources being consumed and byproducts being generated that have to be absorbed. As a growing number of scientists have been pointing out, in many instances, the planet's capacity for resource generation and byproduct absorption are now being overwhelmed.

At present the system is out of balance, with many components of the biosphere showing serious signs of stress. The list is familiar: ozone depletion, climate change, loss of biodiversity, soil erosion and desertification, diminishing fresh water resources, shrinkage of forest cover, and the growing income disparity between and within nations. This pattern must be reversed if major systemic collapses of increasing frequency and severity are to be averted.

The required transformation is unprecedented in scope. It would demand a change in the values we hold, our view of the world, the ways we govern, the structure of our world economy, priorities in the use of technology, and the energy regime that underlies our current civilization. It would impact all aspects and all sectors of human activity. The ultimate objective of such a transformation is to foster a well-functioning alignment between individuals, society, the economy, and the regenerative capacity of the planet's life-supporting ecosystems. The change that is called for has, of course, important implications to the built environment. This is where architecture can play a leading role: by articulating a new vision and design vocabulary, offering new concepts and tools, and directly addressing some of the great dilemmas now facing humankind.

From single structures and the myriad objects associated with their use, to whole urban environments, the challenge of sustainability calls for

6. Michael Ben-Eli, "Sustainability: The Five Core Principles—A New Framework," *The Sustainability Laboratory,* http://www.sustainabilitylabs. org/files/Sustainability (accessed 29 January 2013).

a radically new architecture. The collective, contemporary task of establishing the concept of sustainability as the organizing principle on the planet should, henceforth, constitute the primary impulse in contemporary architectural design.

The Five Core Sustainability Principles: A Framework for Design

Sustainability, as defined above, represents a particular system state in which two primary, interacting variables—in this case population and carrying capacity—are in a dynamic equilibrium. The underlying structure is that of a circular interaction—a loop—whereby these two interacting variables are linked interdependently. They co-create and continuously shape, define, and redefine one another. A particular environment prescribes what kind of population is possible in the first place, and population, in turn, modifies and remakes the environment itself. The long history of the biosphere bears witness to this kind of interaction.

Living organisms and the large complex, dynamic systems that comprise the major components of the biosphere—atmospheric cycles, ecosystems such as rain forests and coral reefs, societies, institutions, economies, urban areas, and whole civilizations alike—all display similar characteristics inherent in circular interactions. All such systems consist of networks of multiple variables, myriad multi-loops and multiple interactions, all co-adjusting and co-accommodating to produce a state of dynamic equilibrium for the whole. In this context, sustainability can be regarded as a type of dynamic stability in which some quantity remains invariant. The invariance in question is the state of equilibrium itself, while the defining elements and detailed forces that produce it change with time.

The set of five core sustainability principles that I developed as part of the work of The Sustainability Laboratory offers a comprehensive framework prescribing the essential conditions for establishing sustainability as an enduring state.[7] The principles are articulated in a generalized fashion, and they can be interpreted in specific relation to any delineation of human activity. Along with their operational implications, these principles can inform a new approach for conceptualizing and reshaping the built environment by enlightened design.

The principles are expressed in relation to five interrelated, key domains, each representing a primary vector of physical or non-physical variables that impact the interaction of humans with the world. The five fundamental domains are the material domain, the economic domain, the domain of life, the social domain, and the spiritual or value domain. Securing an effective sustainability regime requires the simultaneous integration of issues defined by all five dimensions. Let us briefly review the implications.

The *material domain* constitutes the basis for regulating the flow of materials and energy that underlie existence. The related first principle states: "Contain entropy and ensure that the flow of resources through and within the economy is as nearly non-declining as permitted by physical laws."[8]

7. Michael Ben-Eli, "The Cybernetics of Sustainability: Definition and Underlying Principles," in *Enough For All Forever*, ed. Murray, Cawthorne, Dey and Andrews (Champaign: Common Ground Publishing, 2012).

8. Ben-Eli, "The Cybernetics of Sustainability."

The implications for design of the built environment are significant. Enacting this principle would require uncompromising design innovations: striving for the highest resource productivity; amplifying performance per pound of resources with each cycle of use; a complete switch to renewable, clean energy sources; the omni-conversion of waste into a useful resource by implementing closed-loop infrastructures of continuous flows of energy and matter; the establishment of a service, performance-based lease orientation (as distinct from ownership) in managing the circulation of durable goods; and more. If such considerations were to be introduced comprehensively and fully by forward-looking design, they would stand to produce a true, game-changing shift in the world.

The other four domains and their respective principles and operational implications complete the specifications for a new comprehensive design repertoire. Thus, for example, the *economic domain,* which provides a guiding framework for creating and managing wealth, raises questions that inevitably impact and ultimately shape the built environment. What accounting framework is being utilized to measure economic values? Are cost externalities taken into account? Is a measure of well-being and human development embodied in economic cost calculations? What is the true nature of measures and mechanisms that regulate the distribution of resources, their use and allocation? What policies, rules, and regulations are employed in order to accentuate desirable outcomes and eliminate adverse ones? Are such policies piecemeal and fragmented, or do they optimize for the whole?

The *domain of life* provides the basis for appropriate behavior in the biosphere. We are neighbors to many other species and our own adaptive success in colonizing the planet comes at the too-often irreversible expense of many other forms of life. Design considerations related to this domain would primarily involve issues of land use patterns and configurations of spatial design. How does a given plan impact other forms of life? How would we configure an expanding built environment in ways that minimizes overall footprint and reduces encroachment on other species and their habitats? Could we even design to enhance biodiversity in areas of human deployment?

The *social domain,* in turn, provides the basis for social interactions, the nature and quality of which are of prime concern in designing the built environment. Beyond obvious considerations of public space and private experience, there are profound questions that reflect, and could actually help shape, the social order itself. What kind of governance system regulates our urban designs? Who dominates its prerogatives? What channels are open to users for shaping their own habitat? How is access to resources and possibilities determined? And can the built environment be so-designed that by its very nature it would actually educate the public, enhancing beneficial behaviors that promote spontaneous emergence of sustainability practices?

Finally, the *spiritual or value domain* provides the necessary attitudinal, value orientation and acts as the basis for a universal code of ethics. It is fundamental to the quality and coherence of the whole. Considerations of this domain may be dismissed out-of-hand by some, but it is nevertheless of critical significance. Should we allow an egocentric, greedy, predatory civilization to dominate our lives, or should we strive to evolve an aware, self-restrained, inclusive, and nurturing world? Could enlightened design inspire society to move beyond familiar moral and ethical ambiguities that permeate so many aspects of everyday life? How uplifting is the experience of the built environment? Is it oppressive and stressful, or joyful and largely stress-free? Does it enhance well-being and happiness? And to what extent does it encourage the creative fulfillment of full human potentialities?

If the proposition that the sustainability challenge constitutes the primary design challenge of our time is accepted, then the five core sustainability principles offer the necessary framework for change, and constitute a platform for a radically innovative architecture. But what would replace the machine as the contemporary icon? What would the most suitable driving metaphor be for the next revolution in design?

Towards a New Architecture

The growing awareness and interest shown by innovative design circles in seeking direct inspiration from the amazing workings of nature suggests the overall direction. Just as the machine provided the working metaphor and energizing icon for the architecture of the twentieth century, biology and the living organism will offer the appropriate new icon for the built environment of the future. As a symbol, the wonder of the mechanical device will increasingly be replaced by the enormous richness of living systems. Eco-Architecture, or Eco-Design, might accordingly be the appropriate terms for capturing the new organizing concept for the built environment.

Four major trends are currently converging to define a new global context that will redefine the architecture of our time. These trends include the untenable global stresses produced by the unsustainable aspects of the world economy; the game-changing advances that are being made in the material, information, and biological sciences; the historical acceleration of the process of urbanization; and the emergence of a new global consciousness marked by more sensitive awareness of self and others that is beginning to unite people, especially young people, all over the world. These forces are interconnected; they interact, shape, and amplify one another, accelerating change in the process, and opening unimaginable new possibilities with the power of their synergies.

Urban systems offer a prime arena for exploring the implications of these trends in relation to the built environment. The reason is two-fold. First, more than half of the world's population currently resides in urban areas. According to the World Health Organization,[9] cities around the world are growing by sixty million people each year, and by 2050, 6.4 billion people will be urban dwellers. Cities have become the predominant habitat of our species, yet urban infrastructure is woefully inadequate, especially in the mega-cities of the developing countries where much of the growth is taking place.

9. World Health Organization, "Urban Population Growth," *Global Health Observatory*, http://www.who.int/gho/ urban_health/situation_trends/ urban_population_growth/en/ (accessed January 29, 2013).

Second, as actual eco-zones in their own right, urban areas embody all the issues invoked by the sustainability challenge. Cities provide the ideal setting, a veritable experimental laboratory for developing the necessary new design vocabulary. In urban areas, all the questions related to developing an effective sustainability-driven way of life—installing a sustainable physical infrastructure of material and energy flows; inaugurating an economic model that recognizes true social costs; evolving new modalities of governance and public service delivery; implementing strategies for relieving pressure on biodiversity hot spots; and shaping an inclusive value paradigm considerate of happiness and well-being of all—need to be integrated under one innovative design vision.

Driven by rigorous sustainability principles, the new eco-architecture can take us considerably beyond current practices associated with green buildings. These practices are still in their infancy. They are partial and largely fragmented and will not, in themselves, be sufficient to carry the day. Only a major shift in the design paradigm—a true second-order change— can produce the next evolutionary leap. Under these conditions, the built environment will become better aligned with the regenerative capacity of the planet's life-supporting ecosystems and, like a rain forest, it will display in its own structure the same kind of vibrancy, variety, dynamism, intelligence, and adaptive inter-accommodating balance. More than reflecting simple machines, the new house and the new city will exhibit properties of the kind now associated exclusively with healthy ecosystems and life forms in general.

Just like a bird's nest, a beehive, or an anthill, the human built environment is a part of nature. Architecture, in this sense, is a manifestation of evolution, the same process that underlies stages in the complexification of matter, and continues all the way from simple organic molecules, through biology, to human society—its values, organization, culture, and associated technology. In this context, technology itself can be regarded as an externalization of internal genetic and physiological processes. Inspired by the new paradigm, the whole network of humanly created artifacts—all essentially extensions of metabolic, motor, and cognitive functions—would become the subject of radically innovative, integrated design.

Internalizing the sustainability principles in a new design vocabulary and reaching beyond merely superficial design gestures will pose many challenges. If successful, however, technology will everywhere increase performance capabilities and material subtlety, as it moves to approximate the elegant workings of the non-human-made living world. Smart design will vest materials, as well as specific functions and whole processes, with intelligence, making them, like true ecosystems, ever more responsive to their users, to other neighboring structures, to their own integrity, and to the effective functioning of the whole. Single structures and whole complexes will function like gigantic metabolic engines: they will harvest energy directly from the sun and regulate the flows of energy and materials in a continuous infrastructure designed to optimize for the whole. One continuous organism—a world eco-city—with distinctive nodes celebrating unique, local cultural flavors, and linked with rural communities and vast flourishing pristine environments left in the wild, will then form the physical backbone of a new planetary civilization.

Realizing the full promise of a new architecture and the coming revolution in design entails the jettisoning of those weights of convention and burdens of precedence that are holding evolution back. Future possibilities are, to a great extent, limited only by the imagination, and as new creative expressions emerge, the ever-present question, "What next?" should always remain open.

Notes on the Materials

INDIVIDUAL PROJECTS

New Dwellings for Bordeaux
© 2013 Artists Rights Society (ARS),
New York/ADAGP, Paris/F.L.C.

Open-Air School
Netherlands Architecture Institute

Night Shelter for the Homeless
Affonso Eduardo Reidy, *Bauten und Projekte*.
Stuttgart: Verlag Gerd Hatje, 1960, 13.
Nabil Bonduki, *Affonso Eduardo Reidy*.
Lisbon: Instituto Lina Bo e P.M. Bardi,
2000, 37.

Karuizawa Summer House
© 2013 Victor Raymond
Antonin Raymond, *An Autobiography*.
Tokyo: Charles E. Tuttle Company, 1973,
130–131, 133.

Weekend House
Art, Design & Architecture Museum,
University of California, Santa Barbara

Housing at Sunila Pulp Mill
Artek and Artek USA, Alvar Aalto Museum

Jacobs House I
© Frank Lloyd Wright Foundation,
Scottsdale, Arizona/Art Resource,
New York/Artists Rights Society (ARS),
New York

Houses in Space
Amancio Williams Archive, Courtesy
Claudio and Cristobal Williams

House over the Brook
Amancio Williams Archive, Courtesy
Claudio and Cristobal Williams

Jacobs House II
© 2013 Frank Lloyd Wright Foundation,
Scottsdale, Arizona/Artists Rights Society
(ARS), New York
Ezra Stoller © Esto. All rights reserved.

**Building for the Emprezas Gráphicas o
Cruzeiro**
Fundação Oscar Niemeyer

Maison Tropicale
Centre National d'Art et de Culture
Georges Pompidou
Bibliothèque Kandinsky, Fonds Jean Prouvé

Soholm I
Perspective Drawing © Arne Jacobsen
Photographs by Per Munkgård Thorsen/
Lars Degnbol
Realdania Byg

Bachelor Flats
Office of Katz Vaughan Architects

Dexter M. Ferry Jr. Cooperative House
Marcel Breuer Digital Archive, Special
Collections Research Center, Syracuse
University Libraries
Photographs by Ben Schnall

Walker Beach House
Ezra Stoller © Esto. All rights reserved.

Munkegaard Elementary School
Danish National Arts Library, Collection
of Historical Drawings
Photograph by Jörgen Strüwing, Danish
Architectural Press

Cocoon House
Ezra Stoller © Esto. All rights reserved.

Pavilion on the Lagoon Rodrigo de Freitas
Affonso Eduardo Reidy, *Bauten und Projekte*.
Stuttgart: Verlag Gerd Hatje, 1960, 60.

Valéria P. Cirell House
© Instituto Lina Bo e P.M. Bardi, São Paulo,
Brasil
Photographs by Peter Scheier, 1958

Siedlung Halen
© Atelier 5
Photographs by Croci & DuFresne

School of Plastic Arts, National Arts School
Photographs by Daniel Wills

House on a Cycladic Island
Photographs by Lydia Xynogala

House II in Kavouri
Copyright 2012 © Constantinos Decavallas

Vacation House on Aegina
Copyright 2012 © Constantinos Decavallas

**TIMELINE:
SELECTED PROJECTS, 1925–70**

**1928 First & Second Goetheanum,
Rudolf Steiner**
Allgemeine Anthroposophische
Gesellschaft

**1928 San Marcos in the Desert Resort,
Frank Lloyd Wright**
© 2013 Frank Lloyd Wright Foundation,
Scottsdale, Arizona/Artists Rights Society
(ARS), New York
—*Frank Lloyd Wright*
Frank Lloyd Wright, *An Autobiography*.
New York: Duell, Sloan and Pearce,
1943, 314.

1929 Lovell Health House, Richard Neutra
© J. Paul Getty Trust. Used with
permission. Julius Schulman Photography
Archive, Research Library at the
Getty Research Institute, (2004.R.10)
—*Colin Porteous*
Colin Porteous, *The New Eco-Architecture
Alternatives from the Modern Movement*.
London: Spon Press, 2002, 16.

1933 Paimio Sanatorium, Alvar Aalto
Alvar Aalto Volume I 1922–1962. Zurich:
Verlag fur Architecture Artemis, 1963,
36.
—*James Steele*
James Steele, *Ecological Architecture*.
London: Thames & Hudson, 2005, 59.

1933 Schminke House, Hans Scharoun
Peter Pfankuch, *Hans Scharoun: Bauten, Entwurfe, Texte*. Berlin: Gebr. Mann Verlag, 1974, 105.
—*Peter Blundell Jones*
Peter Blundell Jones, *Hans Scharoun*. London: Phaidon Press Ltd., 1995, 76.

1935 Corona School, Richard Neutra
© J. Paul Getty Trust. Used with permission. Julius Schulman Photography Archive, Research Library at the Getty Research Institute. (2004.R.10)

1937 Alfred Loomis House, William Lescaze
Special Collections Research Center, Syracuse University Libraries
—*Jennet Conant*
Jennet Conant, *Tuxedo Park: A Wall Street Tycoon and the Secret Palace of Science That Changed the Course of World War II*. New York: Simon & Schuster Paperbacks, 2002.

1938 Chermayeff House, Serge Chermayeff
ICP Media Ltd.
—*Colin Porteous*
Colin Porteous, *The New Eco-Architecture Alternatives from the Modern Movement*. London: Spon Press, 2002, 83.

1938 Pondicherry Dormitory, Antonin Raymond
© 2013 Victor Raymond
—*Aladar and Victor Olgyay*
Aladar Olgyay and Victor Olgyay, *Solar Control & Shading Devices*. Princeton, N.J.: Princeton University Press, 1957, 189.

1939 Villa Mairea, Alvar Aalto
© Wayne Andrews / Esto. All rights reserved.
—*James Steele*
James Steele, *Ecological Architecture*. London: Thames & Hudson, 2005, 59.

1940 Chamberlain House, Marcel Breuer + Walter Gropius
Ezra Stoller © Esto. All rights reserved.

1943 Ministry of Education, Oscar Niemeyer, Affonso Eduardo Reidy, Lucio Costa and Others
Aladar Olgyay and Victor Olgyay, *Solar Control & Shading Devices*. Princeton, N.J.: Princeton University Press, 1957, 186.
—*Aladar and Victor Olgyay*
Aladar Olgyay and Victor Olgyay, *Solar Control & Shading Devices*. Princeton, N.J.: Princeton University Press, 1957, 186.

1945 Wichita/Dymaxion House, Buckminster Fuller
Courtesy, The Estate of R. Buckminster Fuller
—*Buckminster Fuller*
1929, during the 4D House Exhibition at Marshall Field's department store in Chicago

1946 Kaufmann Desert House, Richard Neutra
© J. Paul Getty Trust. Used with permission. Julius Schulman Photography Archive, Research Library at the Getty Research Institute. (2004.R.10)
—*Aladar and Victor Olgyay*
Aladar Olgyay and Victor Olgyay, *Solar Control & Shading Devices*. Princeton, N.J.: Princeton University Press, 1957, 156.

1947 Mene Grande Oil Company Office Building, Ralph Walker
Ralph Walker, *Ralph Walker, Architect, of Voorhees, Gmelin & Walker; Voorhees, Walker, Foley & Smith; Voorhees, Walker, Smith & Smith*. New York: Henahan House, 1957, 245.
—*J.E. Aronin*
J.E. Aronin, *Climate & Architecture*. New York: Reinhold, 1953, 86.

1948 University of Puerto Rico General Library, Henry Klumb
Enrique Vivoni-Farage, "Modern Puerto Rico and Henry Klumb," *Docomomo* 33, September 2005, 35.
—*Enrique Vivoni-Farage*
Enrique Vivoni-Farage, "Modern Puerto Rico and Henry Klumb," *Docomomo* 33, September 2005, 35.

1949 Maison Curutchet, Le Corbusier
© 2013 Artists Rights Society (ARS), New York/ADAGP, Paris/F.L.C. "Maison Curutchet," *Architecture + Urbanism: Visions of the Real*, March 2000.

1949 Victoria College, John W. Poltock
Aladar Olgyay and Victor Olgyay, *Solar Control & Shading Devices*. Princeton, N.J.: Princeton University Press, 1957, 138.
—*Aladar and Victor Olgyay*
Aladar Olgyay and Victor Olgyay, *Solar Control & Shading Devices*. Princeton, N.J.: Princeton University Press, 1957, 138.

1953 Unesco Headquarters, Marcel Breuer, Bernard Zehrfuss + Pier Luigi Nervi
Special Collections Research Center, Syracuse University Libraries
—*Aladar and Victor Olgyay*
Aladar Olgyay and Victor Olgyay, *Solar Control & Shading Devices*. Princeton, N.J.: Princeton University Press, 1957, 113.

1955 Prempeh College, Fry, Drew, Drake and Lasdun
Aladar Olgyay and Victor Olgyay, *Solar Control & Shading Devices*. Princeton, N.J.: Princeton University Press, 1957, 179.
—*Aladar and Victor Olgyay*
Aladar Olgyay and Victor Olgyay, *Solar Control & Shading Devices*. Princeton, N.J.: Princeton University Press, 1957, 179.

1956 Price Tower, Frank Lloyd Wright
Lantern Slide Collection, The Irwin S. Chanin School of Architecture Archive, The Cooper Union

1957 Universidad Central De Venezuela School Of Architecture, Carlos Raúl Villanueva
Paulina Villanueva and Maciá Pintó, *Carlos Raúl Villanueva*. New York: Princeton Architectural Press, 2000, 113.
—*Paulina Villanueva and Maciá Pintó*
Paulina Villanueva and Maciá Pintó, *Carlos Raúl Villanueva*. New York: Princeton Architectural Press, 2000, 113.

1957 Senanayake Flats, Minnette De Silva
Minnette De Silva, *The Life & Work of an Asian Woman Architect*. Colombo: Smart Media Productions, 1998, 277.
—*Minnette De Silva*
Minnette De Silva, *The Life & Work of an Asian Woman Architect*. Colombo: Smart Media Productions, 1998, 272.

1958 Art Museum in Baghdad, Alvar Aalto
Alvar Aalto Museum
—*Alvar Aalto*
Alvar Aalto Volume III: Projects and Buildings. Zurich: Verlag fur Architecture Artemis, 1978, 153.

1962 Arcosanti, Paolo Soleri
Cosanti Foundation
—*James Steele*
James Steele, *Ecological Architecture*. London: Thames & Hudson, 2005, 135.

1962 US Consulate And Residence, Louis Kahn
Louis I. Kahn Collection, The University of Pennsylvania and the Pennsylvania Historical and Museum Commission
—*James Steele*
James Steele, *Ecological Architecture*. London: Thames & Hudson, 2005, 115–118.

1963 Frey House II, Albert Frey
© J. Paul Getty Trust. Used with permission. Julius Schulman Photography Archive, Research Library at the Getty Research Institute (2004.R.10)
—*Albert Frey*
Jennifer Golub, *Albert Frey Houses I + 2*. New York: Princeton Architectural Press, 1999, 74.

1965 Condominium I, Sea Ranch, Charles Moore, Donlyn Lyndon, William Turnbull + Richard Whitaker
© Donald Corner and Jenny Young/ Artifice Images

1967 US Pavilion at Expo '67, Buckminster Fuller
Courtesy The Estate of R. Buckminster Fuller
—*Buckminster Fuller*
R. Buckminster Fuller, *Inventions, The Patented Works of R. Buckminster Fuller*. New York: St. Martin's Press, 1983, 129.

1969 Chandigarh, Le Corbusier
© 2013 Artists Rights Society (ARS), New York/ADAGP, Paris/F.L.C.
—*Le Corbusier*
Quoted in James Steele, *Ecological Architecture, A Critical History*. New York: Thames and Hudson, 2005, 103.

Index

Aalto, Alvar, 13, 19, 58–63, 179, 180, 185
Africa, 15, 94–99, 106–11, 184, 186
American Institute of Architects (AIA), 190
Amsterdam, 15, 36–41, 189
Angola US Consulate and Residence
    (Kahn), 186
Arcosanti (Soleri), 23, 185
Argentina, Williams work in, 70–81
arid zones, 14, 106–11
Art Museum in Baghdad (Aalto), 185
Atelier 5, 146–51

Bachelor Flats (Katz and Vaughan),
    106–11
Badjara, Domaine de (Le Corbusier), 71
Bo Bardi, Lina, 16, 23, 140–45
Brazil
    Rio de Janeiro, 21, 42–45, 88–93,
        136–39, 181
    São Paolo, 16, 23, 140–45
Breuer, Marcel, 112–17, 181, 184

Castro, Fidel, 153
Chamberlain House (Breuer and Gropius),
    181
Chandigarh (Le Corbusier), 22, 187
Chermayeff House (Chermayeff), 180
CIAM (Congrès Internationaux
    d'Architecture Moderne), 25, 196
Cirell House (Bo Bardi), 16, 140–45
City Beautiful movement, 23–24
climate
    educational organizations on, 165,
        190–91
    geodesic domes and, 22–23
    map, 28–29
    Olgyays' research on, 189–94
    overview and types of, 13–16
    regulation of, 12–13
    solar energy and, 13
    sustainability measurements and,
        196–200
    ventilation and shade for, 14–15, 21–22,
        191–94
    Cocoon House (Rudolph and Twitchell),
        130–35
Columbia University, 165, 190
communes, 22, 203

Congo, Republic of, 94–99
continental zones, 52, 58, 64, 82, 112.
    See also temperate zones
Le Corbusier
    artists influenced by, 16, 46, 141, 159,
        194
    brise-soleil of, 21, 194
    Chandigarh by, 22, 187
    on climate and sustainability, 13, 18, 197
    Domaine de Badjara, 71
    Errazuriz House by, 16, 46
    on health and urbanism, 24, 205
    inspirations for, 207
    Maison Curutchet by, 183
    New Dwellings for Bordeaux by, 15,
        30–35, 205
Corona School (Neutra), 179
Costa, Lucio, 21
Cuba, 152–57
Curutchet, Maison (Le Corbusier), 183
Cycladic Island, House on a (Xenakis),
    158–63

Decavallas, Constantinos, 164–69,
    170–75
Denmark, 100–105, 124–29
Dexter Ferry Jr. Cooperative House
    (Breuer), 112–17
Domaine de Badjara (Le Corbusier), 71
Dover house (Raymond, E.), 22
Drew, Jane, 21, 184
Drysdale, John, 204
Duiker, Johannes, 15, 36–41, 189
Dymaxion House (Fuller), 22–23, 181, 208

Emprezas Gráficas o Cruzeiro Building
    (Niemeyer), 88–93
England, 180, 203, 204
Errazuriz House (Le Corbusier), 16, 46

Finland, 58–63, 179
Florida, 118–23, 130–35
Fourier, François-Marie-Charles, 203
Freitas Pavilion on the Lagoon (Reidy),
    136–39
Frey, Albert, 52–57, 186
Fry, Maxwell, 21, 107, 184
Fuller, Buckminster, 22–23, 181, 187, 208

Garden City movement, 24–26, 204–5
Geddes, Patrick, 205
geodesic domes, 22–2
Goetheanum (Steiner), 178
Gropius, Walter, 107, 181, 199–200

Hayward, John, 204
health, 23–24, 189, 201–6
Hill, Octavia, 204
Homeless, Night Shelter for the (Reidy and
    Pinheiro), 42–45
Hôtel Dieu (Viel), 204
House II in Kavouri (Decavallas), 164–69
House on a Cycladic Island (Xenakis),
    158–63
House Over the Brook (Williams), 76–81
Houses in Space (Williams), 70–75

India, 22, 180, 187
Italy, 19, 23

Jacobsen, Arne, 13, 100–105, 124–29
Jacobs Houses (Wright), 14, 64–69, 82–87
Japan, 16, 22, 46–51
Jeanneret, Pierre, 30–35

Kahn, Louis, 186
Karuizawa Summer House (Raymond, A.),
    16, 46–51
Katz, Bronek, 106–11
Kaufmann Desert House (Neutra), 182
Kavouri, House II in (Decavallas), 164–69
Kelly, Burnham, 190
Klumb, Henry, 182
Kocher, A. Lawrence, 52–57

Larkin Building (Wright), 20
Ledoux, Claude Nicholas, 203
Loomis House (Lescaze), 180
Los Angeles, 24, 178, 179
Lovell Health House (Neutra), 24, 178
Lyndon, Donlyn, 186

Mairea, Villa (Aalto), 180
Maison Curutchet (Le Corbusier), 183
Maison Tropicale (Prouvé), 15, 94–99
Massachusetts, 22, 181, 190
May, Ernst, 19, 25

Mene Grande Oil Company Office Building (Walker), 182
Mies van der Rohe, 208
Migge, Leberecht, 19
Moore, Charles, 186
Munkegaard Elementary School (Jacobsen), 124–29

Nervi, Pier Luigi, 184
Neutra, Richard, 24, 178, 179, 182
New Dwellings for Bordeaux (Le Corbusier and Jeanneret), 15, 30–35, 205
New York, 20, 52–57, 112–17, 180
Niemeyer, Oscar, 21, 88–93, 181
Niger, 95–96
Night Shelter for the Homeless (Reidy and Pinheiro), 42–45
northern zone, 13–14, 58–63

Ogami Lighthouse, 22
Olgyay, Victor and Aladar, 189–93
Open-Air Corona School (Neutra), 179
Open-Air School (Duiker), 15, 36–41, 189
Overy, Paul, 189
Owen, Robert, 203

Paimio Sanatorium (Aalto), 179
Parker, Barry, 204–5
Pavilion on the Lagoon Rodrigo de Freitas (Reidy), 136–39
Petit, Antoine, 204
Pinheiro, Gerson Pompeu, 42–45
Poltock, John W., 183
Pondicherry Dormitory (Raymond, A.), 180
Porro, Ricardo, 152–57
prefabrication, 19, 31, 95
Prempeh College of Ghana (Fry et al.), 184
Price Tower (Wright), 184
Prouvé, Jean, 15, 94–99
Puerto Rico, 182

Rancière, Jacques, 194
Raymond, Antonin, 16, 46–51, 180
Raymond, Eleanor, 22
Reidy, Affonso Eduardo, 42–45, 136–39, 181
Reverse House (Olgyays), 190
Rio de Janeiro, 21, 42–45, 88–93, 136–39, 181
Rudofsky, Bernard, 12

Rudolph, Paul, 22, 118–23, 130–35
Ruskin, John, 204

sanatoriums, 179, 206
San Marcos in the Desert Resort (Wright), 178
São Paolo, 16, 23, 140–45
savannah zone, tropical, 42, 88, 94, 136, 152
Scandinavia, 14
Scarpa, Carlo, 23
Scharoun, Hans, 179
Schindler, Rudolph, 24
Schminke House (Scharoun), 179
Schütte-Lihotzky, Grette, 19
Sea Ranch Condominium I (Moore et al.), 186
Senanayake Flats (De Silva), 185
Senegal, 106–11
Siedlung Halen (Atelier 5), 146–51
De Silva, Minette, 185
Siple, Paul, 190
Soholm 1 (Jacobsen), 100–105
solar power, 22–23
Soleri, Paolo, 23, 185
Space, Houses in (Williams), 70–75
Sri Lanka, 185
Steiner, Rudolf, 178
subtropical zones, 14–15
    Bo Bardi, Cirell House in, 16, 140–45
    Decavallas, House II in Kavouri in, 164–69
    Decavallas Vacation House on Aegina in, 170–75
    Raymond, Karuizawa Summer House in, 16, 46–51
    Rudolph and Twitchell, Cocoon House in, 130–35
    Rudolph, Walker Beach House in, 118–23
    ventilation and shade for, 14–15, 21–22
    Williams' House Over the Brook in, 76–81
    Williams' Houses in Space in, 70–75
    Xenakis' House on a Cycladic Island in, 158–63
Sunila Pump Mill Housing (Aalto), 58–63
sunshades, 14–15, 21–22, 191–94

sustainability
    criteria for, 17–27
    health and, 23–24, 189, 201–6
    measuring, 196–200
    principles, 211–13
    urbanism, 24–26, 201–6, 213–14
Switzerland, 146–51, 178

Telkes, Mária, 22, 192
temperate zones, 14
    Aalto, Sunila Pump Mill Housing in, 58–63
    Atelier 5, Siedlung Halen in, 146–51
    Breuer, Ferry Cooperative House in, 112–17
    Le Corbusier and Jeanneret, New Dwellings for Bordeaux in, 15, 30–35, 205
    Duiker, Open-Air School in, 15, 36–41, 189
    Frey and Kocher, Weekend House in, 52–57
    Jacobsen, Munkegaard Elementary School in, 124–29
    Jacobsen, Soholm I in, 100–105
    ventilation and shade for, 21
    Wright, Jacobs Houses in, 14, 64–69, 82–87
Tenon, Jacques-René, 204
Thermoheliodon device, 192
tropical zones, 14–15. See also subtropical zones
    Katz and Vaughan, Bachelor Flats in, 106–11
    Niemeyer, Building for the Emprezas Gráficas o Cruzeiro in, 88–93
    Porro, School of Plastic Arts in, 152–57
    Prouvé, Maison Tropicale in, 15, 94–99
    Reidy and Piheiro, Night Shelter for the Homeless in, 42–45
    Reidy, Pavilion on the Lagoon Rodrigo de Freitas in, 136–39
    ventilation and shade for, 14–15, 21–22, 191
Turnbull, William, 186

UNESCO Headquarters (Breuer et al.), 184
Unwin, Raymond, 204–5

urbanism, 24–26, 201–6, 213–14
Usonian house (Wright), 14, 19, 65
utopianism, 203–4

Vacation House on Aegina (Decavallas),
    170–75
Vassar College, 112–17
Vaughan, Reginald, 106–11
ventilation, 14–15, 21–22
Victoria College of Egypt (Poltock), 183
Viel, Charles-François, 204
Villa Mairea (Aalto), 180
Villanueva, Carlos Raúl, 185

Walker, Ralph, 182
Walker Beach House (Rudolph), 118–23
water elements, 76–81, 196
Weekend House (Frey and Kocher), 52–57
Whitaker, Richard, 186
Wichita / Dymaxion House (Fuller), 181, 208
Williams, Amancio
    House over the Brook by, 76–81
    Houses in Space by, 70–75
wind power, 21, 22–23
Wisconsin, 58–63, 82–87
Wright, Frank Lloyd, 19
    Jacobs Houses by, 14, 64–69, 82–87
    Larkin building by, 20
    Price Tower by, 184
    San Marcos in the Desert Resort by, 178
Wright, Henry, 190

Xenakis, Iannis, 158–63

Zehrfuss, Bernard, 184